St. Jude Momma

~

A Love Story

Sarah Bucciero

Sarah Bucciero

DEDICATION

This book would not have been possible without the love and encouragement of so many people. I am forever grateful for those who have walked this journey with me. Some of them have been there since the beginning and some have joined me along the way. They are Carter's storytellers. They are the reason that his story continues to be shared and to be told. I couldn't do this without you.

Most importantly, thank you to Melissa Woodridge for being my mentor and guide on this journey. You are the original St. Jude Momma. While I hate that we met each other in the lobby at St. Jude, I love that you were our neighbor and became such a wonderful friend - there are no coincidences.

To Carter – Thank you for giving my life purpose and passion. You taught me more in three years than I have learned in a lifetime. You are never far from my thoughts and you are always in my heart. You are my dragonfly. You are my pixie dust.

To my St. Jude Family (the doctors, nurses, staff, other families) – Thank you for loving my little boy and for your continued love and support. I truly consider you all family.

To Mason - Thank you for being the reason I got out of bed every morning on the darkest of days. You will never understand the magnitude of my love for you or how you saved me from drowning so many times after Carter was gone. You are the best big brother Carter could have ever had.....

To Porter - Thank you for taking my breath away. You are the silver lining in this story.

To Mom and Dad - Thank you for the life lessons you instilled in me before this journey ever started. Thank you isn't enough.

To Kelly, Emily, and Renee - Thank you for your help, guidance and encouraging words while being the first to read this story.

To Mike Todas - Thank you for designing the cover of this book and for designing the Carter ((HUGS!!)) logo. It is everything I ever imagined and I am so blessed by your creativity and talent.

To my Springfield Middle School family and FMSD friends – Thank you for your continued love and support over all of these years.

And to Paul – It isn't the journey that we wanted or chose, but I am thankful you've been on it with me.

Prologue:

This is the book I never thought that I would have to write. It is my love story. A story of love that will last forever in my heart, but one that I only was able to embrace here on earth for a few short years. It is, essentially, the Caring Bridge journal that I kept while on the journey.

This story began long before he was ever here. It's hard to pinpoint the exact moment it started. Did it begin when we were trying to get pregnant? Did it start when the doctor told me I needed to try and be finished having children by age thirty-five? Was it when I had a miscarriage and then got pregnant when the doctor gave us the go ahead? Or maybe it was when the nurse gave me a little more Pitocin to speed up the delivery and he arrived way too quickly, causing an alert in the hospital and resulting in the nurses and doctor running down the hall, just in time. It's all a part of his story and happened before he ever arrived.

Carter Joseph came into this world on May 27, 2009 at a dizzying speed. He was a day past his due date and there weren't any beds available in the hospital for my induction. I was told that I would be put to the top of the list since he was measuring large. His older brother had arrived just eighteen months before at nine pounds and almost twelve ounces. When the phone call came from the hospital, I quickly answered while renting movies in hopes that it was my turn to meet my little prince. My husband came home from work and we calmly and carefully drove to the hospital. It was anticlimactic in comparison to my first pregnancy.

I arrived at the hospital about 4:30pm and six centimeters dilated. I was given an epidural immediately. Pitocin was started and we waited. About 7:30 the nurse increased the dosage. At 7:43 pm the nurse had me push and realized that this little guy was going to make an appearance quickly. She paged the nurses and doctor and they stampeded down the hallway, arriving out of breath and washing up quickly. I was told not to push anymore. The doctor could tell that the umbilical cord was wrapped around the baby's neck. I pushed a second time per the doctor's orders at 7:47 pm and Carter Joseph entered the world, the umbilical cord around his neck and the color of his skin a deep purple.

The cord was cut and the nurses went to work. I prayed. I prayed harder than I had ever prayed. I didn't want to lose my baby. I wanted him to be healthy and perfect. I needed to hold him and care for him. The others in the room cheered him on and finally someone told me to talk to him. I did, trying not to cry. He needed to hear my voice they said. So I did. I told him that he could do it, that I needed him to breathe. And just like that, he started to cry.

Carter was a fighter from day one. As he got older, he battled ear infections and respiratory infections on a weekly basis. At six months old he had ear tubes placed. At eighteen months old he got a second set of tubes and had his adenoids out. It was at that point that he seemed to get better, the distance in time between his illnesses got longer. We had turned the proverbial corner.

And that's when everything changed.

****

Part One

~

The Beginning

It's hard to start this story. Not because of the story itself, but because my life was a chaotic blur before it came to a sudden stop. My husband was commuting weekly for his new job two and a half hours away. I was playing single mom during the week, working full time with boys who were two and three years old. When my husband came home on the weekends, we attempted to do things together as a family and catch up on everything that didn't get done during the week. Our lives seemed full and happy. Chaotic and overwhelming, yes, but happy.

In mid-September, our son Carter woke up with croup. I knew it was croup because my boys had it on a regular basis during allergy season. With the seasons starting to change, I wasn't surprised that Carter was barking like a seal.

I was sick, too. Bronchitis hit me hard and I called my mom to come down from Virginia to help. I didn't know how I could handle being sick and care for a sick child on my own. It seemed daunting.

In the days that followed, the croup disappeared, but it turned into an ear infection and a respiratory infection. It was the first ear infection since Carter's new ear tubes were placed in April. It was the longest he had gone without an ear infection since he was three months old.

On the fifth day of the antibiotic regimen, Carter vomited, just once. I will never forget it. He came running towards me in the hallway crying. As he ran, projectile vomit came flying towards me onto my freshly cleaned hardwood floors. I play that day in slow motion in my mind over and over again. It was the day that everything started to change. After a few tears and cleaning up, Carter seemed fine. That night he complained that his neck hurt, but we rubbed it and he didn't complain again.

My mom literally had just left to head back to Virginia right before Carter vomited. I was so upset that she had gone and now I had a child who was vomiting. It hit me in that moment that this was the reason why so many people lived close to family.

The next day Carter and his brother, Mason, went to daycare. I went to work. My husband was two and a half hours away at his new job. Everything seemed normal. But then, it happened again. Mason and Carter were sitting on the sofa watching a show while I put dinner together. I remember hearing Carter cough and thinking that the bark was gone. Mason jumped up and started screaming. Carter started crying. He had thrown up again, this time all over the leather sofa and himself. I scrambled for paper towels and tried to reassure Carter that he would be fine. In my mind, I was convinced he had developed an allergy to the antibiotic. It had been a while since he had been on it. So, it made sense somehow.

The next morning Carter and I went to the pediatrician's office. We switched antibiotics, hoping to see immediate results. But two days later, Carter was still throwing up, one time a day. So we went back to the pediatrician's office where they determined he must have reflux. Carter was taken off of the antibiotic and started his new medicine.

My Facebook post from September 28, 2011 read, *" wants to figure out what is making poor Carter sick....my poor little guy is lethargic, no fever, but vomits 1x a day after not eating anything all day long....thought it was the antibiotic, but now I'm not so sure...oh – and after he vomits, he feels fine and nothing seems to be wrong...."*

I hoped that there would be results, I wanted there to be results. I do not do well with vomit. Carter kept vomiting. It occurred most frequently in the morning, but occasionally at night. He wasn't eating at daycare and becoming less and less interested, wanting only to cuddle or rest on the bean bag chairs. I was convinced he had a blockage in his tummy.

About a week into this vomiting chaos, I was determined to get answers. It was a Sunday and Carter and I headed to the ER where I explained the scenario to the doctor on call. He did a liquid challenge test- that meant that Carter got to eat a popsicle while watching television. He passed the test because he kept the popsicle down and didn't vomit. The doctor told me that everything was just fine and that my little guy's tummy was just upset from all of the meds. We went home. I felt defeated and angry having just spent money on an unnecessary ER visit.

Monday morning Carter walked into my room and announced, "Mommy! Look! I all better!" I was elated. I was relieved that I was simply an alarmed and panicked mom.

Tuesday morning arrived and Carter didn't get sick again. I felt like we were making progress. I went to work and the boys went to daycare. Mid-morning I received a call from daycare. Carter had vomited and I needed to get him as soon as I could. I remember leaving work and thinking that it would be the last time I would be leaving. It was an odd feeling and I pushed it aside mentally thinking that I was being paranoid.

I picked Carter up and we went home. I called the pediatrician and specifically requested a doctor that I felt comfortable with and knew Carter. For some reason, that was important to me at that moment. We started out once for the office and Carter vomited again before we got very far. So I turned around, headed back home to change him and got on our way. I was scared. I was angry. I knew it was time to demand tests and scans.

While I knew and loved our pediatrician, I wasn't expecting her to say that Carter needed to be admitted to Jeff Gordon's Children's Hospital across the street. He had lost two and a half pounds in less than two weeks which was about ten percent of his body weight and a reason for alarm.

Every mother feels that their child is special the moment they are born. When Carter was born, and then lived through his battle with the umbilical cord, I knew that he was special. He was the answer to the prayers I whispered to God in the middle of the night for a healthy baby. It was an added bonus that he was born a little boy and would be best buddies with his older brother, Mason.

Long before anyone ever told me that Carter was special. I knew it with every ounce of my being and soul. The first time I held him in my arms, I dove deeply into his eyes and melted. There was something he was trying to tell me with his eyes. I tried to understand. Had he been here before? Was he an old soul? His dark gray eyes captivated me for hours on end in the beginning of his life, causing me to ponder and wonder about my little boy. Perhaps it was a mother's love for her child, perhaps it was because Carter was to be my last child, or perhaps I was simply in love with my little boy.

I had never been to the hospital inpatient before with a child. I had no idea what to expect. I don't remember all of the details of getting Carter registered, but they knew we were coming and we were sent up to the children's area of the hospital. We took an elevator and Carter started screaming and crying. A man in a tie looked at me like I had a demon child. I don't think that Carter had never been in an elevator (or one that he remembered) and it scared him in ways that I didn't know possible. He hated elevators after that trip. It took until the end of his journey to get him over that fear.

Once admitted, the doctor told me she thought Carter had a virus. He was running through the halls and she figured he needed fluids and we would be gone in the morning. I called my husband, still almost three hours away, and convinced him that he needed to come home. I made arrangements for Mason to get to our neighbor's home after daycare until Paul, my husband, could pick him up. He would come to see us in the morning after dropping Mason off back at daycare.

I slept that night in the hospital bed with Carter. I didn't have a change of clothes. I didn't have toiletries. I remember thinking that my day had not gone as planned. And, for whatever reason, the hospital gave him a full-sized bed instead of a crib. We cuddled up and fell asleep. I slept in my clothes, my work clothes. I had no one to bring me toiletries or night clothes. I was thankful that I had worn a comfortable outfit to work that day. Sometime in the middle of the night, Carter started squirming and I knew that he was hurting. The nurses came in early and not long after he vomited all over me.

Paul arrived and I could tell he was still trying to process the situation. He is an engineer and the quieter of the two of us and more balanced when I'm emotional. He brought clothes and toiletries so that I could change and clean up.

As the vomiting increased, Carter slept more and more and was talking less and less. I spent my day trying to research his symptoms, talking to friends about their own thoughts, and trying not to be jump to the worst conclusions. He was basically comatose, his eyes closed and resting the majority of the day. He only woke up to vomit. I knew that he was in pain because he was grinding his teeth, just like he had as a baby with ear infections.

I thought that Carter had a blockage in his tummy, something that was preventing his food from being digested. I told the doctor I wanted a MRI or CT scan and she looked at me as if I were a monster. She told me that MRIs weren't done on children under the age of three because they could possibly cause cancer.

At one point I needed a break, I needed to be clean and to have something other than hospital food. Paul spent the day with Carter. While he was there, Carter vomited a dark liquid. Paul got ugly with a nurse and doctor and the dark liquid was tested. It was blood.

A pediatric gastroenterologist was called in to look at Carter and order some tests. She wanted to do an upper GI. Carter and Paul were wheeled down into the depths of the hospital building and I was left navigating a

9

maze. I remember feeling panicked that I couldn't get to Carter. I knew that Paul was with him, but I was angry and frustrated and feeling lost, literally. By the time I caught up with them, they were trying to get Carter to drink a syringe of barium. But he couldn't keep it down, as soon as he would drink some, he would throw it back up. They were able to get a few images even though he could barely keep the liquid down.

The images showed that Carter's stomach wasn't working. The food or liquid he ate just sat in his stomach and wasn't being emptied into his intestine. The doctors explained that this was neurological. He was scheduled for an MRI and spinal tap at 9pm that night. The doctor reassured us that she thought it was meningitis without a fever. I had no reason to believe it was something terminal or something that wasn't fixable. I just wanted answers to make my little boy all better.

Paul went home to be with Mason. My mom had returned from Virginia to help again. They were at the house. I was alone at the hospital, but since the doctor thought Carter had a virus I didn't see the need for anyone to stay with me.

At this point I hadn't heard Carter's sweet voice in two days. I knew he was in pain because he was grinding his teeth like he had done when he had ear infections as a baby. I told the nurses this as I stuck my finger into Carter's mouth for him to bite. I was certain that he was going to break his teeth from the awful noise that came from his mouth. He bit me so hard that I cried. I didn't want my baby to hurt.

Carter was sedated and rolled into the MRI as I sat with a *People* magazine. It was a Thursday night. Hawaii 5-0 was on the television in the waiting room. I think there was one other person in the room with me, but I was restless and couldn't focus. I just wanted answers.

A nurse came out much more quickly than I had anticipated. She told me that they didn't have to do the spinal tap because they found something in the MRI. My stomach sank. I didn't want to think it was a brain tumor, but a nagging voice in my head kept telling me to be prepared for those words. I pushed the voice away, not wanting to acknowledge my suspicions. The nurse told me the doctor would explain and that Carter was already on his way up to the room.

As I approached the nurse's station, the doctor was sitting at the desk. She was on the phone and hung up as I stood there.
"What did they find?" I questioned.

"You mean no one has spoken to you?" She looked at me in disbelief.

She came out from behind the desk and took my hand. I don't know that I had ever had a doctor take my hand prior to that moment. I felt like all of the nurses were watching me in the hallway. The doctor led me to Carter's room. The nurses fell in line behind us. We walked in the room and everything had been packed up. It didn't register because I was more concerned about seeing Carter sleeping in his bed and his pale color.

The doctor explained that Carter had a brain tumor. An astrocytoma it what she called it. She had scribbled it on a piece of scrap paper for me. My world stopped. I wailed, my knees buckling. Tears streamed from my face as the nurses held me up so I wouldn't collapse. The doctor kept talking but the only thing that registered was "emergency surgery" and that we were "going to Levine immediately."

I was alone. My husband was at home asleep with our older son. I couldn't get in touch with him and I was at a loss as how to do so. The police were contacted in our town to go knock on the door until he answered. In the meantime, a neighbor went to do the same thing. I told her to ring the doorbell until Paul answered the door.

Paul finally called me after what seemed like forever. I told my husband in his Tylenol PM induced state what was going on and he could barely process the information. I remember telling the doctor that Paul had reacted better than I thought he would, but how exactly does one react to hearing that their child has a brain tumor?

I got in touch with my brother in New Jersey who had just returned from the ER with his son's broken arm. I remember wishing that Carter had a broken arm. I alerted as many family members as I could before leaving the hospital, the others would have to wait for the ambulance ride.

I headed to the chapel quickly before we had to leave. I needed to have a chat with God. I begged and pleaded with Him. I promised that I would go wherever I needed to go in order to make Carter better. I prayed and I cried. Part of me died that night, but part of me was born. I remember wanting to stay in the chapel. I remember thinking that it had to be a bad dream. But I also remember being ready to fight and wanting to fight.

Carter was loaded in the back of the ambulance and I sat up front calling more family members. I updated Facebook with a vague, *" Long night ahead – please continue to pray....really, really hard."* I told the ambulance driver that I hope he didn't think I was being rude by making the calls in the front seat. He explained that he didn't and that unfortunately he was accustomed to hearing calls like the ones I had to make.

There was construction between Concord and Charlotte. Traffic was awful, even at 10:45pm at night. I spoke to more family members. The ride felt eternal.

We arrived at Levine Children's Hospital and were sent to the PICU. I had never been in a PICU before. Levine was less than five years old. I remember because it opened about the time my first son was born. I will never forget my mom saying to me that it was wonderful that Charlotte was going to have a children's hospital, just in case we needed it.

Carter was wheeled in ahead of me and I didn't initially see the mob of doctors, nurses, fellows, and others. The lead doctor wanted a quick version of what had happened over the past days and stopped me at the doorway.

Within moments, I could hear Carter calling for me. I hadn't heard his voice in two and a half days. I remember walking into the room and seeing the mob. I felt like I was in a television hospital show. I tried to process what was happening and began crying. I didn't understand how we could be in the PICU and how Carter could be talking to me so suddenly. The doctor explained that Carter was on a steroid to reduce the swelling in his brain. Since he was responding, they made the decision to postpone emergency shunt surgery. Carter just wanted to know why I was crying.

I didn't sleep that night. Carter was exhausted and slept well. I tried to sleep on the sofa in the PICU room, but it was more like dozing in and out of various states of consciousness. Carter woke up early wanting to cuddle with me. He had a crib and so I climbed into it awkwardly, trying my best to hold my baby boy and comfort him. He didn't like the crib and so one of the nurses was kind enough to order a bed for us. We had to vow never to leave him unattended in the bed because they were worried he would fall out and get hurt. In my mind, I couldn't imagine leaving Carter's side even for a moment.

Our nurse that night was a man by the name of Trent. He was fabulous. I remember asking his advice. I still follow it to this day. He told me that I was now running a marathon. Sometimes I would take it moment by moment, others step by step, and still others breath by breath. He told me to take care of myself, too. Carter needed me to be strong – mentally, emotionally, and physically. You can't be sick around a cancer patient and Carter was going to need me to be healthy.

First thing in the morning, I posted on Facebook, "*My dear, sweet friends- it breaks my heart to have to post this..... Our worst nightmares have been confirmed- our sweet baby Carter has a brain tumor called Astrocytoma. We have been transferred to Levine Children's Hospital in CLT and we're waiting to see the neurosurgeon.... Please lift us up in prayer.*"

Shortly after this post, my Facebook account exploded with comments and prayers. It was overwhelming emotionally. It's one thing to know that you have friends, it's another to know that you're loved and that people are praying for your child. I felt loved, really loved. I knew that Carter was being lifted up in prayer, and that was a priceless gift.

"I am forever thankful for each and every post, tag, and email that you all have sent. Please know that I have read each one and each one has touched my heart. Carter will have surgery in the late morning to biopsy the tumor and to try and relieve pressure on the brain. We had planned to take the boys to Disney on Ice tomorrow and I will take Mason and then join Paul at the hospital - it will help keep my mind off of the surgery and I will be there before it is over. The waiting kills me.... We should have the results on Monday of the biopsy.....thank you for all of your love, support, and prayers..... You are amazing."

That same day, Carter underwent his initial brain surgery to relieve the pressure in his brain. I had promised to take Mason to the Disney on Ice show around the corner from the hospital. It was a little bit of normalcy and helped me keep my mind off of the fact that my baby was having brain surgery. I needed the distraction. It had been planned for months and I needed to spend some time with Mason. He needed his mommy, too.

The problem was that I missed what ended up being Carter's first haircut. It wasn't something that I had ever thought about until I had a text from Paul saying that they were going to need to cut Carter's hair for the surgery. The nurses had to cut his hair where the surgeon was going to cut. My sweet baby had been bald until recently. His hair came in shockingly white, making him look even more angelic. The nurses put his hair in a Ziploc for me. They understood.

I was there when Carter woke up. I had returned from the ice show and was greeted by our priest who had spent the day with Paul and our family waiting in the ICU waiting room. I climbed in bed with him and snuggled because he was in so much pain. My dad and I have an extra enzyme that metabolizes morphine quickly, and it became obvious that Carter had it, too. My baby was in excruciating pain and the doctor quickly determined that a stronger pain medication would be necessary. I sang to him. Over and over again, I sang to him. I sang the songs that I sang to him as a newborn infant. I sang to him hoping that it would take away the pain. I sang so I would feel his pain. I sang and sang.

Sweet Baby Carter is finally resting peacefully - he didn't respond to the morphine originally and so they were able to find a med that worked better for him. This is the best I've seen him sleep in a while.....Tentative plans for another trip to the OR on Monday to try and get a tissue sample. ((HUGS)) to you all for all of your love and support.....my friends ROCK!

The PICU is an interesting place. You have children fighting for their lives. You have children who will recover and those who won't ever leave the floor again. It has an intensity on the floor that isn't explained by words, but by feeling. It feels like an electric pulse, perhaps because of the machines humming in the background behind every door or perhaps because of the power generated by the emotions of parents, grandparents and close family friends. It isn't somewhere you want to be or visit, ever. Carter wasn't in the PICU long, but it was long enough.

The first few days were a blur. Cold showers in a bathroom at the end of the hall were the highlight of my day. It was surreal. I was trying to keep things as normal as possible for Mason, who was just four and didn't understand the sudden change is his normal schedule and life. I was trying to be a warrior for Carter, and trying to be a mommy for Mason. I was running on adrenaline and exhausted.

10/9/11
We are an army of thousands of prayer warriors at this point - thank you, thank you, thank you for your prayers, love, and support. I have never felt so loved and supported in my life and I'm blessed to have you all standing behind me........HUAH!

10/9/11
Carter will have surgery tomorrow to get a tissue sample - don't know what time yet. Keep the prayers coming please!!!!

10/10/11
Change of plans: 3D MRI at 1pm to get a better image of tumor and location. Keep those prayers coming please!!! HUGS!!!!

10/10/11
The doctor STILL hasn't shown up, so I'm calling it a night. I need some beauty sleep! I will go to bed tonight knowing that I'm embraced in your love and support....for which I am forever thankful.

10/11/11
Biopsy probably tomorrow - God asks us to be specific on our prayers, so that is my prayer right now... Since the tumor is inoperable - a benign tumor would be ideal.

10/11/11
I'm posting to answer a lot of questions - sorry that I'm not getting to each of you individually, but I hope that you understand. Time is something I have very little of these days!

Carter's tumor is a low-grade Astrocytoma located in the thalamus and hypothalamus which is near the pituitary gland. This is a region where they don't operate because it controls too much and is too risky. This means that the tumor is inoperable. The MRI yesterday was 3D and essentially created a road-map for the biopsy surgery tomorrow (better than going in blind). The surgery tomorrow will be a needle biopsy where they drill a small hole in the skull and insert a needle to obtain the tissue sample. Once we know if the tumor is malignant or benign, we will sit with the oncologist and determine a plan of treatment.

I hope that this answers some questions - please keep them coming, just know that I will most likely answer them as a group! Keep those prayers coming! I'm forever grateful for each and every prayer that is offered! ((HUGS!!))

10/11/11
Meant to post this the other day and forgot.....I never would have thought that Carter's first haircut would be for surgery. SO thankful

for the wonderful nurses here who cut a few of Carter's golden locks and saved them for me. Brain surgery is one hell of a first haircut! At least they only had to cut the top......

10/11/11
Two funny moments to post about: 1) love my dear friends who have been visiting and never bothered to tell me about the 1/2 inch long hair growing out of my chin!! 2) Mason and I watched DWTS last night and the Footloose dance - I told him it was my favorite and he was mesmerized.... Then proclaimed it was his favorite too!

No one talks about the havoc that having a sick child causes on a marriage. Paul and I were literally passing each other at the hospital. Sometimes we got to see each other for a bit, other times we didn't. We tried to keep life as normal as possible for Mason. He went to daycare and he spent time with either Mommy or Daddy. We told him that Carter had a "boo-boo" in his head and that the doctors were trying to fix it. He seemed to understand and just wanted Carter to be better.

10/12/11
Carter is sleeping quietly right now. He had a great day! He played in the toy room and was up most of the day (vs. sleeping a good bit of it). He will not be able to eat after 11pm tonight - so I'll get him up about 10pm to eat some more pizza. He is my pizza eating champion! His surgery is at 8am and I'm sure that we'll have an early morning. They postponed the biopsy until tomorrow because the OR schedule was full and they couldn't squeeze him in.......Thank you for your continued prayers, posts, emails, gifts, and love - I am eternally thankful for each and every one. They give me strength, courage, and knowledge that I am not alone in this battle. Thank you my dear, sweet friends.....I love each and every one of you! ((HUGS!!))

Carter was moved to the eighth floor of Levine. He quickly started flirting with the nurses and got accustomed to the bandages, needle pokes, and constant beeping of the machines. Elisa was our primary day nurse and Carter loved her dearly.

It was about this time that I realized Carter was suffering from white coat syndrome. It's basically a fear of doctors entering the room when he was inpatient. I'm not sure what it stemmed from, maybe from an event when I wasn't present perhaps, but he freaked out every time a doctor showed up to talk to us or needed to check on him. It was awful. My baby boy would go from elated to a petrified state instantaneously when someone with a white coat walked through the door.

10/13/11

About this time last week I was being moved from the imaging waiting room to the recovery waiting room - praying that the doctors would find an answer to my baby's illness.......how was that a week ago? It feels like it was just a moment ago.......I have an episodic memory and I keep hitting replay........

10/14/11

Thank you everyone for your prayers and love. Carter had a good afternoon yesterday and was able to play in the toy room on his floor. He also went up to the roof where there is a children's garden for some fresh air. Seeing him act like a typical two year old is so refreshing!

Please join our Prayers for Carter FB page, too. The photo is the same as the one posted here...I'll try and post the link later.

Just so you are aware - Paul and I are switching nights at the hospital each night so that at least one of us gets a good night sleep (or better than the hospital at least!). I will try and update this page as frequently as I can - it seems that I have the most time when Carter is sleeping.

Love to you all - I am blessed with the best friends in the world and I cherish each and every prayer that is being sent our way.

((HUGS!!))

10/14/11

Heavenly Father - I can now see how everything in my life has brought me to this point. I am strong because of you. Everything I have ever been through has prepared me to be strong and fight. I will fight this with every ounce of my being for our little boy. You are my Commander in Chief and I am fighting with an army of prayer warriors behind me. We will win this battle for Carter. Winning is the only option. In your name I pray, S.

10/14/11
Carter is resting - it was a good day. He has some swelling over his right eye from the surgery, but they don't seem concerned about it. He went to the roof garden again and jumped in the puddles.....When we were resting in his bed later, he was talking to me about sharing his new toys with Mason and said to me, "Mommy, you're happy!" I told him that he makes me happy and I was so glad that he had a good day. I think that he smiled today more than he has in a long time........it made my heart happy.

10/14/11
Sweet Carter is sleeping - It is easiest for me to write when I know that he is resting well and I can try to think clearly.

Thank you all for everything. I have never felt so loved and supported in my life. It makes this journey so much easier. Everything in my life has prepared me to be strong and to fight for my little guy. I understand now why God has put me through the trials and tribulations. Don't get me wrong - I've led a blessed life and I am forever thankful for it......but now I just have a deeper appreciation for all the potholes that I've hit along the way. This is more like a sinkhole - but even sinkholes can be fixed to be as good as new!

Right now we're just waiting for the biopsy results. My prayer is that the news we've already received will be wrong. I pray that the tumor is not a stage 3, I pray that it is benign, I pray that it will be operable. A sweet friend reminded me today that doctors are not God and that it is God himself who will determine the results of the biopsy.

Tomorrow our sweet Mason will come to see Carter for the first time since Carter was admitted to the hospital. Carter is VERY excited to see his "bruder" and is eager to show off his balloons and new toys. He even said that he'd share with Mason! Carter and I had a little chat tonight and it was so sweet. We were both smiling and Carter turned to me and said, "Mommy, you're happy!" It warmed my heart. I told him that I was happy because he was feeling better and was talking to me. I cherish our little chats.

Tomorrow will be a big day. There are friends from Locust and Fort Mill who are running in the Levine Children's Hospital Hopebuilders 5k Run/Walk for both Carter and other children that we know. It means so much to know that they will carry light blue balloons for my little guy. Next year, Carter and I will walk together.

Tonight my dad is driving from Cincinnati to be here. He and mom will switch so that Mom can go back to VA for a few days. My father-in-law and his wife are also here to help us. My brother-in-law and sister-in-law will be coming down tomorrow for the day to help, too. ALL HANDS ON DECK!

Thank you to all of my neighbors and local friends who are preparing meals for us each night. I have never needed to receive meals and didn't realize what a blessing they were until now. I so appreciate each and every one.

And thank you to each and every one of you for your love and prayers. I have never felt so loved and supported in my life and for this I am eternally grateful.

I'll close with something that my great-grandmother used to say and which has been echoed by my father throughout my life......"Love is the golden cord dropped down from heaven which binds us together." I have a totally new appreciation for this saying now.......I am forever bound to you all with love.

Sweet dreams.
-S.

I couldn't stop crying. In between the posts, the emails, and the texts. There were tears, lots of them.

I let myself become truly vulnerable to emotion and let it envelope me for the first time in my life. I cried the tears that Carter didn't know how to cry. I cried the tears for his future. I cried tears of fear. I cried tears because of the unknown.

It was Carter who calmed me. He was the one who would look at me and say, "Why are you crying Mommy?" He was the one who told me it would be fine.

Carter was the strong one who giggled and ate pizza like a champ. The steroids he took made him a fierce eater for the first time ever. He had been a pretty good eater before, but now he craved pizza at all hours of the night.

It was during this time that I had a dream. Maybe it was more of a nightmare. I saw myself at Carter's funeral. It was in Cincinnati where my grandparents were buried. Everyone around me was angry. It scared me in a way that I cannot explain. I had dreams that had come true before, and this was one dream that I didn't want to come true.

I told Paul the next day about the dream. I told him that I had to tell him so that the dream didn't come true. He understood what I was saying. He didn't want the dream to come true either.

I will never forget Paul holding me after I told him. It was the foreshadowing of an awful story.

10/16/11
Tomorrow is a big day......we should hear the biopsy results. Praying for answers and a plan.

I will be strong and fight this for my little boy. Winning is the only option.

((HUGS!!))
S.

10/16/11
Heavenly Father - I feel your embrace. I know that you are with me holding my sweet Carter close. Help me to be patient. I want to fix this and fix it now.....and I know that isn't how this whole thing works.......and I'm really, really sorry that I asked "What else?" a few weeks ago.........can I take it back? I really wasn't trying to challenge you......more like ask why it was all happening.......In your name I pray, S.

10/16/11
Just ordered Halloween costumes for the boys....Mason will be a dragon and Carter will be my Knight in Shining Armor.

I ordered these costumes late at night from a website that had costumes that were way out of my budget. I remember thinking that this could be Carter's last Halloween and I wanted to make it special. I wanted to make it memorable. I wanted it to be a night that we wouldn't forget.

10/18/11
Yesterday the doctors confirmed everything that they were speculating: the tumor is a grade 3 malignant anaplastic astrocytoma glioma. It amazes me that these doctors were able to determine the type of tumor without the biopsy, but the biopsy simply confirmed their diagnosis. We will have the tissue sent out to both St. Jude and Duke for a second opinion and to put Carter on their radars.

Paul and I have decided to begin Carter's aggressive chemotherapy here in Charlotte at Levine because we love the doctors and because after much discussion, we are not certain that putting Carter in a clinical trial/study right now is the best option. We want to see if the tumor will respond to the chemo first before making our sweet Carter a guinea pig.

Thank you for all the love, support, and prayers. I know that God is with us every moment of the day and I feel His presence.

The good news is that Carter will be coming home today. I am one happy momma......

Love to you all!

((HUGS!!))
S.

10/19/11
Carter came home yesterday! It feels so fabulous to have our family together under one roof. Carter is still on steroids and is very grumpy and VERY hungry. His pizza cravings have now expanded to Bojangles biscuits and Teddy Grahams! We are in the process of weaning him off the steroids......

Please know that I am eternally thankful for each and every card, meal, gift, guest book post, message, donation, etc. I don't think that I will ever be able to catch up on the thank you notes. Please know that I will try to respond to each email, but it might be a while before you get a response!

Tomorrow (Thursday), Carter will get a few little stitches out of his head. These are sutures from the biopsy. We will meet next Thursday with Dr. Chad, our pediatric oncologist. The following week we will meet with Dr. H., our neurosurgeon. I will keep you posted as things progress.

10/19/11
Tomorrow Carter will get the stitches in his head out. He has been a grumpy little boy today and I will be thrilled when he is off of the steroids! He has become a little chunk with an appetite that won't stop! And he was my skinny boy!

We are teaching Carter to say, "No big deal!" to help get through the rough patches......I pray that it will help him!

I am overwhelmed by the generosity of both my dear friends and complete strangers.....we received cards, gift cards, a prayer blanket, a cookie arrangement, and a dump truck full of snacks today! Not to mention an envelope full of cards created by children who have never met my little guy. I am blessed to have such a wonderful network of friends. With or without these wonderful tokens, I am forever thankful for each and every one of you.

I feel God's presence every moment of each day. I am a survivor. I am a fighter. I am a believer. I know that with each and every prayer God is fighting to heal my Carter and make him healthy. I am eternally thankful for each and every prayer that is said.

I think that I forgot to tell you all last week......I was in Target with my mom and the cashier was a nice older lady. There was a woman who was waiting for us to complete our transaction to exchange some slippers (she picked up the wrong size). Mom said something about the cashier being closed and we needed to go to the next one, but the cashier said that we could go through. She thanked us for noticing that her light was off. I don't remember most of the conversation, but I remember telling her that my brain was mush because my little boy had been in the hospital and had just been diagnosed with a brain tumor. This kind woman literally stopped the transaction and said, "Let's pray." She said the most beautiful prayer to heal Carter, right there in the check out line.

The woman who was waiting was also in tears for me. I apologized when we were finished to her, but then she apologized to me and said that she was so sorry to hear about Carter. I am surrounded by angels. God's grace is infinite.

I will forever remember feeling God's presence as a young child. I've always known that He was with me, but sometimes it has been harder to feel His presence than others. It is now that I am embraced in His love. Carter literally has people all over the world praying for him, for which I am eternally thankful.

I am at peace with this situation. I do not question. I do not worry. I know that we will win this battle for my baby boy. I find solace in the prayers, messages, posts, and gifts. God has prepared me for my entire life to deal with this situation. I have been collecting angels in heaven since my first loss at age four......these angels are protecting my Carter and fighting for him. I know that they want him to win this battle. Winning is the only option.

(((HUGS!!))
S.

10/20/11
Today Carter got his stitches out. He was happy at the doctor's office. He gave the nurse and surgeon kisses. It made me happy. This is my little boy.

He was not so happy when I ate a Chick-fil-a sandwich and he got Chicken tenders.....what was Mommy thinking????!!!

When we returned from our doctor's visit - our entire neighborhood had blue bows on the mailboxes to honor Carter........and Noelle and Chris had delivered a Thomas cake courtesy of Wal-Mart (Chris is a manager) for our little guy! It was consumed quickly by everyone! I couldn't stop crying. I am forever and eternally thankful for all of the gifts that are sent our way..... I have never felt so loved. I am forever thankful for the prayers - they are coming in from around the world and they continue to awe me........THANK YOU!!! And I am wondering what our daycare is up to........

Some people are calling me an inspiration......I don't know about that.....I'm just Sarah. God has prepared me for this journey and I will face it. I am nothing without God, my friends, and my family. I am eternally grateful for every gift of kindness......You all make me whole and make me strong.....God has prepared me for this journey.......it has been a lifetime in the making....

All I need is a miracle, all I need is YOU........

((HUGS!!)))

10/21/11
It was a long day. Carter was out of sorts. Mommy didn't feel well (side-effects of flu shot?). I was so thankful for some time outdoors to be in the sunshine and visit with my fabulous neighbors. Carter drove his truck a little bit and coerced our neighbor Cindy for some snacks. He repaid her with hugs and cuddles!

Tomorrow Pop-Pop and Grammie leave to go back to PA. I am forever thankful for their help and presence here over the past two weeks. My dad will leave on Sunday and my mom will arrive on Sunday (they'll wave to each other on the road!). Our family has been incredible about offering to help. Many family members have offered to come stay for a few days and/or a week.......I am eternally thankful. It helps so much having extra hands around. I have a new appreciation for the saying, "many hands make light work."

I need to get Mason to bed. Poor thing hasn't had a normal bedtime since this all has happened. Trying to keep things "normal" isn't as easy as it sounds - but we're certainly trying! We definitely have a new normal around here.......

So many people have commented that I amaze them or that I'm such a strong person.......you obviously haven't seen me cry in the middle of Target or CVS! I find my strength in God and in you all - the words, the wisdom, the prayers, the everything! You all are a blessing in my life and I am eternally grateful. You all give me strength.

I thought of my Aunt Peggy today - she's not really my Aunt Peggy - but a lifetime friend from when we lived in Barrington. Several years ago she made a comment about the fact that I learned how to network at age three and I never stopped expanding that network......I am forever thankful that I have such an incredible network of friends.... you all are amazing.......we'll have to play The Six Degrees of Sarah sometime!
Love to you all!

((HUGS!!))

10/22/11

Heavenly Father - You are amazing. I see your work in everything now. The phone calls, the prayers, the gifts, the fundraisers. I am forever humbled by your grace and mercy. Thank you Father for the angels who are at work in my life. I know that you hear our prayers because I can see your work being done. I am eternally grateful for each prayer that is sent to you.

Heavenly Father, please heal my sweet Carter and make him whole. I know that he is your child and that he is on this earth for a purpose. You give me strength. You give me purpose. You are in my heart and in my life. In your name, I pray. Amen.

Today was an extremely humbling day. I was contacted by the CEO of St. Jude and spoke with not only him, but the Director of Clinical Research. Angels are at work in my life. I know that God is at work in my life. What are the odds that I would receive a personal invitation to St. Jude from the CEO himself? I am constantly amazed by God's presence in my life. This is yet another example.

There are angels all around me. They bring us dinner each night, prepare fundraisers for Carter's medical bills, make donations to his fund, and most importantly, surround us with prayer.

Just in case you're wondering - I don't wear make-up anymore.....what is the point when you know you will cry so many tears of joy that it will be washed off by the end of the day?

I don't think that I've mentioned this, but when I was pregnant with Carter, my good friend Amy's little boy was diagnosed with a kidney tumor (Willm's tumor). His name is Bo. Bo is a special little boy to me because he was born early - on the day I was going to throw his mom a baby shower. Amy was a sister to me when I knew no one in SC and she accepted me with all of my faults (and there are many!) When Bo was diagnosed with the tumor, I prayed and prayed for him. I even sent him a Super Bo cape to help him get through the chemo process. When Amy heard my Carter's diagnosis, she sent Carter a Super Carter cape - complete with a note from Super Bo.......Amy and I have cried together. What are the odds that two friends would have children with tumors? Bo is a survivor and he and his parents are believers - that alone gives me strength. They are an inspiration to us.

I did something that I've never done before in my life today. I wrote someone in the Clemson Tigers organization (maybe Dabo's admin?) to thank the Tigers for having a winning season this year. I know that it sounds goofy - but this is the first year that we haven't had season tickets (so it makes sense that they are undefeated!). I simply wanted to tell the team that I am forever thankful for their fighting spirit. It is a bright spot in our week when the Tigers win.....something that gives us hope and strength. I know that it sounds silly - but when you've had tickets for almost 15 years and the team hasn't had an incredible season......and then they are winning when your son is battling the fight of his life.......it gives you hope. Winning is the only option......I think our Tigers get that now!

Friends - thank you for being angels in our lives. I will never be able to thank you, but my promise is that I will pay it forward forever.......and if you know me well enough, you know that I always keep my promises!

((HUGS!!))
Sarah

It was a pretty humbling experience to receive a phone call from one of St. Jude CEOs. It's one of those moments that I will never forget. He actually left me a message and left his cell phone number for me to return his call. I remember thinking that St. Jude must be a pretty amazing organization if the CEO was calling and extending personal invitations.

I didn't know anything about St. Jude at that point. I thought it was an institution where children were guinea pigs for experimental treatments. I had never paid attention to their ads on television. I had never been involved in their fundraising. It was just a place in Memphis to me. And, until that day, a place that I never thought that I would go.

10/23/11
God bless our cleaning lady who was here for almost 8 hours today.....please send her a prayer or two - she will probably need it in order to recover!

Not much to write today......Carter was grumpy but not as bad.....just a few more days of the steroids. He played outside for a little bit with Mason - I'm sure that the fresh air did him some good. I will post a few pics that my dad took yesterday .....love my little Chunk!

Paul went to SC tonight to be at work thru Monday. My mom is here this week to help. We are attempting to keep things as normal as possible - but it's hard. I know that it sounds awful, but just having a clean house helps. It's the little things that keep me grounded.

I need to get some sleep. This is one tired momma! ;) Sweet dreams my friends, sweet dreams.

((HUGS!!))
Sarah

10/25/11
Sorry that I missed writing last night (Monday). I managed to fall asleep while putting Mason to bed......obviously I needed it!

Thursday we will go back to Levine - Carter will have a physical to establish benchmarks of health. Before we can start chemo he must have another MRI, a spinal tap, and have a Hickman port placed in his chest. Lots to do in a short amount of time!

We are currently working to have all of Carter's records sent to St. Jude for review. We will know more once they have reviewed his information.

I am constantly reminded that God has a sense of humor. He obviously likes to see me scramble to get our house ready to be shown. For those of you who aren't aware, Paul took a job in Greenwood, SC on June 1. Our home went on the market shortly thereafter and never had a single showing until last week. Coincidentally it was on the same day we were given the biopsy results. Last night I received word from our agent that there was going to be a showing today at 11am. The house was clean (our cleaning lady was here for eight hours on Sunday - God bless her!) - but it was cluttered and needed some help. I put out an SOS on Facebook last night and within minutes my neighbors were volunteering and organizing a "Clean Team" to help! Many hands make light work - and this was once again proven. Thank you to my neighbors once again who came to my rescue! The house was spotless and in show house condition by the time they left (in about an hour and a half!)!

I am constantly being reminded of God's grace. Today I went to the bank to withdraw some funds for Carter's bills (yes, they're already starting to arrive!). One of the tellers handed me a deposit slip for $700 and told me that the donated monies had arrived in the mail yesterday. I burst into tears and I think that most of the tellers were crying with me. I am forever thankful to all of you for your generosity.

The first 400 Prayers for Carter bracelets arrived today and SOLD OUT! It is baffling to me to think that 400 people will be wearing bracelets for my little guy......and this is just the first shipment! More bracelets will be arriving soon!

I told a friend tonight that I have always hated asking for help. I've always tried to be the person to help others and not ask for help in return. God is teaching me to accept help......and to realize that it is not a sign of weakness or of being inept. Accepting help is accepting that others love you........and I cannot begin to express how loved I feel.

I do not want to be remiss in thanking all of the churches that have added Carter to their prayer lists. I cannot keep track of them all! Our Prayers for Carter page on Facebook reached over 900 members today! Heavenly Father - Can you hear me now? I am forever thankful for each and every prayer warrior who is a part of our army.

I am sure that I have posted this before - but I want to post it again.....my great-grandmother used to say that "love is the golden cord dropped down from heaven that binds us together." I feel that cord wrapping us all together tightly every day. Perfect strangers, best friends, and everyone in-between.

((HUGS!!))

10/26/11
Today was a day. It was a wretched day. It was an amazing day. It was a gift from God.

My day started at 4am when Carter woke up telling me he was hungry. He was soaking wet (another steroids side-effect), so I changed him first and got him a sippy. I then put him in bed with me and Mason. I was lazy last night and let Mason sleep in my bed since Paul was out of town and I was exhausted from waking up in the night with him the previous two nights. Carter kept asking if the "sunshine was awake" and I was trying to keep him quiet so Mason wouldn't wake up........something of a challenge to say the least. Somehow I managed to wedge myself in-between each of the boys......and while they slept soundly, I merely dozed in and out of sleep. Sleeping is not an easy feat when you're being kicked and hit from either side.......

So I was a grumpy momma when I finally dragged myself out of bed and rushed to get Mason to school (looking like a hot mess). There was a day and age when I wouldn't have dreamed about leaving the house without make-up, a shower, or a matching outfit.......now all of that is optional.

Oddly enough, Carter was in a really good mood this morning. Eating like a champ (eggs, roll, sippy, and Chex for b'fast). I also noticed that he was speaking a lot more and a lot more clearly today. Perhaps it's a benefit of almost being off of the steroids? He wanted to go to Wal-Mart with me (and my mom), so we set out on a field trip of sorts. I figure that I'll take him just about anywhere right now because he will be confined to home in the near future.

Anyways - on our way to Wally World we drove down the main street here in Locust. For as long as I can remember, there has been a disabled man in town who uses a type of Hove-around to maneuver the sidewalks in town. As I was driving, I noticed that he was stopped (unusual since he is usually moving on the sidewalks) and there was a Styrofoam container on the ground. I immediately said something to Mom about the gentleman needing help and turned the car around and parked as close as I could to the man's location. Mom got out of the car and asked if he needed help. The man explained that he had dropped his sandwich and that he couldn't reach it on the ground. Mom promptly picked up the container and asked him if he needed help getting repositioned and he asked her to help with his straps to buckle him in to the chair. I don't know this man's story, but he has lost his legs beneath each knee. He was appreciative of the help.

Mom simply explained that so many people have been good to us with Carter's battle that we were just paying it forward. The man immediately offered up a prayer for Carter. It dawned on me that here we were trying to help the man and he turned around and prayed for Carter. Simply remarkable.

Another bright spot was when a neighbor brought dinner tonight. It was a new neighbor whom I had never met. I looked like I had been hit by a Mack truck, the house was a disaster, and Carter was whining like a champ........and she took it all in stride - either that or she is a really good actress! I told her that I felt like I was in a bad commercial ....probably for Calgon!

It was shortly thereafter (I think) that I got a call informing me that we would have another showing for the house tomorrow morning at 10:30am.........If you haven't seen me freak out, I'll have to video tape it for you at some point. It's not a pretty picture! This is a blessing because it is a second showing to the people who looked at our house on Tuesday. I'm trying to remind myself that this in God's hands, not mine.......and also I'm realizing that the three St. Joseph's statues in my yard are probably getting headaches after being there for three months!

But the best part of the day didn't happen until about 9pm. Paul had just arrived home from Greenwood, Mason was getting ready for bed, and then the phone rang from an "unknown" number on my cell phone. I answered it thinking that it was my friend who has a police officer as a husband and regularly calls from an "unknown" number. It wasn't my friend. It was Coach Dabo - Head Coach of the Clemson Tigers Football Team!!! I was shocked and tried to hold back the tears ....Never in my wildest dreams did I think that the little note I sent would spur a phone call from Dabo himself! I just was writing the note to thank the team for winning and for giving us hope!

Turns out that Coach has read some of my journals here, too.......including the one that states that I stopped wearing make-up because of the tears........clearly goes to show that you never know who might be reading your posts! I am forever thankful for the phone call .....poor Paul will be forever jealous! Coach is a class act and I love my Clemson Tigers more than ever now!

Heavenly Father - there isn't a doubt in my mind that we're going to win this battle for Carter. My army of prayer warriors is growing and we are strong. With you as our commander, we will succeed. Winning is the only option!

I love Pinterest.com - it is a favorite of mine......and long ago before any of this chaos entered my life I pinned this from Proverbs......it meant something then, but it has even more meaning now.

"She is clothed in Strength and Dignity, and she laughs without fear of the future." Proverbs 31:25

((HUGS!!))

S.

10/27/11
(A note from my dad)

I would appreciate your help in acknowledging the efforts of several neighbors of the Bucciero family. Last Thursday (10/20/11) while Sarah was at the doctor's office having Carter's stitches removed, they sprang into action and decorated the entire neighborhood with beautiful blue bows to honor our sweet Carter. Needless to say, when Sarah pulled into the development and saw these decorations, she was awestruck and began to cry. I must tell you, she was not the only one in her family to have this reaction, I can attest to that personally. There is great truth in the statement that life is not measured in the number of breaths we take, but rather in the number of times our breath is taken away!

In those first moments that I navigated the neighborhood, I quickly came to understand and embrace the fact that these blue bows are the symbol of Carter's journey, and the many people that are traveling by his side, to provide strength and encouragement. A symbol is simply an outward and visible sign of an inward, spiritual grace. These bows symbolize so much more than great hope. They demonstrate the great love and prayerful supplication of the community of faith. Each time Sarah or Paul sees one of these bows, they know that someone, somewhere is praying for Carter, asking God to heal this child.

Virtually every mailbox in Locust Valley is adorned with one of these magnificent blue bows. There are bows on the street signs. There are bows on the entrance walls to the development. There are still more bows on the house railings.

The photos that I am adding show you just how beautiful these bows are, all over the neighborhood! Sarah, and all of her family as well, would like to acknowledge how meaningful this effort is to all of us, and how deeply we appreciate the work of all involved.

Gary Betz (Sarah's father)

10/29/11
My baby is wired.....literally. Carter is doing well with the addition of his Hickman port......Mommy on the other hand tries not to cry when she looks at it! Carter pointed out to me today that he had wires.....he seems to wear them as a badge of honor for the moment. I pray that this doesn't change once he learns that there will be medicine put through them.

Mason actually has accepted the wires pretty easily, too. *phew!*

I had to change the dressing on the port today because the bandage came off. Actually, the bandage didn't come off but rolled onto itself and became entangled in the wires. Not an easy first changing ....

In the beginning, Carter had white-coat syndrome in the hospital.....then he got over the white-coats and he came down with blue-glove syndrome........So, what did Mommy have to wear tonight in order to change the bandage around Carter's port? Blue gloves. If you heard the screaming down the street, it was probably due to Mommy wearing blue gloves......OH, and Mason decided that he wasn't thrilled that Mommy couldn't give him attention simultaneously......so Mason was screaming and crying, too. Gimi (my mom) was trying to get Mason to calm down........it was a zoo. Somehow I managed to stay calm and change the bandage......all while realizing that there was a tube inserted into my baby's chest.

For those of you who don't know, I'm a teacher. I taught middle school for many years (both 7th and 8th grades). I left the middle school environment to teach with the adult high school program at the local community college. I teach. I am not a nurse. I never wanted to be a nurse. I never wanted to be a doctor. I don't like the sight of blood. I am allergic to formaldehyde, which immediately eliminated me from certain biology classes. Guess what? I'm learning to be a nurse. I'm learning to be a doctor. By the time this journey is over.......I might consider either nursing or medical school!

I have the Clemson vs. GA Tech game on right now......I am worried that I jinxed the team by speaking with Coach Swinney earlier this week. I'm praying for a better second half..........C'mon TIGERS!!! Carter's going to win this battle........we need you to win, too!

Today was normal in most ways. I went to Target. I went to Costco. I took Mason to a birthday party and then to a Halloween party. I wore make-up for the first time in weeks (for Coach Swinney!).......If you didn't know that my baby had a brain tumor and was getting ready for the fight of his life, you would have thought that we were just an ordinary family.

It's half-time, I need to get Mason to bed - it is WAY past his bedtime.......just one last thing - THANK YOU to the Locust Bojangles and their manager Gregory for being so wonderful to us. Prior to all of this, I would stop for my morning caffeine and grits before heading to work each morning.......so I knew the staff pretty well.....when they found out about Carter, they were devastated and have totally been a God-send when my little guy wants biscuits, fries, and chicken supremes! Nicole, Karen, Gregory, and Jeff have all been amazingly supportive.........Locust is so fortunate to have such a wonderful Bojangles team!

'night, 'night......sweet dreams.......GO TIGERS!!!!!

WINNING IS THE ONLY OPTION!!

((HUGS!!))

10/30/11
The expression, "When it rains, it pours...." has a whole new meaning tonight.......It looks like we have sold our home. This is a blessing. This is a curse. I am in shock. Really. Our house has been on the market since June 28.......we didn't have a

showing until the day that we were anticipating Carter's biopsy results........No one sells a house in less than six months anymore......except for us! Pray that it goes through........or wait, pray that it doesn't go through????? I don't know what to ask God for at this moment.......And yes, we lost money....but not the way some people have lost money in this economy.......I'm good with our selling price. Greenwood, SC - here we come!

I went to church this morning and I was able to talk at length with Rev. Cox. I need to add that getting to church by 9am is something of a miracle in our house. I was able to go by myself because Mom and Paul stayed home to watch over the boys. It was a miracle that I woke up early enough to get to church (it's a good 30 minute drive). Rev. Cox has been so supportive and amazing throughout this entire ordeal. I am forever thankful that God sent her to our church in time for our paths to cross. Today was the last day for our interim assistant rector - Gary, he was the one who first visited Carter and prayed over him while Carter was at Jeff Gordon's Children's Hospital (Rev. Cox was on vacation)........I am forever thankful for our church family. Both of our boys were baptized there as infants - it will forever be a part of our lives.

By the way - someone said something to me about "bad things happen to good people" and that may be true......but God takes care of GOOD people.....just a thought......

Not much more to write tonight. I cannot believe that Halloween in tomorrow. Where did October go? The last time I checked I was being admitted to Jeff Gordon's because Carter had some type of GI issue.......

Love you all! ((HUGS!!))
S.

11/2/11
I am so sorry that I haven't written in the past three days......I have been overwhelmed and now I am exhausted.
I honestly barely remember Monday.....I do remember that I was surprised by a check from the Friends4Michael Foundation. Thank you to the mystery angel who referred us to this organization.
I know it was Halloween and that my nerves were fried by the time we were finished trick-or-treating. I can't tell you what I did during

the day......I just know that I wasn't certain if I'd make it out trick-or-treating because I was so tired. Thank goodness for adrenaline! Carter and Mason were two happy little boys as they drove from door to door in their motorized truck. I am so thankful that we had this toy car because Mason did the driving and Carter did the riding. They drove up to each driveway, got out, and hustled their little bodies up to the doors of our friends. And yes, we went to every house in the neighborhood! Carter's outfit was a size 4 and barely fit - but his "Sir Carter" cape covered any gaps in his costume...and I thought that it was going to be big on him! The little guys were elated with their loot.......My knight in shining armor melted my heart ......and my dragon cuddled up with me at the end of the night. Best.Halloween.Ever!

Tuesday was another chaotic day. It is a fun task trying to keep a two year old from eating until a 2pm procedure! We got Carter up at 6:30ish and he ate a TON before 7am......but it didn't stop him from asking for goldfish as we walked back to the prep room for his spine MRI. I am a huge fan of Carter's new Hickman port because we had such a positive experience yesterday. He walked back to the prep room with me and was a little nervous when the nurse started cleaning his port. She allowed Carter to help clean it and this made the experience much better. The nurse quickly checked to ensure that the port was working and then gave him Propofol. Carter said, "Look Mommy - it's working!" and then promptly passed out cold! No more waiting for the meds to take effect! *phew!*

I had to leave Carter and Paul at the hospital because I was told that I "HAD" to pick Mason up at school on Tuesday afternoon about 4:15. I arrived about five minutes late and noticed that the entire parking lot was full.....so full that I had to park on the grass! I figured that they must be giving kids away! To my amazement I was greeted by a "SURPRISE" from all of the kids at the daycare, the teachers, close friends, and two gentlemen I had never met. These men were from a local foundation. A good friend from daycare referred our family to the foundation because it was established to help teachers with cancer or teachers with dependents who have cancer. One of the men lost his mother, to cancer and his friend helped him establish the foundation. The woman who passed taught in Cabarrus County where I taught for just over a year after Carter was born. These angels presented

me with a $2000 check to help with Carter's medical expenses. I
am eternally grateful for their generosity.

My cousin-in-law (new term that was coined today!) arrived on
Tuesday. A perfect example of how overwhelmed I am - I thought
that she would be arriving at 9:45 PM and she actually arrived at
9:45 AM!!! So thankful that she is here- she has made life much
easier......

I will update you on the events of today tomorrow .....it's 11pm and
I can barely keep my eyes open.

((HUGS!!))
Sarah

11/4/11
How can it be Friday? Where has the week gone? Wasn't
yesterday Halloween? It's amazing when you get sleep how much
time you lose.......I managed to lose my journal time! ACK!

So - I told you about Monday and Tuesday ......and I'm going to be
really vague about Wednesday......it was fabulous because an
"Aunt" was here and we got to do some much needed catching
up. It was horrible because it was the day after Carter's spinal tap
and spine MRI. Needless to say - don't ever schedule a home
inspection the day after a spinal tap and spine MRI.......especially
when the buyer will be present. Carter literally screamed all
morning and when the Advil didn't help, I panicked because I
couldn't figure out if he could have Lortab ......so I spent most of
the morning on the phone with the nurses. Our "aunt" spent most
of the morning helping me clean and straighten so it didn't look
like a total bomb went off in our house........No, I haven't managed
to recover from the first house showing where everything got
stuffed in my dad's van.......or the second showing where it got
stuffed in my mom's car and my car.......or the third showing where
it went back into our cars for the second time. So now that the
inspection is done, I'm praying that the appraisal goes through so
that I don't have to put the house back on the market and deal
with this all again........oh, and irony of ironies......the man buying
the house works for the company where Paul used to work.....and
would have been his boss. I'm guessing that God has a sense of
humor?

Thursday was better for Carter. Still some pain in his back, but more tolerable. We had a check-up at the oncologist's office - they are wonderful there. The ladies are so good to him and he loves the attention. Ms. Lana is Carter's favorite......she helps Carter get the treats! Ms. Jessica helped teach Mommy (again) and Daddy how to change the connections on Carter's Hickman port and the dressings. It's totally different changing everything on your child vs. on a doll!

Today Carter had his hearing check. This is necessary because a side effect of chemo is hearing loss. Today established his benchmark hearing as "normal". Ms. Edie was incredible and had some need toys to help Carter through the test. Today was also a big day because I was able to talk to St. Jude about Carter's possible treatment there. My contact was wonderful and helped me think through a lot of logistics and questions. I am praying to know more first thing on Monday morning. I will keep you posted.

Tomorrow morning (Saturday) I will get up at the crack of dawn and drive to Greenwood, SC to look at 17 different homes in attempt to narrow down a few for Paul to look at so we can hopefully find a home there. Did I mention that we have to be out of our house here in Locust by December 14th? What's humorous to me is that I actually thought that this would be the year that I had my act together for Christmas.........now I'm thinking - not.so.much.

Thank you again for your continued prayers, support, donations, gifts, and love. Thank you for spreading the word about Carter's Prayer Warrior Army and invoking prayers for my little guy. I know that God is working. I see his messages to me and I see the work that He is doing all around me. He is working not only for me, but for others, too. I read the emails, I hear the stories, I know that God is good.

Heavenly Father, I lift my heart up unto you.......

((HUGS!!))

These first few weeks I operated in survival mode. I did everything I could just to exist and be strong for Carter. It was a constant state of chaos and I felt like I didn't have answers to important questions. My mantra became, "This too shall pass." I convinced myself that Carter was going to beat the tumor. I refused to say the word "cancer" in front of him or in front of anyone. I didn't want to give the word power.

11/5/11
I am indulging with a peanut butter pie that a fabulous friend made for me yesterday........I deserve it! Might even have some for breakfast tomorrow morning. It. is. THAT. good!

*Today I went to Greenwood to look at houses. I think that I looked at about ten houses, but only one stood out. It was the first house that I visited at 10am ....It.Is.Perfect. However, I realize that there is another family who lives in the house and I will not rush them out of it! And of course, I pray that it is God's will that we move into it. It is in move-in condition. It overlooks the water. Very little would need to be done to it. If God wants us to move into this house. He will make it happen. *sigh* Now I get to hurry up and wait again!*

Let me explain something. I don't have to buy a house. I will not be a wretched buyer that makes everything on their terms and makes life complicated for another family. I will be patient. I will be kind. I know that if it is God's will, it will happen........if it was meant to be, it was meant to be........so. be. it.

OH - and less I forget.....I wore make-up this morning. I cried at lunch when I found out that the owners of the house could move at anytime because they own several homes in the area. I STILL can't manage to keep make-up on throughout the day. GO.FIGURE! And Coach Swinney - I'm sorry, I'm trying!

Not much else to say..........nada mucho. My daddy will arrive tomorrow to help us out. And yes, I still call him "Daddy" - makes life confusing around here for Mason and Carter......by the way, please add my daddy to your prayer list - he has gone into atrial fib a few times since Carter was initially admitted to the hospital (just a coincidence - and yes, he's a cardiac patient). He has been able to convert back to normal rhythm, but it's a little unnerving to say the least.....he will be changing medicines soon to hopefully keep it under control. I need him to be healthy - so please say an extra prayer for him.

It's 11pm and I need to head to bed. My sugar high has worn off. Since it's day-light savings, I am going to lose an hour of sleep -

children don't get day-light savings.......I think that all parents should write Congress to protest!

((HUGS!!)) and love to you all, my sweet friends.
S.

11/6/11
Heavenly Father - Tonight I pray that tomorrow will bring answers. Will we be headed to St. Jude? If so, when? Help me be patient. Amen.

When I was a little girl, I knew that God had already planned my life out. I don't know how I knew this, but I'm guessing it was from Sunday school or from something someone important said to me. I used to have visions of God and His file cabinets. You see, to me God already had written my life plan and He could look at it whenever He wished ....all in His great, big file cabinet. The past few weeks I have thought about this file cabinet and wondered about my visions as a child. Only God has a key to His file cabinet for each one of us.......Only He knows what He has planned for each of us. Everything that I have experienced in my life makes sense now.......but only God knows what the files contain.

When I was in college I took a creative writing class my sophomore year. I enjoyed creative writing, but I used it as an outlet......not as a career goal or as a way to impress people. Sophomore year of college was a difficult one. Just a few weeks into the year, my Grandpa Mason passed away. He died of lung cancer. In fact, he came to live with us in April when my Mimi was ailing and was finally diagnosed with Alzheimer's. In May, my mother took my grandfather to the doctor for a physical and it was determined that he had lung cancer at that point in time. I remember that summer vividly because I watched a powerful man fade before my eyes.

I remember my goodbyes to my grandpa - he was in a hospital bed sleeping. The picture of him sleeping is still vivid in my mind. I knew that it was the last time that I would see him alive. Grandpa was only the second grandparent that I had lost and the only grandfather I had ever known. He was diagnosed in May and he passed in September.

I wrote a lot about death during my creative writing class, because that is how I was dealing with the loss of my grandfather. I was criticized by the teacher for only writing about death for our assignments.......at the time I thought that he was insensitive for not realizing the association when he criticized me in front of the class. I now know that the professor just didn't understand why I was in the class. It had been God's plan for me to be in the class and to use it as an outlet for the pain I couldn't express to anyone at the time. Sophomore year changed me, from beginning to end....but that was the plan all along.

I am a Christian. I was raised in the Episcopal Church. During my junior year of college I was lost. Sophomore year had left me friendless and alone - or so I thought. Junior year I started going to a Bible study group at VMI with a few good friends and started to broaden my Christian perspective. I am forever thankful for that experience because it helped me understand how other denominations worshiped. Until then, I just didn't know.

After we first moved to Locust, I started calling it "Deliverance" because my life was less than perfect and I seriously doubted why we had moved here. No matter how I tried, it never seemed to get better. This past summer, after hearing many false rumors about my family being circulated, after having people tell me that I was a horrible person for considering their community "Deliverance," and after many other trials and tribulations - I decided to curtail my relationship with many of these neighbors....Seriously, nothing is more crushing than sitting on your deck in the summer only to hear people talk about you in negative ways at the pool across the street. I needed to protect my family and myself. It was a lonely summer. Once Carter was diagnosed, all of these trivial issues fell to the side and my neighbors and friends surrounded me with love, prayers, support, and grace. I am thankful for their forgiveness, love, prayers and support that surrounds me now. Locust calls itself the "City with a Soul".......now I understand.

Tomorrow will be a big day on many different levels - I will keep you posted. To be continued........

((HUGS!!))

11/7/11
CARTER AND I ARE GOING TO ST. JUDE TOMORROW FOR TREATMENT!!!

Part Two

~

St. Jude

11/9/11
*Sorry that I haven't written - and this will be quick because I'm
waiting for Carter to wake-up in recovery......*

*Yesterday morning Carter and I flew to Memphis on Delta flight
2996. I had nightmares of Carter screaming the entire way to
Memphis and when we got on the plane, I realized that we were in
the VERY.LAST.ROW. I was certain that this meant that my
nightmares would be confirmed and that entire flight (which was
full) would hate me by 8am CST. My prayers were answered
(ONCE AGAIN!) and Carter was a ROCK STAR on the flight! He
kept all the people around us laughing and only had a brief
moment of screaming when I had to take him to the potty with
me.....which I am sure was humorous for anyone listening outside
the door! Carter earned his wings and spoke with the pilots when
we left the plane (we were the last ones off). The woman sitting in
front of us thanked me for teaching her some ways to keep her
little one calm for their trip in the near future. She then told me that
her husband had been recently diagnosed with liver cancer, but
that she thought we needed prayers more than they did.....*

*Once we arrived at St. Jude - our schedule didn't stop. It was
exhausting and emotional....we are staying at the Memphis
Grizzlie House since Carter is outpatient for the time being.*

Gotta run - Carter is in recovery!
((HUGS!!))
Sarah

I will never forget the day we arrived at St. Jude. The flight went so
much better than I expected. We arrived in baggage claim and there was
a driver to meet us. I walked through the doors of the hospital and a
nurse named Bridgette was there to show me around and get me to all of
the appointments. She never left my side that day and it made such a
difference. We met with doctors and nurses all day long. I remember
being upset that they hadn't left a time for Carter to nap. I was exhausted
and emotionally spent by the end of the day. I wondered how I ever
thought I could be in Memphis by myself with Carter.

Sarah Bucciero

11/11/11
This is hard. Really. Hard. I am trying to be strong, but it is harder than I ever imagined. I don't know what I need. I don't know where I am. I just don't know.....and that is hard for me. Really. Hard. The problem is that I just don't have a clue. My schedule changes by the moment. Appointments are made. Appointments are canceled. Plans are made. Plans are canceled. It just makes it hard to function.

I'm finally learning my way around St. Jude......it's not that big of a hospital, but it is a maze. St. Jude is actually a compound of sorts....lots of buildings surrounded by a gate. It is probably comparable to Fort Knox! We have a room at the Memphis Grizzlie House which is the short term housing. We will be moving to the Target House on Monday after Carter is discharged from his chemo.

I didn't realize how accustomed I had become to Levine.....the nurses, the staff, the kids movies loaded on the TV, the kitchen......even the carts to haul all of our stuff.....It's hard making the adjustment, but I know that I will get through it. I need to remember that I am at one of the top hospitals in the country and that overrides any of the petty stuff.....

The good news is that Carter has charmed his way into the hearts of just about every person that has met him here. He waves to strangers, blows kisses, and talks incessantly. He has mastered how to check vitals and knows how all the machines work. It shocks everyone that he has a brain tumor.....He even tells everyone that he is "perfect!" If he doesn't end up becoming a doctor when he's older.....he'll probably run for office.

Please keep praying ....I'm fairly certain that we're a million members strong at this point!

((HUGS!!))
Sarah

What I didn't write about was the fact that I had forgotten to take Carter's stroller. I had never travelled with a little one before and we didn't use it too often at home. It was an epic mistake. I ended up carrying him through a good bit of the airport. Thank goodness when we arrived at St. Jude they had little red wagons that he could ride in through the hallways and even over to the Grizzlie House where we were staying.

I somehow failed to pack enough diapers, too. What I didn't realize was that St. Jude would provide us Pull-Ups every time Carter was admitted, but we hadn't been admitted yet.

That night we boarded the St. Jude Shuttle for the first time. It was cold and dark, but I needed some basics for us in our room, including diapers. I remember telling the shuttle driver that I was new and that I hadn't done this before. He gave me a card and told me to call when I was ready to be picked up.

The Kroger near St. Jude is not in the best part of town. It was nighttime and I was scared to death. I would have been scared to death in the daytime, too. I quickly got the few things we needed and checked out. I remember that there was a University of Tennessee dental student (I could tell from his scrubs) checking out in front of me. He had TONS of ramen punctuated with a twenty-four pack of cheap beer. I remember wanting to say something to him, wanting to ask him to wait with me outside the grocery, but I didn't.

Instead, Carter and I stood outside, waiting and waiting for the shuttle. It felt like forever. I remember crying and Carter wiping my tears, telling me that everything would be fine and not to be sad. I remember telling him that I would be strong for him, that I would make sure that I protected him and kept him safe. I think my words were meant more for myself than for him. If I said the words aloud, I might actually believe them.

These first few days were a whirlwind of emotions. The hardest part of my day was usually then end of it, and I always seemed to meet with Trish, our line nurse. For whatever reason, Trish and I seemed to have an unspoken understanding of one another. Sometimes there are people you meet who just understand you from that initial moment, Trish was one of them.

Carter loved Trish. He loved her more than any nurse that he encountered at St. Jude. She made him laugh and she tolerated my tears, and I think that Carter had an understanding that this made her special. I could let my guard down with Trish and cry. I would be strong all day, but when we met with Trish to do Carter's line changing, I would cry. I will never forget her asking me why I cried, she thought that I was upset with her and that was the furthest thing from the truth. I cried because I felt comfortable with her, because she understood me.

I will never forget the afternoon when Trish was helping me change Carter's line dressing and Carter passed gas. She immediately giggled and said, "Did you sit on a duck?!" Carter thought this was the most hilarious accusation and started belly laughing hysterically. This made me laugh hysterically through my tears. And that made Trish laugh hysterically. It became a running joke with us any time that Carter "sat on ducks" throughout his journey and always included giggles.

11/12/11
Carter started chemo yesterday at about 3pm and it will go until about 3pm today......YOUR PRAYERS ARE WORKING! GOD IS AT WORK! I can feel Him all around me and I know that God is working because Carter has responded well to the chemo (as of this point). Just a few messy diapers and a temper tantrum from time to time (but hey - he's a two year old!).........

Thank you for your continued love, prayers, and support. I need them now more than ever. I have no doubt that Carter will win this battle. He is a special little boy and has won over the hearts of so many with his smile, his laughter, and his goofy little self!

((HUGS!!)) to you all for being my prayer warriors and praying for us .....I know that God hears us. There's no such thing as a busy signal to heaven!

Heavenly Father - thank you for blessing me with such wonderful friends....those that I know personally and those that I only know as a name. Someday we're going to have a MASSIVE party for Carter to celebrate his health and for him to meet all of his prayer warriors.......might need to rent a convention center at this point! ((HUGS!!))

11/12/11
CLEMSON WON!!!!! WOO HOO!!!!! Thank you Tigers for giving us HOPE! TIGERS WIN - CARTER WINS!

((HUGS!!))

11/13/11
Just a quick update tonight.....it's past my bedtime and this momma needs to get some sleep!

I feel guilty just leaving Carter to go get a meal. I usually try and go when he is napping or when there is a volunteer here (or nurse) to play with him in the toy room or go on adventure through the halls (there are murals on every wall, and LOTS of things to discover).

This is a special place and you can feel God's presence through the halls and amongst the staff........I pray that others can feel it, too.

Carter is doing well. The first round of chemo is over and as long as his ph levels are good tomorrow, we'll go "home" to our new housing in the Target House. The side effects have been minimal - please keep praying that this continues to be the case......he is definitely grumpy and not eating as well, but these are issues that can be dealt with easily!

I am forever thankful to my friends in Memphis and to all of those who have reached out to me here. Yesterday, the underwriter for our new home in Greenwood, SC came by with gifts and goodies for us. I had never spoken with her, but she heard our story from our mortgage lender and wanted to help. Today, Stacy, my college friend, came by and spent time with us and brought goodies, too! I am blessed with fabulous friends - both those that I've met and haven't met. It touches me every time I hear from someone I have never met. It is humbling to know that total strangers are praying for your child and are willing to help in any way they can..... You all are my angels......

Just to elaborate on the aforementioned thought.......I don't think that I mentioned it here, but we bought a house in Greenwood, SC. It was the first house that I saw and the best price and least amount of work. Thank you God for helping me find it. Paul has only seen the inside of the house from a Skype that I did from my phone......thank you Lord for technology! We will be moving there just ten days before Christmas......or actually - Paul and Mason will be moving there just ten days before Christmas.......

Heavenly Father - thank you for the many blessings of this life, for the friends known and unknown, for the angels that surround me both near and far. Please continue to heal my little boy and shrink the tumor that harms him. Amen.

((HUGS!!))

11/15/11
Carter is napping, so I thought I'd write.

I'm having a hard time dealing with being angry right now. It's not about Carter being sick, it's more of the petty stuff. For instance - Target House wants residents to be sanitary, but they don't provide cleaning products.....and the bus to Kroger isn't until Wednesday.....and we moved in on Monday......so how in the world am I supposed to keep this place clean????

Please don't misunderstand - I am forever thankful for Carter's wonderful care here at St. Jude......but there are a lot of logistical nightmares for single mommies who don't have a car. Mine should arrive the week of Thanksgiving.

Today is Mason's fourth birthday. It is killing me that I'm not with him. I'm angry that I can't be there - I constantly question whether it was the right decision to come to St. Jude - especially when things seem to go wrong (which seems to be a lot). I'm praying that my Mason doesn't feel like his mommy abandoned him. I don't want him to feel alone.

Many of you have asked about Carter's treatment. He is on a protocol called SJYC07 (St. Jude Young Child 2007). He had a high dose of Methotrexate (24 hours worth) on Day 1. He will have a dose of Vincristine on Days 8 and 15. On Day 8 he will also have a dose of Cisplatin. On Day 9 he will be given Cyclophosphamide. Not fun for any child......and especially not fun for a two year old.

I need to mention that Carter has a new girlfriend. He's going after the "older" ladies now.......little man is obsessed with his nurse Robin who helped him through the first two days of our stay. Today we went up to the inpatient floor just so he could say hello and give her some love. It is the sweetest.thing.ever. I must add that I think that several of the other nurses are jealous.....

I need to run and attempt to get some laundry run (thank goodness I happened to have a travel size of detergent because otherwise I wouldn't have clean clothes!)........nap time is the only time that I can get anything done anymore!

Heavenly Father - Please help me to be patient and to see the good around me versus letting the petty stuff irritate me. Help me learn to ask for help when I need it.....and allow the angels around me to do their work (because they are magnificent in so many ways!). Father God, I lift my heart up unto you.......and I feel your warm embrace in return. Amen

((HUGS!!))
Sarah

11/15/11
To my son Carter,

You are an inspiration to us all. From the beginning you have been a fighter. Your spirit and drive to learn, be competitive and your will to succeed are unmatched. Despite the challenges, you continue to make us laugh and love you even more. I think of you often each day as I look at my Prayers for Carter bracelet which I proudly wear everyday. I cherish our conversations and will forever remember the day we bring you home as WINNING IS THE ONLY OPTION! I can't say thank you enough to all the people praying for us and the endless support from friends, family, and those we have yet to meet.
ALL MY LOVE,

Daddy

11/16/11
I went to bed last night realizing how blessed I am.......it is an amazing feeling and the darkness that had overwhelmed me since arriving here was lifted. God was just showing me everything that I needed to understand the journey we're taking.......and with His guidance, we'll make it to the finish line! WINNING IS THE ONLY OPTION!

Have you ever stopped to see the angels around you? It is amazing to see them at work.......I encourage you to look for them - it is so easy to get wrapped up in the business of life and fail to see angels.......They are here doing God's work - whether it is something little or something big........but they are constantly working - and I'm thankful for each and every one of them. I'm convinced that God has surrounded me with angels!

I mentioned last night on Carter's FB page (Prayers for Carter) that Carter has a new buddy name Chase. Not only is Chase from Prosperity, SC, but he's a Clemson Tiger, too! Chase is battling his second round of cancer and needs our prayers. Chase really is a great young man and his mom has already taught me so much.

I need to run and get a few things done before Carter wakes up.

((HUGS!!))

11/16/11
I meant to include this quote in the journal entry that I just wrote.....it was included in an email that my mom sent me......and it is so very, very true. ((HUGS!!))

"May today there be peace within. May you trust that you are exactly where you are meant to be. May you not forget the infinite possibilities that are born of faith in yourself and others. May you use the gifts that you have received, and pass on the love that has been given to you. May you be content with yourself just the way you are. Let this knowledge settle into your bones, and allow your soul the freedom to sing, dance, praise and love, it is there for each and every one of us."

11/18/11
Sorry that I haven't updated. I hope that tomorrow things will be less stressful. I am totally overwhelmed and totally exhausted. I'm headed to bed.....please pray that tomorrow will be a quiet day for us.

((HUGS!!))

11/19/11
The past few days have been a whirlwind......

Thursday was supposed to be a slow day and it turned out to be insane. Thursday was the annual gingerbread-decorating event here at St. Jude. While we waited in line, Rick Shadyac, the CEO of St. Jude/ALSAC, walked through the hallway where we were lined up and started saying hello to everyone and shaking hands. I'm fairly certain that many of the people were clueless about Rick's position with St. Jude. In fact, the woman next to me asked him about the role he played at the hospital. She had no idea that he was the CEO! Carter was sitting in a red wagon (transport of choice in the hospital) and Rick bent down to say hello to him. I made mention to Carter that he needed to thank "this nice man" for helping bring him to St. Jude. Rick looked at me and said, "Is this THE Carter?" It was priceless to me. He immediately shook my hand and we had a quick chat in the midst of the hallway and he promised to follow-up with me. Rick Shadyac is an amazing man. I feel blessed to have met him, but even more blessed to know that he has taken the time to contact me and remember Carter.

Carter later created a "lollipop" to put outside the gingerbread house that decorates the hallway outside of the cafeteria. All of the participants received a green chefs hat and coat. I will try and add the pictures later. He looked so sweet and did a great job putting the candy decorations on the lollipop.

After several appointments we learned that we would be admitted to the hospital for chemo on Thursday night instead of Friday morning. This would have been fine, but there was a major disconnect in the communication line as to when we were to be admitted. Needless to say, Carter and I rode the bus SEVERAL times on Thursday night and were finally admitted about 9pm. It was 11pm before we got to bed and a long night. It is very difficult being at the mercy of the bus system with a two year old......

On Friday, Carter was full throttle and charming his way through the hallways. Beth, his nurse, is his new girlfriend. The second dose of chemo was given (Cysplatin) and it is the nasty stuff. This is what will make his counts fall, lose his hair, make him sick, etc. I'm praying that God will envelope Carter in his loving embrace and shield my sweet boy from as many of these side effects as possible. The nurses and doctors say that the worse of these side effects will hit either Thursday or Friday, just in time for Thanksgiving. Please pray for my little boy.....

Carter also won the heart of Lauren Alaina from American Idol (third runner-up) yesterday. She's a beautiful young lady and she took some amazing pictures with Carter yesterday. OH - and the photographer's name is Peter (Carter knows it by heart). Peter told me that I'll be able to get the pictures in a few weeks. At this rate, Carter is going to become a poster child for St. Jude. He loves the camera, attention, and charms everyone around him!

Today was another crazy day. It's hard just trying to keep up with Carter these days. He has impressed everyone with his vocabulary (stethoscope, blood pressure machine, temperature, and seriously) and his ability to remember most everyone's name.......and if he doesn't know your name - he isn't shy about asking it! Carter woke up with dry heaves this morning. This afternoon he woke up vomiting and did so several times sporadically until he went to bed. The vomiting scares me. It's the first time he has vomited since being diagnosed and it brings back the memories of Sept./Oct. when he vomited for eleven out of twelve days. Vomiting will never be "just" vomiting again. Tonight Carter sleeps peacefully as a cocktail of Benadryl, Zofran, and Ativan seeps through his body to fend off the poison that will heal him.

I am forever thankful for my sisters from college here in Memphis. They have brought me groceries, food, presents for Carter, and reminded me that I belong to the best Old Girl Network ever! One sweet classmate even contacted an Episcopal church here in Memphis that isn't far from St. Jude and put me in touch with the assistant rector. It's hard to feel alone when you've got college sisters helping you!

Today was also the St. Jude Give Thanks Walk. Carter had at least two teams walking for him (that I know of) and one was built just three days before the walk. One of the teams walked in Charlotte and the other team walked in Columbia, SC. Together they raised approx. $1000 for St. Jude in Carter's honor. Next year, Carter will be walking (or riding in the stroller!) next to me. He will be a healthy little boy just finishing up his oral chemo and still charming everyone around him.

Tonight I was reminded that I am never alone. Christ is standing right beside me on this journey. I needed to be reminded of that tonight when Carter got so sick. It is hard to have a sick child, but it is even more difficult to do it when you're far from home and far from your family.

Tonight is just the first part of a rough journey.....but with God by my side, I will make it. If Carter can fight, so can I! WINNING IS THE ONLY OPTION!!!

((HUGS!))

11/20/11
Looks like we'll be heading back to Target House later today. Carter's vomiting subsided - thank you for the prayers! Prayer is even better than medicine!

I have to admit, it scares me to head back to the Target House. This is when Carter's counts will drop, his hair will fall out, and when the vomiting will occur. My prayer is that God will make me strong.

As part of my mommy training here I am learning how to change Carter's port dressing and flush his lumens. I will also have to learn how to give him shots of medicine to help boost his counts. I'm not looking forward to these things. I am not a nurse and I never wanted to be a nurse. In fact, I am incredibly grateful for all of the amazing nurses here......they do a job that I could never, ever do.

I now belong to an elite club of mommies who have children with brain tumors......and I belong to an even more exclusive club of mommies who have children at St. Jude. It's not a membership that I ever sought out - but I'm thankful that I have other mommies to help guide me through this process.

More later - Carter is awake!

((HUGS!!))

11/20/11
Unfortunately I didn't get to finish my thoughts earlier and now it's past my bedtime......

I mentioned the elite club to which I now belong......another member is a friend that I met by email at the beginning of this journey by the name of Sally. She has a son who had a brain tumor that was removed, but unfortunately it has returned. Please add her son Taylor to your prayer lists. Sally is an incredible support for me and I am blessed that she has shared her experience. The other day she sent me this piece and it has resonated in my soul.......I want to share it with you all, too.

Be at Peace.
Do not fear the changes of life, rather look to them with full hope as they arise.

God, whose very own you are, will deliver you from out of them.

He has kept you hitherto, and He will lead you safely through all things; and when you cannot stand it, God will bury you in His arms.

Do not be afraid of what may happen tomorrow; the same everlasting

Father who cares for you today will take care of you then and everyday.

He will either shield you from suffering, or will give you unfailing strength to bear it.

Be at Peace...and put aside all anxious thoughts and imaginations.

-St. Francis de Sales

St. Francis de Sales managed to beautifully state the very thoughts of my heart. I am not afraid. I am at peace. I have put all anxious thoughts and imaginations aside. I know that God will heal my son. I know it with every breath I take and with every prayer that I whisper. I am not worried about tomorrow, I know that God will hold me in His embrace and carry me through many tomorrows. He is giving me the strength to bear the suffering of sweet Carter. I know this because I know the Lord. Believe and it shall be done.

WINNING IS THE ONLY OPTION!! If Carter can do this.....then so can I.....

((HUGS!!))

Thanksgiving arrived and the idea of gratitude took on a new meaning. I was so thankful to have Paul and Mason with me and that they brought my car to Memphis. I was so thankful for the Cracker Barrel Thanksgiving dinner that we ate in the comfort of our Target House apartment. I was so thankful for every moment of the day.

Thanksgiving was a blur. I remember having to go to the hospital for appointments in the afternoon and spending time in the medicine room. Carter broke the g-shot needle twice and so the medicine was put into an IV and administered that way instead.

What I remember most is that we were together as a family and it felt so good to have both of my boys with me, so I could love on them together.

11/24/11
Heavenly Father - Thank you for showing me what to be thankful for on this glorious day. Thank you for the family that surrounds me, the giggle from Carter's belly, and the fabulous care that Carter is receiving. Amen.

I have always been thankful for the blessings in my life. But this year, I am especially thankful. God has opened my eyes and shown me so many other blessings.

I am thankful for the nurses, doctors, and support staff at St. Jude - they are amazing in so many ways. They are not only caregivers at this point, but family.

I am thankful for cold showers and bus rides, because they remind me that I am blessed enough to have a car to drive and warm water running through the pipes in my home.

I am thankful for gray hair, because it means that I might look wise to someone.....even if I'm not.

I am thankful for the many people who have donated to Carter's fund, known and unknown and the thousands of Carter bracelets that have been sold. I am especially thankful for those who wear the bracelets and pray for my little guy.

I am thankful for all of the fundraisers that are being done to help raise money for Carter's medical bills and expenses. For people coming forth and generously offering to donate commissions and for the creative ways that they are generating money for the fund.

I am thankful for being overweight - because it means that I have enough to eat and that I am blessed with food on my table.

I am thankful for the chemo that runs through Carter's body and makes him grumpy and vomit - because it means that it's fighting Carter's tumor.

I am thankful for friends who send cards, packages, make meals, text, send emails, and read this site.....because it means that we are loved. They are the fairy godmothers and godfathers in our lives and we are eternally grateful for them.

And most importantly, I am thankful for Carter - whose very presence on this earth is a gift from God. I am thankful for every giggle that he makes, every tear that he cries, and every kiss and hug that he gives.......

I am thankful for this journey that I am taking.......whether I want to take it or not, it is a meaningful and amazing journey which I will be able to share with the world once I am finished.

I am thankful that God chose me as Carter's mommy and that He feels that I am capable to deal with the task of getting Carter well again. I truly believe that this didn't happen to me, but that I was chosen.

Dear friends, gather close with your family today and tell them how much you love them. Be thankful for all of the potholes in the road on your journey in life. It's the potholes that help us appreciate the smooth road when it's before us.
Most importantly. Give. Thanks.

((HUGS!!))
S.

11/26/11
Dear Coach -

Carter had a blood transfusion, chemo injection, and g-shot today. ....and did it with a smile on his face. He is a winner! Nothing would make him (and us!) happier if the team would beat the socks off of USC. WINNING IS THE ONLY OPTION!!!!

((HUGS!!))
Sarah
p.s. I wore make-up just for the team today......

11/26/11
Paul, Mason, Grammie, and Pop-Pop just left to drive back to NC. I'm sad.....really sad. Not only are they leaving me, but they will be leaving Locust soon for Greenwood, SC. I remember driving away from the house and praying that it wouldn't be the last time that I saw it. Unfortunately, that will be the case.

I have a Love/Hate relationship with Locust. It isn't anything that I haven't been honest with people about......I'm a city girl and from the start it was hard for me to adjust. Locust was my Deliverance for the majority of the five years that we lived there. This was in part because my life was awful while I was there for a variety of reasons which I won't elaborate on....but I had friends who refused to talk to me because I thought this way - but this was my reality for a while......

That being said, my two babies were born in the house where we live now. It is where I imagined Carter being born on the side of the road on our way to Pineville CMC ......and as it was I was 6cm and hadn't had a contraction when we arrived to be "induced" (which was just breaking my water!).

It is where I taught a few and was remembered by many (jury is still out as to whether this was a good thing!)

It's where I can hear gun shots from my bedroom during deer hunting season and where the sound of Mr. Chad's truck at all hours of the morning is comforting.

It's where my boys can ride their miniature truck through the neighborhood streets and race with the Gator and police car......

It's where I can work at Stanly Community College and meet just about every police officer.

It's where Charlie of Charlie's Hardware knows my name and knows when my daddy comes to town that he spends his money there vs. in Northern VA.

It's where people invite you to their churches when they first meet you.....

It's where I can stand in front of the Locust Zoning and Planning Board and appeal the need for sidewalks in a community that doesn't really need them.

It's where Kelly Pickler frequented....and yes, she was a waitress at the Sonic fifteen minutes away.

It is where the town manager, the mayor, and the head of city works will meet with a neighborhood on a Saturday afternoon to address the needs of a neighborhood.......and give you a hug at the end of it.

It's where you can walk into the ABC store and feel like you're best friends with the employees and manager.

It's where your dentist is your neighbor and your little boy doesn't have a problem going to his first "REAL" appointment because he knows Mr. Jason.

It's where I can go to Wal-Mart and see people - even if I am trying to be incognito.

It's where neighbors put blue bows on every mailbox in a neighborhood and adopt your son as their own.

It's where dinner is delivered without question for two months. And every night - it is delicious!

It is where your children are loved at Locust Child Development Center - and you can't imagine anyone else taking care of them. And where the other families are part of your family.

It is where the Tiger Lily creates a float for your son in the local Christmas parade at the last minute and where they sell my favorite Tyler Candle.

It is where you can walk into the Bank of Stanly and cry with the tellers because they understand how humbled you are by the deposit slips.

It is where the receptionists at the Barker Vet and Diamond Electronics talk to you because they want to hear about Carter's story......

It is where you meet best friends because they own local stores.

It is where the sweet people at Dunn Rite Cleaners know your name and your children's names.

It is where there are only a few places open for lunch on Monday.

It is where the Mexican restaurant looks like "Dora's House."

It is where the staff at Bojangles is family.

It is where the Fresh House will make time to bag 10 more bags of fruit cobbler for you on a Sunday afternoon because you need them on short notice.

It is where you can go to the local pawn shop and you are treated like a princess.

It is where people pray for you, whether they know you or not.

Locust is "A City with a Soul" and I didn't see that until Carter was in the hospital......now I get it.

I won't have the chance to say "good-bye" to our home before we move in a few short weeks to Greenwood.....but that doesn't mean I won't be back.....and it doesn't mean that I won't always remember the unconditional love from the people of Locust. There is no greater gift.

Carter had a blood transfusion, a chemo treatment, and a G-shot today......and he managed to come out of it like a rock star.......and in my heart I know that it was from all of the prayers that are going up for him.......thank you friends. Thank you.

((HUGS!!))
S.

11/27/11
Late last night Carter spiked a fever and we returned to the hospital. When the ANC count is 0 it means that he has no immunity to infection - and because he had a fever, it meant that there was some sort of infection beginning. We rushed to the hospital about 2:30am and were admitted promptly. The fever is gone as of now but Carter will remain in the hospital until he has gone 48 hours without fever and his ANC counts have started to increase (anything above 1000 is good!).

Please pray that the fever doesn't spike again and that we're able to return to Target House soon.

((HUGS!!))

This was what the doctors and nurses warned me about, the fevers. I was ignorant to think that they wouldn't happen to us, that Carter would somehow be able to avoid them. I was wrong.

When we got to the Medicine Room at St. Jude, the fellow from E Clinic was waiting for us. Dr. Ross was a favorite of ours. He asked me how I knew that something was wrong and I explained that we had gone to bed normally and that Carter started being agitated in his sleep. At first I tried to avoid heading into the hospital, thinking that he had too much to eat or that he had a bad dream. It was unavoidable. I had to take Carter in once his fever hit 101. It was inevitable.

I had another cancer mom warn me about having a packed bag by the door, just in case. Fortunately, I had listened to her and our bag was packed and ready to go. Not having to pack in the middle of the night was a blessing.

11/27/11
Today is Carter's 1/2 birthday......he is officially 2.5....It's hard to imagine that this little guy is only 2.5 - hasn't he been in my life forever? Happy 1/2 birthday little man! Six months from now we'll

be in Greenwood doing oral chemo ......and you'll be three years old!

Love you Baby Bear.......

11/28/11
Carter had another blood transfusion today. His ANC is still zero and his hemoglobin dropped below 8 again.......and it was obvious that Carter didn't feel well. He vomited first thing in the morning and then was just grumpy.....He was able to take a three hour nap this afternoon and woke up a different child.

Today was a big day because Carter wore his mask for the first time and roamed the halls. Patients with an ANC of zero may not leave their rooms without a mask.....we've spent a lot of time in our room since we arrived early Sunday morning because Carter refused to wear one. Just imagine trying to sit in a small room with an active two year old.......Wearing the mask is a feat worth celebrating!

My prayer is that this means his ANC is rising and that we will be able to return to Target House. I am going to attempt to decorate a little bit for Christmas in the coming days and see if I can make the place festive. The room is bare because we cannot have rugs or drapes (fabric holds germs) .....and the pictures on the wall are minimal. I found a beautiful Christmas train at the St. Jude gift shop which I intend to purchase this week........it will be a special reminder in the years to come of our stay at St. Jude during Christmas.

I'm not sure if I have mentioned this before, but Carter will be coming to St. Jude for the remainder of his life. He will be tracked to help other children and the researchers here determine a myriad of information. So when I refer to St. Jude as family, I mean it. We will be forever a part of the family here in Memphis.

I know that Carter has a purpose on this earth and I believe it is, in part, to help the doctors and researchers here at St. Jude. I know that God will heal Carter and we will celebrate the miracle of his life. I believe that we were led here for a purpose - much more so than "just" Carter's healing. God is planning something bigger - I don't know what it is, but I feel it every day in so many incredible ways. God is in control. He is the ultimate healer.

Sarah Bucciero

((HUGS!!))

11/30/11
phew! We're back at Target House! Carter's counts continue to rise and I can tell that he's feeling better! I will write more tonight once he goes to sleep - right now I'm just trying to get caught up on everything!

((HUGS!!))

11/30/11
If you'd asked me four months ago where I'd be right now.....I'd tell you Walt Disney World. You see, I had wanted to take the boys last spring.....but for a variety of reasons, we chose not to take them.....I will never live my life putting off anything ever again. Carter and I spent almost the entire week in the hospital. We should have left with Paul and Mason on Saturday for a voyage to WDW....instead, we checked into St. Jude with a fever.......when you are undergoing chemo....a fever isn't "just" a fever.....it's a life-threatening illness that needs to battled with intensive antibiotics.

Paul and Mason are in Greenwood and Locust. We have tentatively rescheduled our WDW trip for January.....and I'm praying that it will take place. When you plan a vacation six months out, you never think that a brain tumor would side track your voyage......but in this case, it did.

Someone in the past few weeks told me that St. Jude was a magical place during Christmas and we're slowly seeing the transformation. Target House became a festival of Christmas lights while we were gone a few short days. Christmas trees are showing up in unlikely places around St. Jude.

Many of you may see the Christmas commercials for St. Jude on TV. Please know that these children are real and that we've met many of them already. A very special little girl named "Hope" stars in one of these specials - Carter loves her dearly. Please keep her in your prayers. She will be able to go home for Christmas!

And as we enter the season of Christmas - please think of those who do without.....for whatever reason. I truly believe that my journey to Boston shortly after college graduation was an education in serving those without. The Junior League provided me an opportunity to serve a women's day shelter on Newberry St. that I remember fondly for so many reasons.

One of those reasons includes buying dinner for a man asking for money. I told him that I didn't believe in giving him money - but that I believed in filling his belly. In the pitch cold of Boston we trekked to a local restaurant and I told him to order whatever he wished - told him to order extra to take home if he wanted. When the food arrived and he was served, I marveled in the hunger that embraced his body. He inhaled soup, salad, and entree......and ordered more to take with him. The meal cost me just a few dollars.....but the experience was priceless. The man told me that I was an angel that night......and I laughed at his proposal. I was just doing what God would have wanted me to do.....I embraced someone without and gave him something worthwhile.

I also remember visiting Chicago during the Christmas season when I was still in elementary school. I think that I was in either third or fourth grade because I remember the dress coat that I wore. I had never seen the homeless, the needy, the street savvy. There was a man begging for money and I gave him a dime that was in my pocket as we walked by.......I don't know if that dime made a difference, but I still think of the experience and hope that it did.

Please know that I am not a martyr. I have plenty of flaws and those who know me closely, know them well. My prayer is that if everyone were to open their eyes to those in need around them that no one would actually be in need. Perhaps I am naive in my train of thought - but it might help someone, somewhere.

Heavenly Father - as we enter this holiday season, please help us see those in need and those without....please help us open our hearts and minds to give and support one another .....both monetary and not.....Father God, help those who have forgotten the true spirit of Christmas find it once again and find You in their hearts. In Your Name, I pray.

((HUGS!!))
S.

Sarah Bucciero

12/1/11
Today has been a tough day. Poor little Carter has been downright mean and awful.....something that I've rarely seen before. I keep telling myself that it's the chemo, but it doesn't help. Carter is a triple threat right now - he's 2.5, undergoing chemo, and exhausted from being in the hospital. I'm praying that he'll at least get caught up on the sleep and that factor can be eliminated. Carter has a little buddy named Luca here who is diagnosed with liver cancer. Luca has completed his chemo and has a scan on Tuesday to see if the cancer is gone. Please say a prayer for him - I know that it would be the best gift ever for them to go home for the holiday season.

Thank you to each of you who have left guestbook messages here. They are a bright spot in my day. I hope to print them out at the end of this journey and put them in a book for Carter to read someday. I know that it will eventually help him understand the journey we've taken.

I'm exhausted......sleeping in the hospital did absolutely nothing for me and I'm trying to keep up with everything. I will write more later when my brain can function clearly once again.

((HUGS!!))

What I didn't write was that Carter had bit me so hard that I screamed and scared the nurses. The bite drew blood. It wasn't because he wanted to bite me, it was because the chemo made him so angry and so mean. As a two year old, he didn't know how to deal with it. Fortunately, that was the only time that he ever bit me. Our wonderful friend, Ashley, from Child Life gave Carter a doll that he could hit and bite when he got angry. It only happened once or twice again, but it saved me from being bitten!

12/1/11
Tonight the Eric Trump Foundation held a dinner for the residents of Target House. I didn't realize that Eric was the son of Donald Trump until after the dinner. He was extremely personable and very sweet to Carter. His foundation will announce a $1 million dollar donation to St. Jude tomorrow....almost enough to run St. Jude for one day!

I've decided that there needs to be a reality show called "The Real Mommies of St. Jude".......I think that it would be much better than The Jersey Shore or The Real Housewives......seriously - you want drama, we got drama.........not the back-stabbing kind, but the heart wrenching, blood curdling, make-you-wanna-cry drama.........and no, I have no desire to star in it......I was a thespian in high school, but that's "pretending" to be someone else.....this is having to live it.

I noticed this afternoon that some of Carter's hair is starting to fall out. I know that means that the chemo is working, but I'm not ready for my little guy to lose his beautiful blond locks. Everyone loves his hair.....he looks like a little Einstein the way it sticks straight up. I refuse to cut it because I know that it won't ever be the same. I have been told that his hair will most likely change color and possibly become curlier.......so my prayer is that his hair will turn either strawberry blond or red and be curly.

Heavenly Father - please make me strong to deal with Carter's grumpiness and anger. Help me be strong to get him through this ordeal. Grant me peace in knowing that the chemo must be working if my little guy is feeling so awful. And please tell Satan that he better hide - he doesn't want to mess with a St. Jude Momma! In your name, I pray ~S.

((HUGS!!))

12/3/11
It is Saturday, so we must be in the hospital again! We have spent every weekend in the hospital since arriving at St. Jude. It almost has become something to joke about ......what are you doing this weekend? Umm.....we'll be in-patient at St. Jude.....either getting chemo or fighting a fever.....take your pick! Certainly nothing glamorous or jet-setting about hospital food and the lack of sleep on the weekend .....but certainly time well-spent getting my little boy well!

The good news is that Carter's ANC counts were 4000 yesterday (Friday) which allowed him to be scheduled for his second round of chemo. Yes, I know that it isn't "Day 1" again......but we're starting this next round of chemo early in hopes that Carter will be healthy for Christmas while Paul, Mason, and my parents are here in Memphis. Besides, the sooner we finish the chemo - the sooner we get to go home (which won't be until spring!).

So - today is "Day 1" again......and we'll be in the hospital probably until Tuesday. This is the big dose of chemo which needs to clear his system before we can head back to Target House. This month we'll receive chemo on December 3, 11, and 18 (or at least that's what my feeble mind thinks at the moment).

I keep trying to write and I keep deleting my sentences - this tells me that I am exhausted and that I need to give my brain a mental break.......so I'll write more later.

((HUGS!!))

12/3/11
Dear Coach -

Praying for the Tigers tonight! I'm not wearing any make-up either.....when I wear it, y'all don't do so well! Don't want to jinx you tonight!

WINNING IS THE ONLY OPTION!!!

((HUGS!!))
S.

12/3/11
It's gotta be the make-up......I look awful without it, but if it keeps our Tigers winning.....might need to make the sacrifice!!!

Thank you Tigers for giving us HOPE! WINNING IS THE ONLY OPTION!!! Congratulations on the ACC Championship!
I am smelling ORANGES!!!

((HUGS!!))

12/4/11
Carter is having a much better day today.....which means that Mommy is having a much better day today.

Yesterday Carter was just exhausted. He had a nurse who insisted that we change his diaper in the middle of the night and I kept telling her that he was sleeping and that I didn't want him changed (he wasn't on chemo at the time and so it was unnecessary). She finally wore me down at 6am and I told her that I would do it.....well, Carter woke up screaming bloody murder and the morning went downhill from there. I was hit, kicked, and bit to the point of bruising. Let me note that this was not one of the regular nurses that we see......I had never seen this nurse before.

I was so thankful to see the weekend nurses arrive at 7am for the day shift. They are fabulous and treat Carter so well (as do the weekday nurses!).

Carter started his chemo and got a dose of Benadryl which allowed him to nap for five hours straight! I was so excited that he got good sleep. It makes such a difference (for both of us!). Carter woke up happy, had dinner, played a little, and promptly went back to sleep for another twelve hours! My little guy was exhausted!

Last night, while Carter was sleeping, I was able to watch a little of the Clemson/VA Tech game. There is something about HOPE that pulls you in and envelopes you.....whether it is a football game, a sick child, or a special wish......The Clemson Tigers have given us HOPE since the beginning of the season - which was almost simultaneous with Carter's illness. For the first time in 20 years they have earned an ACC Championship title.........and in my mind, they did it for Carter! Thank you Tigers!

This journey has been hard, but it is made easier by the kindness of loved ones, friends, family, and complete strangers. I have had so many complete strangers extend such beautiful gifts of love and support to us. In my mind, they are no longer strangers - but friends whom we just have never met. We are receiving all sorts of magical letters, presents, and love from strangers from afar. I am eternally grateful for everything that everyone has done for us......from both people we know and from the people we don't know. It is the most amazing feeling to have packages arrive unexpectedly, to have people say "we want to do this for you", and to know that your little boy is loved by thousands of prayer warriors.

I hope you all don't mind my babbling here sometimes.....this is a good place for me to put down my thoughts and feelings as I go through this journey. I have so many things that I want to say and I'm still trying to sort out how to say them. As an English teacher, I am hesitant to write publicly without editing first......but I keep reminding myself that when I had my students write their journals every night, I preached, "it's not what you write, just write something." It's the idea that thoughts are being generated and written down.......not necessary that they are profound or perfectly written.

ACK! Carter's awake....gotta run!

12/5/11
I mentioned that Carter's hair was starting to fall out last Thursday.....I'm letting it fall out naturally instead of brushing it out or pulling clumps out. Carter said to me the other day, "My hair hurts, it's falling out." He hadn't even seen the hair on his pillow that was left behind. This morning he said to me, "I need a haircut." It's hard to see Carter has a 2.5 year old anymore. I tend to see him as this wise old man in the body of a little boy.

Carter's hair thins out day by day and reminds me that the chemo is working. I haven't cried about it falling out, but it saddens me. Of course, Carter didn't have a whole lot of hair until he was two - so it's more that it saddens me that he's going to have to start all over again! My friend and fellow St. Jude Momma, Rachel, mentioned in a post that she thought of the hair falling out much like that of a phoenix. This analogy makes so much sense to me. Carter will be a healthy little boy after the chemo has finished. God will make certain of it.

Many of you may have read in earlier posts about the sale of our home and our move to Greenwood, SC. To say that the move has been convoluted is an understatement. Paul closed on the house last Friday (I signed POA papers and overnighted them) and the moving company will arrive on Wednesday to pack and load the truck in Locust. Paul will close on the house on Friday and then (I think) the moving company will arrive on Monday (this was the plan last time I heard). Please say a prayer that everything goes smoothly!

I worry about our older son, Mason. This journey has not been easy on him. His mommy and brother are gone. He's leaving his friends, school, and neighborhood. We've told him that he's going on an adventure (cue the Dora music!) and that everything will be fine. My prayer is that he is as resilient as his little brother.....

Carter is awake - gotta run!

12/5/11
Tonight, as I put Carter to bed, it dawned on me that Carter looks much like he did as an infant - no hair and a sweet little angel.

Many of you may not know, but Carter was born really quickly. I was to be induced on his due date (a bed finally opened at CMC-Pineville). Paul and I arrived at 3:05pm and Carter was born at 7:44pm (and yes, he was 9 pounds 4oz). When the doctor checked me upon my arrival, I was 6cm and 100% effaced and hadn't had a single contraction. Needless to say, inducing meant simply breaking my water. I think that I only pushed twice......and they actually had me NOT push through a contraction so that the doctor and nurses could sprint down the hallway. Carter was born so quickly that the umbilical cord was wrapped around his neck and he was literally the color purple. Paul, who is color blind, even commented later that he knew that Carter was purple. Carter's heart was beating, but he wasn't breathing. Everyone was talking to Carter and urging him to fight - but I was praying silently. I remember praying to God not to take Carter away from me - that I would do anything to keep him.

Finally someone told me that I needed to talk to Carter, too - and I remember barely choking some words out....something to the extent of "C'mon little guy, you can do it - fight!" Slowly, with the help and encouragement of the nurses, doctor, and Paul and me, Carter started breathing. I remember thanking God for hearing my prayer and for the gift of Carter.

Carter is a fighter and I am still whispering, "C'mon Carter - you can do it - fight!" And I'm still praying to God - confirming that I will do anything to keep my Carter. This time, I have heard God whisper back that Carter will make it and that Carter will win this battle once again.

It's a pretty amazing feeling when you hear God whisper back to you. It takes away all doubt. It takes away all fear. It takes away all of the pain and sorrow. Sometimes I think that God whispers back and we don't always hear Him. I have vowed to listen more closely to hear those whispers. God will heal Carter - of this, I am certain.

Heavenly Father - You alone know our hearts and know our prayers, secrets, and desires. You alone know our fears, our joys, and our battles. Your love is precious and inspires us to rejoice in the gift of your son, Jesus Christ. Thank you Father God for being the little voice in our head that whispers back and answers our prayers when we need to hear them most. In Your name, I pray - Amen.

((HUGS!!))

12/6/11
The good news is that we're back at Target House. The bad news is that we're back at Target House with a toddler who has to have IV fluids. This means that Carter has a sack with a bag of IV fluids in it. Whoever had the bright idea that it was smart for a 2.5 year old little boy to be checked out of the hospital with fluids obviously hasn't met Carter! I'm sure that it's wonderful for most patients, don't get me wrong......but my little guy wants to play with the pump, the fluids, etc. etc. He wants to run and play and now has essentially a leash between himself and the carrier of the fluids (read me).

I'm praying for a good night's rest. I am grumpy and we have to be back at the hospital at 8:30am for more appointments until noon tomorrow. The fun.never.stops.

((HUGS!!))

12/7/11
It has been a terrible, no good, horrible kind of day.

It started out by snowing. It wasn't supposed to snow. We got about three inches. I don't have gloves, a hat, or a warm coat. To top it off, I don't have a snow duster to get the snow off of the car. I improvised the best that I could.....

Carter was in an awful mood. I should know by now that when this happens it means that Carter is going to vomit. It wasn't until Carter vomited all over my back while we were in triage having vitals taken and blood drawn. I pack extra clothes for Carter......now I will need to start packing extra clothes for me, too!

It doesn't help that there is a pit in my stomach just knowing that the moving van arrived in Locust today to pack and load the house.

My day did have an incredible bright spot - a wreath from a store on Etsy arrived for my little guy. It is fun and festive and perfect for our door here at Target House! I will hang this wreath every year for my little guy and say, "Remember when?"

Another bright spot was when I met Meri, Josiah's mommy. After Carter was diagnosed, Paul and I were looking for "signs" to go to St. Jude. My friend and colleague, Sheila, brought one such sign to me. She had received a solicitation letter from St. Jude with Josiah's picture and story. You see, Josiah has the same exact type of tumor that Carter has and is about the same age. Today when I realized that Meri was Josiah's mommy, I immediately started to cry. It just overwhelmed me - here was the little boy that I had read about......I feel blessed to have met Josiah and his mommy (even if Carter was being a grouch today!).

It looks like we'll be admitted for day 8-9 chemo tomorrow night to pump Carter full of fluids before the chemo is administered. Can't let the weekend nursing staff down - gotta make our appearance!

I need to head to bed....praying for a better day tomorrow.

12/8/11
It's late. I'm tired. Carter is resting peacefully (while receiving blood to boost his hemoglobin) and I'm ready to attempt to get some sleep. I'm just waiting for a nurse to find me a pillow (they seem to be all out?) so that I can sleep.

I'm praying that Carter starts to feel better. It's hard when he doesn't feel well. He articulates so much, but he doesn't know how to express that he is nauseous or not feeling well. I'm learning that when he's grumpy it is only a matter of time before he vomits. He vomits about once a day at this point (from the last chemo dose).

I'm praying that it will subside. The hard part is that we can't simply stay at Target House and let him watch TV on the sofa. We're at the hospital literally every day for blood work, neuro-oncology visits, and other random appointments. And no, we don't have a choice in the matter.

Tomorrow is the closing on the house in Greenwood. Please pray that everything goes well - I'm scared to death that it won't based on a few crazy things that have happened. Praying that it isn't a sign of some-sort and just the incompetence of some overworked secretary. Nothing like a little additional stress.....obviously God thinks that I can handle it.......

I've been on an emotional roller coaster just knowing that the moving truck is in Locust. I'm praying that Mason understands all of this chaos ....my heart breaks for him. I'm already mentally planning Carter's third birthday party for the Great Wolf Lodge in Concord so we can have a reunion with our Locust friends and so I can get some closure.

Speaking of Locust, I think it's one of the last places where a physician will pick up the phone, call a patient (me) and say, "Call me if you need to chat!" Um, yes - I will be doing that as soon as time permits) How am I going to find a new doctor like that????

I finished about one-third of all the Christmas cards I sent out and they were put in the mail......just two-thirds to go! And yes - I put the new house return address on them, so if the new house doesn't close, I'm out of luck!

OK - I'm off to find a pillow so I can sleep.......where's a pillow pet when you need one?
((HUGS!!))

12/9/11
*I think that today officially qualified as the best day of the week. Carter was so much happier today.....or at least this morning. I can tell that the blood transfusion made a huge difference. He is such a happy little boy when he feels well. And when Carter feels well, this momma is definitely less stressed! *phew!**

That being said - Carter had his chemo this morning and early afternoon and by dinner time, he wasn't feeling so well. I know that the side effects from the chemo mean that the chemo is working, but it doesn't help my mommy paranoia from going into overload.

We only have one more dose of chemo for this round and we'll be one-third of the way done with our St. Jude chemo!!! WOO HOO!!! It also means that Carter will have an MRI after this round is complete. AND it means that after the next round we will be halfway finished with our St. Jude visit!

So many people have been telling me how positive I am and what an inspiration I am ....I really wish that you could see me the majority of the time. I'm stressed, I'm frustrated, I'm grumpy and overwhelmed......and if Carter doesn't feel well, Mommy doesn't feel well! Just know that I'm not Little Miss Sunshine the majority of the time......I'm definitely not at my best these days....but I'm trying and I know that I have Prayer Warriors behind me and I have God in front of me and together we're all going to get through this.......

It's funny, because I've always thought of time as a lifetime......six months at St. Jude is just really a blip on the radar as far as time is concerned, even though it may seem like forever. It is just a second of my life and even smaller than a second in Carter's life.

Today we bought a home in Greenwood, SC. The moving van packed everything up and it will arrive there on Monday morning. It's killing me that I'm not there to help Mason with this transition and to say good-bye to our Locust friends. I've been told that many in Greenwood already know that we're coming and know our story. I'm praying that we are able to find friends as wonderful and as loving as we have had in Locust.

An old Chinese proverb says that the journey of a thousand miles begins with a single step. We took this step in coming to St. Jude and again, we are taking another first step in moving to Greenwood.

One of my favorite quotes is from Dicey's Song by Cynthia Voigt. I honestly can't remember it perfectly right now - but it's when Gram is saying good-bye to Dicey. Gram says something to the effect of, "When you leave, you'll take a piece of me with you, because you're a part of my life now and you always will be." That's pretty much how I feel right now about leaving Locust......it will always be a part of our lives and I will forever have a piece of each of the people I've met there as a part of me.

((HUGS!!))

12/10/11
Carter had a rough morning. He is vomiting. This is called "break-thru" because he is on Zofran regularly for the nausea and when he vomits, it "breaks thru" the medication. We then gave Carter Ativan and he still had "break-thru" so we added Benadryl. Little man is sleeping like a champ now.

Carter and I had a little chat as he was getting ready to nap. I told him that I hated the fact that he was throwing up, but that it meant that the medicine was working. I then told Carter than Mr. Jesus was going to make Carter all better. Carter then told me that Mr. Jesus was going to make me all better, too. HE IS SO RIGHT! I immediately got weepy and just held my little man. Jesus is going to make it all better for both of us. I know it.

((HUGS!!))

12/10/11
The nurses have all told me that I would hit a true "low" at some point and I think that it has been today/tonight. I am so thankful for our nurses. They are wonderful. We laugh together and they let me cry when I need to cry. I've done a lot of crying today.

Carter hasn't been this sick since he was at Jeff Gordon's in Concord (where we were first admitted for treatment). He has vomited at least six times today, maybe more but I've lost count. He hasn't vomited like this since then. It scares me and I know that it scares him. Not to be too graphic, but Carter won't let himself throw up and swallows a lot of the time. I know it's because it scares him. I do everything that I can to be calm and supportive, but he knows that vomiting means that he's sick......and he doesn't want to be sick.

Little man has spent much of the day in bed. We've had the lights out and the TV off. He has just wanted warm blankets and for Mommy to hold him. I've been praying so hard for him to feel better.

The nurses tell me that it is the Cysplatin that is making him so ill. It has nasty side effects and vomiting is one of them. I keep telling myself that it means that the tumor is shrinking and that God will give us a miracle......but it's so hard to see my baby lethargic and pale white. If we can just make it through this round, we will have another MRI and I am convinced that God will show us that the tumor is shrinking and that Carter is getting better.

Tonight, in Locust, our neighbors are gathering for a Christmas party and Paul, Mason, and my mom are saying goodbye to everyone. I so wish that I could be there. Tomorrow they will leave for Greenwood and start the next chapter in our lives.

Heavenly Father - Give me strength to fight this battle for my little guy. Make me strong and grant me courage to look this monster in the eye and make it back down. Wash me with your mercy, bath me in serenity, and cleanse me with grace. I know that you will heal my little man. I know that you will rid Carter of this tumor and that he will be well again. Please grant me patience, for I know that all things are done in Your time. I lift my heart up unto You. Hear my prayer Heavenly Father. Amen.

((HUGS!!))

12/11/11
Carter is sleeping right now. He vomited once this morning. The doctors have said that we can go back to Target House if Carter drinks on his own and can keep it down. They have stopped the fluids to see if it will help make him thirsty and want to drink.

Please pray that Carter drinks liquids when he awakes and is able to keep it down. Thank you for all of your words of encouragement. I so appreciate them. I think that each time Carter vomits from now on I'm going to imagine that he is vomiting the nasty tumor out.........

((HUGS!!))

12/11/11
We are back at Target House.....Carter got sick as we walked through the door. I am praying that it is a restful night. We have an 8am appt. at the hospital and then another from 9:30-12:30......If I

can just get through this week, it will be Christmas and Paul, Mason, and my parents will be here.

I think I can, I think I can......With Christ I know I can, I know I can.......

((HUGS!!))

12/12/11
Heavenly Father - When I am weak, you lift me up. Thank you for the angels and cheerleaders in my life. They are your voice in human form. Thank you for sending them my way when I need them most. Father God, hear my prayer.

Today was another wretched day for Carter. The chemo is taking its toll on my little guy. He has something called mucusitis which is essentially the breakdown of the esophagus lining (from the chemo). It creates a thick wall of mucus in the throat, making it difficult to swallow. Carter loves milk and liquid yogurt, but they are not the best things for him to have right now......I know first-hand from cleaning up what feels like a gazillion vomit messes. Might be treating myself to a car wash and detailing for Christmas......until then, Febreeze will take away the stench!

Anyways - This means that Carter needs to drink liquids like water, apple juice, and Gatorade....none of which taste good to him right now. I broke down and bought Carter a small sweet tea today. He's not really supposed to have it. Sweet tea (or tea of any sort) can harbor bacteria (tea leaves aren't cleaned before they are crushed) and that bacteria can cause illness in cancer patients. I just wanted my baby to be able to drink something and keep it down.....and to have it taste good. Of course, none of the doctors have told me this first-hand......so I can do a lot of praying that Carter won't get sick and play ignorant, right? The dilemmas a mommy faces!

Carter and I went to Arkansas today. We spent a whole five minutes there. I thought that the trip across the bridge would be a fun change of pace for my little guy. I had never seen the Mississippi River before and I never had been to Arkansas before either......crossed two things off of my bucket list.

On the way back - Carter threw up (albeit on a towel that he is draped in for every car ride now). You can't stop on the bridge .....it was a LONG trip back into Tennessee.....all five minutes of it.

So many times I feel like if there were video cameras rolling I would be the star of a hilarious sitcom. I can almost hear people laughing at me......she did what?!? A long time ago I learned that it was easier to laugh at myself....I guess that's part of the reason why I'm so goofy. I'm thankful that I've learned this skill at this point in my life.....at least I can laugh at my failures.....because they are too numerous to count! I think that God blessed me with this skill because He knew that I would need it now more than ever.

So the good news is that the next chemo dose will be out-patient. I think that it will be done on Friday. This means that Carter's ANC counts will bottom out probably on Saturday and we'll have to be ready to go to the hospital if he has a fever. My prayer is that Carter will be healthy for Christmas. Although I've heard St. Jude spoils the patients who are in-patient for Christmas......I just want my little guy to be at Target House.....so that we have some sense of normalcy.

Speaking of normalcy.......2/3 of my Christmas cards are finished, most of the Christmas presents are purchased (need to get going with a few), and just a few more to ship! WOO HOO!!! Here's to being normal and to actually keeping up with the holiday season!

OH! The moving van delivered all of our things to the new house in Greenwood today......sounds like all went fairly well....and most of the furniture even fits in the house!

Heavenly Father - Thank you for the giggles, the sillies, the crazies. Help me to continue to laugh through the tears, the vomit, and the whining. Send me guidance with smiles and hugs. Thank you for the snorting, the sound effects, and the goofiness that helps me remember the joy in my life. I know that you have a sense of humor, for I have seen it dear Lord. Thank you for sharing it with me when I need it most. Amen.

((HUGS!!))
Sarah

12/13/11

I know that God hears our prayers for Carter because Carter's ANC counts were 22,200......these are the highest that I've seen them! Little man felt a lot better today and it was obvious.....he still vomited twice - but I was able to handle it because Carter was in such a good mood for most of the day.......It makes life so much easier when he's happy!

Lots to tell, but it will have to wait until tomorrow. I'm one tired momma!

Thank you Lord for this fabulous day. I rejoice in Your name. Amen.

12/15/11

Did you know that 46 children a day are diagnosed with pediatric cancer? There is an organization called 46 Mommas who shave their heads each year to raise money for St. Baldrick's - these are all mommies of children who have cancer. Chase's mommy was one of the original 46 women who shaved their heads ....this year, they shaved their heads in front of Congress to advocate for pediatric cancer funding

It has been a whirlwind of a few days. Carter has started to feel better - the vomiting has subsided for the most part (36 hours vomit free!). While he has been feeling better, he hasn't been feeling necessarily great. He has been tired and grumpy. Both of which could be side effects of the chemo and also due to the fact that his hemoglobin dropped. Today Carter not only received his last dose of chemo in the round today (WOO HOO!), but he also received another blood transfusion. This time next month, we will be celebrating being halfway through the chemo here at St. Jude! Carter's ANC count was 3300 today, so I'm anticipating it being zero tomorrow - if this occurs, it will be the same pattern that occurred last cycle. Please pray that he does not get a fever and that we do not have to return to the hospital for in-patient treatment.

When we were hospitalized last week, the resident doctor realized that Carter's ear tubes were working their way out. Today we met with the ENT and confirmed that the tubes were indeed either out or on their way out. We are going to go ahead and have another set of tubes put in because I don't really want to have a 2.5 year old child undergoing chemo treatment with ear infections - call me crazy! I don't know when this minor surgery will occur, but I will let you know.

I know that Carter will have an MRI soon because this round has now been completed. I know that it will be once his counts have rebounded ....so maybe sometime right after Christmas. My prayer is that the tumor is shrinking. I've been told not to expect much, but I'm praying for a miracle. Wouldn't it be a testament to our prayer if the tumor had significantly decreased in size? My God is a powerful God and I know that if it is His will, this will happen.

On Tuesday night, employees from Target headquarters in Minnesota flew down to Target House to help host a dinner event (how awesome is that?). Each family received a roll-up blanket and there were crafts for the kids. Carter decorated a Christmas plate and some Christmas cookies. He was feeling well enough to work the room and make friends with all of the pretty ladies from Target.

On Wednesday, Carter was not feeling 100% but we made it to the Target Wish Upon a Star Carnival/Party. Target set up a HUGE tent in the parking lot of St. Jude and each child got to pick out a toy (Carter got a ride-on Mater!), a t-shirt (for mommy), a $10 gift card to Target, and a goody bag of little favors. There was live music (Carter is in love with guitars, so this was a huge hit!) and food to eat. And of course, Carter's favorite photographer, Peter, was there. When Peter took Carter's photo, Carter (without prompting) put his hand on his fist, opened his mouth like an "O" and looked up at the massive stars which hung from the ceiling.......Peter snapped the pictures and of course, Carter requested to see them! The photo was BEAUTIFUL......can't wait to get it to post for you all to see!

Last night was the first night in forever that Carter really slept through the night......which means the first night that I have actually gotten some decent sleep in a long, long, long while! I am praying for a second night of such bliss!

Tonight Carter ventured over to our neighbor Chase's room. Upon arriving I mentioned Chase's haircut and asked Carter if he'd like a haircut like Chase's. Carter promptly agreed and after Chase's mommy showed Carter the clippers, he sat down in my lap and allowed her to shave the remaining fuzz off of his head. I started to tear up a little - not because I was sad, but because I was so overwhelmed with how easy it was .....no tears, no fighting, nothing! Carter continues to amaze me....

On a different note, someone made a comment to me the other day to the effect of me being mad at God about Carter's tumor. How can I be mad at God? I may be mad, stressed, or frustrated at other people or situations, but I cannot be mad at God. He has prepared me for this journey. He has given me the strength that I need each day to be strong for my little boy. God has provided me a multitude of angels who have humbled me with gifts of all varieties. No, I'm not mad at God and I don't imagine that I will ever be mad at Him. I find peace in knowing that God chose me for this journey and that Carter will be well again.

Heavenly Father - You love us. You love all of us. No matter what our faults, no matter what our mistakes, you love us unconditionally and for that I am eternally grateful. Your love embraces us in the happy times and the sad times - but it is always there. Father God, let us see the love that surrounds us each day, in both those things that seem trivial and those that are not. Help us to love thy neighbor as thyself. For You so loved us that You gave us your only son. Help us love you with our full heart, dear Lord. In Your Name, I pray. Amen.

The picture that Peter took at the Target Wish Party later became the picture used for the month of January in the 2013 calendar. I knew that it was a special picture when it was taken. In my heart, I think that little man knew it, too.

12/17/11
I am on a mission tonight to finish my Christmas cards! Just a few left to go......and I need to add a disclaimer - if you don't receive a Christmas card from me this year, please don't take it personally. I ordered 100 cards and realized that I ordered too few....and then I realized that I hadn't updated my address book this year (usually do it in July and obviously that didn't happen!). Some of you may

even get two because there were times when I couldn't remember where I stopped and where I needed to start again.......

Carter has continued to feel well. We went to the Memphis Zoo for a short walk this afternoon and we were able to see the Giant Pandas. Many of you may not know this, but I have a thing for pandas.....in third grade I had a year long project with Mrs. J. We had to choose an animal on the endangered species list and write a research paper (complete with bibliography) and then write a story about the animal. My story was titled, "Patty The Performing Panda." I still have it nestled somewhere in my files. Needless to say, the pandas were not performing today, but chomping away on bamboo. Carter was fascinated and wanted to pet them. I bought him a stuffed panda to pet instead. It seemed like a fair compromise!

We ran over to Target House Two this evening where the local Optimist Club showered Carter with gifts - knit hats, coloring books, crayons, and a toy helicopter......Carter was more than pleased. If Carter wasn't spoiled rotten before his diagnosis, he certainly is now! Packages arrive daily from friends both known and unknown with Christmas cookies, candies, and goodies.

It is such a gift to have Carter feeling better. Two weeks of him feeling rotten really took a toll on me (and him, too!). He is such a joy when he feels well. I'm praying that he'll continue to feel well and that we'll be able to avoid a fever when his counts are low. Please keep sending up those prayers! Gotta stay out of the hospital during Christmas!

Off to finish the Christmas cards.....

((HUGS!!))

12/18/11
God is in control. I get it. That doesn't mean that I like it however.

Today started as a normal day. We got up. We got our stuff together. We came to the hospital. Carter was fine when we were in triage. He loved on one of his favorite nurses, Candice. He got a toy from the treasure box. Carter was even feeling good in the medicine room when he had to get a shot. He didn't like it and he screamed bloody murder, but he got something out of the treasure box and was happy. Carter was even somewhat content eating Fruit Loops (at this point I don't care what he eats as long as he's eating!) in the cafeteria. It was a pretty good day....I should have known better.

When we went to the clinic to get the test results of Carter's blood it showed that his hemoglobin was critically low. This probably explains why his hands were so cold yesterday night and this morning. The doctors want his hemoglobin above 8 and today it was at 6.7.....not good. Carter's platelets were also low. So our good day took a nosedive quickly.

We were then put in a room in what essentially looks like an emergency room, lots of small rooms around a central nurses station. Carter became irritable and wanted to go (who wouldn't?) and so I convinced him that we needed a nap. Almost two hours later the blood and platelets still hadn't arrived for the transfusion. Carter awoke with a vengeance and Mommy was less than happy. The nurse took Carter's vitals and confirmed my worst fear. He had a fever. This meant more blood tests, including a prick to his arm......it took three nurses and me to hold him down and get the bare minimum of blood needed for the test.

So, we've been admitted again .....we almost made it through a weekend without being in-patient. I am still at a loss - how did Carter start the day off so well and end it so poorly? We will have to be in-patient until the fever has been gone for 48 hours and his ANC counts are above 500 and show that they are rebounding. This means that the earliest we'll be back to Target House is Wednesday at this point (if the fever breaks tonight).

Good news - the Christmas cards are finished. They aren't sealed and they weren't put in the mailbox, so maybe this last group will get out in time to actually arrive by Christmas. Oh well. I tried.

I have one last set of Christmas presents that I need to ship. Again, I tried. Hopefully they'll understand.

Dear God - Fevers stink when your child is neutropenic....I know that you're in control, but really? Can I just have a break one time? Pretty please? I mean it is Christmas and all. All I want for Christmas is for Carter to be healthy and to be at Target House so that we can have Christmas as a family. Do you think you could work on that for me? Maybe call in a favor to Santa for me? I'll even forfeit my Christmas presents if Carter can just be well (I'm probably not getting anything but underwear and socks - but I'll gladly donate them to someone in need if it will be a bargaining chip!). Father God, watch over my little one and heal him with your loving touch. Amen.

I just wanted life to be normal, but when you're waging war against a pediatric brain tumor - normal is relative. The Christmas cards, the holiday season, the anything and everything…...but nothing was normal about our life that Christmas season. As much as I tried, as much as I prayed....it wasn't normal, and it wasn't going to be normal anytime soon.

12/19/11
The fever is gone! WOO HOO!! Carter has slept a good bit of today because he's been so tired. I think that the fever and a rough night's sleep left him exhausted. I'm just thankful that he's getting some sleep. When you're admitted for a fever, the blessing is that you have a little more space....less poking and whatnot.

I also found out that the MRI has been scheduled for December 30th at 9:30am. Please pray for a miracle. Please pray that the tumor is gone. I know that we'd have to continue with the protocol that we're on, but it would make a fabulous belated Christmas present.

I'm exhausted and need to get some rest. I cannot wait for Paul and Mason to arrive on Wednesday morning. I know that Carter is excited for them to come, too. He is constantly saying, "I want Daddy!" I think that Carter is bored of me right now!

More tomorrow. ((HUGS!!))

12/21/11
REJOICE! Paul and Mason have arrived! Paul drove through the night last night and they arrived at Target House early this morning. They came over to the hospital first thing and brought McDonald's for breakfast. Such a luxury! Paul got to spend some time with Carter this morning and Mason and I checked out the construction site while eating lunch (watching bulldozers is much more interesting than lunch!).

Prior to driving out to Memphis last night, Paul and Mason made a stop in Spartanburg, SC where some of Santa's elves delivered a stash of Christmas presents for Mason and Carter! One of my former students, Sarah, and her family and friends raided Santa's workshop and brought the goodies to Spartanburg from Concord. Sarah is an amazing young lady and also did a fundraiser for Carter at Central High School. It's an amazing feeling to have a former student embrace my little guy in such an incredible way. I am forever thankful to her and her family and friends!

While Paul and Mason were driving to Memphis, I was blessed with a Vietnamese dinner from our dear friends Rachel and Nick. Their son, Luca, is one of Carter's buddies. Luca is "across the pod" here in the hospital and recovering well from some surgery. His parents got carry-out and brought me some, too! I felt spoiled not having either Dominos or hospital food! I am thrilled to report that little Luca is getting to go home to Mississippi! What a wonderful blessing during the holidays! We will miss them dearly, but will keep in touch forever. LOVE YOU LUCA!

It looks like Carter and I will be staying one more night here at the hospital. Little man spiked a fever after he received blood yesterday. His blood work continues to be negative for any infection (THANK GOD!), but the doctors just want to make sure that nothing is brewing. God is teaching me that I cannot heal Carter - only He can and He will do it on His time, not mine. Carter's awake....need to run!

I yearned for normalcy during this time. I wanted it to be a typical Christmas holiday season. I didn't want to acknowledge that I was in the hospital with Carter. I didn't want to acknowledge that it might be Carter's last Christmas. I wanted everything to be the same or as close to the same as possible. I was exhausted trying to keep up. I bought Christmas presents, worried that the boys wouldn't have a nice one. I made sure that all of our extended family had Christmas presents, because that was my normal. I made sure that all the Christmas cards went out. I made sure that there was a Christmas tree in our room, a wreath on the door, and whatever else it was that made the season feel normal. Because in my heart, nothing about this Christmas was normal.

12/23/11
I need to write quickly. Paul has taken Carter to bed. Mason is sitting in the sofa fold out (our bed) eating Goldfish and watching Cars 2 (the movie of the moment!).

Tomorrow Carter and I will head to the hospital for labs and a doctor's visit. I'm praying that his ANC counts will top 2000 so that we won't have to return on Christmas Day for his G-shot. It would be an amazing Christmas gift not to have to go to the hospital on Christmas Day.

I cannot tell you all how humbled and overwhelmed I have been with all the cards, presents, financial contributions and gift cards that have arrived throughout this Christmas season. When I wrote earlier in the season about giving, I in no way intended for anyone to give to us - just to give to someone who was in need. We have been blessed with so much this Christmas season because of our friends - those known and unknown. It is an amazing feeling to open the mailbox and to see a stack of cards where there should not be any. It is an overwhelming feeling to have the front desk call and say that there are packages (day after day!) for Carter - when there shouldn't be any......I'm blessed with the most amazing and incredible friends in the world. I cannot thank you enough.....when I have time, I will list names and specifics but I don't have enough time right now......I didn't have a whole lot of hope for this Christmas season because I had planned such a magnificent one at home.....but God has delivered and I am forever thankful for the angels who have helped Him do so!

Every day is an amazing blessing. With Christmas Day approaching, I am forever thankful for this journey and all that it has taught me. I will never forget the love and support that has been given to us as we've walked each step of the way.

I hope to post more tomorrow, but in case I do not - Merry Christmas my dear friends! Please know that we love each and every one of you and wish that we could somehow, someway be with you during this Christmas season. Your love and support has helped get us through this journey and we are forever humbled by it.

Father God - Your mercy is great. Your love is infinite. Your kindness is seen through so many small acts - you are the parking spot that appears, you are the smile in the grocery store, you are everywhere and for that, I am grateful dear Lord. In your Heavenly Name, Amen.

((HUGS!!))
Sarah

12/24/11
BEST CHRISTMAS PRESENT EVER!!!! Carter's ANC is 7300 - tomorrow may be the first day since we've been at St. Jude that we don't have to go to the hospital for something (we'll find out later today!)!!!! GOD IS GOOD!!!!
This is my Christmas miracle!

12/24/11
My dad, "Grandy" to Mason and Carter, wrote this and asked that I post it for him. ((HUGS!!))

Last year, the Rev. Leslie Chadwick, an Episcopal priest, mused out loud how she should begin to tell the Christmas Story to her two and a half year old son

In her sermon on Christmas day, she observed that John's gospel begins with the translated words, ""And the Word became flesh and lived among us . . ." However, a literal translation is., "And the Word became flesh and pitched his tent among us."

That puts the birth of the Christ Child in a very different perspective, especially when you consider that many of the homeless that live among us pitch tents to shelter themselves from the cold and darkness of the winter night.

In her words,

"Jesus became flesh that he might reach us. He pitched his tent with us in the darkest, least safe places. He came to shine light into those places. He sat with sinners, healed the sick, wept over the dead, and risked his life to teach us how to love each other. He had no illusions of security. He taught that those who try to save their lives will lose them and those who lose their lives will be saved. He showed us in his death and resurrection that God's light shines in the darkness, and the darkness will not overcome it.

I come to the end of John's prologue aware that there is no adequate way to tell the story of God's great love for us. Words fail. But the Word does not. In the end, you have to experience love to believe it. God knew and still knows that you have to see, hear, touch, taste, and feel love."

In the days after the October 6 diagnosis of Carter's tumor, I have come to witness God's love in so many, miraculous ways. I have seen friends and family, known and unknown, reach out to give strength, courage and support to Carter and his family as they embark on this most difficult journey.

I have heard many of the prayers that Sarah's "Prayer Warriors" have lifted up to God, asking Him to heal Carter and restore him to good
health.

I have been touched both emotionally and spiritually, in the most profound way, by the many ways that friends, many whom none of us have ever met, have undertaken projects to help with Carter' needs.

Most certainly, I have shared the never ending stream of delicious food, prepared with great love, by friends in the Locust community.

But most of all, I have felt God's love in this journey, in ways I have never experienced in my lifetime. The community of faith is ever present, to graciously and lovingly remind me that this path is not one that Carter will walk alone

.
How do you share the miracle of Christmas with a child? I am sure there are many answers, but the one that comes to my mind is very simple, "one day at a time. .."

Christmas is many things, but it's essence is expressed so simply in this verse:

Out of the silence,
The Word made flesh . . .

Out of the darkness,
The Light of the World . . .

Out of uncertainty,
God's redeeming promise . . .

Out of the Virgin's womb,
God's love incarnate . . .

May the Peace, Joy and Hope of the Christ Child dwell deep in your hearts this Christmastide, and may He sustain and nurture you each and every day in the New Year.

12/24/11
Tonight we went to church to celebrate the birth of our Lord, Jesus Christ. I cried from the first hymn to the last "Thanks be to God" - even hugged the associate rector during communion (I'm sure that it is some sort of faux pas, but I think that God understands). Just when I thought I'd composed myself, I'd start crying again. The poor woman in the restroom was so excited that Mason might be in her Sunday school class next year - and I broke down telling her that I didn't want to be here next year! I think that she understood, but I couldn't talk enough to explain! The people around us were patient and kind to Mason and Carter who would not be quiet (Mason STILL wants to see Baby Jesus!). We even met someone from Greenwood, SC! *phew!* All of that in about an hour!

REJOICE! Christmas is here! REJOICE! For our Lord has delivered us a magnificent Christmas present - Carter doesn't have a doctor's appointment tomorrow and it's the first day since we've been in Memphis for this to occur! I know that it is not a coincidence! GOD IS GOOD and He has heard our prayers!

Merry! Merry! Merry! Christmas to you and your loved ones!
((HUGS!!))

In my heart, I knew that I needed to be at church on Christmas Eve. I thought maybe it would bring some normalcy back into my life. It didn't. If anything, it made me realize just how abnormal my life had become. I cried literally from the moment the music began until we walked out the door. The tears flowed and no matter how I tried to make them stop, they wouldn't. It wasn't anything that I anticipated, it wasn't anything that I wanted....but the tears flowed and flowed and flowed. Perhaps it was because I felt so close to God that night. Perhaps it was because I was praying for normalcy. Perhaps it was because I just wanted a break from all the chaos.

12/25/11
It's only 8:30pm here - but it feels much later. It has been a miraculous day, my dear friends! MERRY CHRISTMAS!

Let me start by explaining that this is the very first day that Carter and I haven't had to go to the hospital since we've arrived here in Memphis. This may not sound like a major ordeal, but it is to me (and to Carter, I'm sure). I cannot tell you the stress that surrounds going to the hospital - especially when Carter doesn't feel well!

The blessing of today is that Carter has felt fine! He enjoyed Christmas to its fullest - and that in itself is a present to me.

This morning started at a healthy 8am - much better than years past! Mason woke up first and barely even noticed the HUGE stack of Christmas present that Santa and his elves managed to send our way. He finally looked up from playing with his train and said (in a totally calm voice!), "OH MY! Look at all these presents!" It took everything I had not to totally burst out laughing! He then ran to where Paul and Carter were sleeping and urged them out of bed. I don't think that Carter was totally on-board with waking up at that point, but he did and was excited once he realized Mason's excitement. Carter loves his big brother - and if Mason is excited, so is he!

We literally opened presents for a solid 1.5 hours before taking a break for breakfast. After breakfast - the boys opened presents for another 1.5 hours.........and I was afraid that these children would have nothing this year?!?! (Please take into account that each present must be meticulously evaluated before the next could be opened!) What a miraculous blessing that they have opened so many marvelous gifts from so many wonderful friends and family (aka Santa's Helpers). I am eternally thankful for all of you. You have made my Christmas.

After the first three hours of gift opening, I was given a HUGE box by Paul. It seems that my dear friends in Locust planned an awesome surprise for me. My bestie, Deidra, and other bestie, Candice, managed to pull off the biggest surprise of them all. After my post about Locust (back in late November), They took it upon themselves to visit each of the locations I mentioned and have them donate something for a huge basket of goodies. I seriously think that this was one of my best presents ever! There was a "Hope" sign from Charlie's Hardware, my favorite Tyler candle from The Tiger Lily, a bottle of wine from Dennis Vineyards, and so many other amazing presents to remind me of Locust. Candice outdid herself by creating a photo-book of all the places I had mentioned and our Locust Valley family. I will treasure it always! Needless to say, I started sobbing immediately upon opening the box.....and while opening each present.....and while reading the photo-book.......and after......what a priceless gift from my amazing Locust families. I love you all.

About the time that I finished up opening the basket....and had started feeding the boys lunch, there was a knock at the door. The Target House manager and staff delivered a shopping cart (LITERALLY) of toys and goodies to us. There was a Schwinn tricycle for Carter, goodies for Mason, and even some things for Mommy! WHAT A SURPRISE! I'm definitely going to have to switch my loyalty to Target from Wal-Mart after all of this!

And no, I didn't get socks and underwear for Christmas! But Paul got boxers and pj pants! I got the Panini maker that I have been asking Santa for the past five years! And here I thought I would be the one getting socks and underwear!

The boys took their nap (well - Mason pretended to nap!) and then we took them to the Peabody Hotel for Christmas dinner. This was an amazing experience for Mommy (and for the boys!). There are ducks that swim in the water fountain in the lobby of the hotel and not only were we able to see them, but we were able to see them parade out of the lobby and up the elevator to their Duck Palace on the roof! Mason was totally mesmerized by this experience and cried when it was over. We met the Duckmaster, Anthony, up on the roof (where the ducks live) and got to see an amazing sunset over the Memphis skyline and the Mississippi River. What a perfect way to end such a wonderful experience!

I believe in miracles. I believe in the birth of our Savior, Jesus Christ. I believe in the Spirit of Christmas. I believe in the healing power of our Lord. I believe that Carter will be healed. This

Christmas has shown me more than ever that God is with us, every moment of every day. He is with us when we least expect it and when we want it most. My God is a good and righteous God which gave his only begotten son to forgive us of our sins. Heavenly Father, thank you. Thank you for this amazing Christmas gift. Thank you for choosing me to be Carter's mommy. Thank you for this journey. Thank you for your love and grace.

Merry Christmas dear friends. Merry Christmas.

((HUGS!!))

12/27/11
PRAY HARDER. PRAY LOUDER. WINNING IS THE ONLY OPTION!

Something good will come of our MRI on the 30th.....God is whispering in my ear......He will provide!

12/27/11
Celebrate normal my dear friends. You don't know how fabulous it is until you've lost it. Even when life is crazy, celebrate it. Don't worry about being the Mom Taxi or Coach Dad, celebrate that you can be either. Love it. Live it. Share it with your children. ((HUGS!!))

12/30/11
Heavenly Father - Today is the day! Please show us a miracle - show us that the tumor is gone or that it has significantly been reduced. Bless me with strength to get through today and for the answers that are coming our way. I know that you do all things in Your time dear Lord, perhaps, just this once - we could have the same schedule? Heavenly Father, embrace me in your loving arms and cradle me with your grace. I lift my heart up to you dear Lord. Amen.

Carter is currently undergoing an MRI of his brain and spine. When that is finished, they will do a spinal tap to ensure that the spinal fluid is clear of any tumor cells. It will be early afternoon before he is finished and then hopefully we will get the results later this afternoon.

Carter asked for Chex-Mix all morning and I had to get creative with ways to avoid food and drink. All things considered, he did pretty well.....I will be prepared with a sippy and Chex-Mix when he wakes up. He was sad when his "buddy" (his port) got a drink of milk (Propofol) and he didn't - but Carter was asleep before the Propofol even was finished being administered.

The good news is that Carter has felt well for the holiday season. It was such a blessing to see him play with his big brother Mason and his daddy! If it weren't for Carter's bald head, you wouldn't know that anything was wrong with his health. He's a happy little boy who wants to play and explore - and who desperately tries to keep up with big brother! I am praying for so many answers today. I know that God provides them in His time. I just want my baby boy to be healed. We have been so blessed in so many ways on this journey, but ultimately it's Carter's healing that will be the ultimate blessing of them all!

WINNING IS THE ONLY OPTION!

((HUGS!!))

When Carter was finished in recovery, I was told to go directly to the clinic. The nurses told me that they didn't know why. I showed up in E Clinic in tears, hardly able to breathe. Carter was still groggy and half-asleep, swaddled in blankets in the little red wagon I pulled. The receptionist got me back into a room and held me. I couldn't talk, I knew in my heart that something was wrong, something was very wrong.

When your doctor shows up to see you and it's obvious he has been crying, your world shatters into pieces without him ever saying anything. The tumor had grown. The protocol wasn't working. Carter's brain was swelling due to the pressure and he needed emergency shunt surgery.

12/30/11
Well - this day certainly did not go as planned......Yes, Heavenly Father, I know that you are in control and will provide the miracle we need on Your time........I hear you, loud and clear!
I knew something was wrong when they told me they didn't do the spinal tap. That is the same thing that happened at Jeff Gordon when the original MRI was done. It was, in a sense, deja vu.

I drove Carter to LeBonheur Children's Hospital (which is just down the street) and a top children's medical facility. They are a top ranked neurosurgery institution, so I didn't have any worries......We were admitted quickly and Carter had a CT scan (I actually laid on the bed with him for it - how wild is that!?) and the nurse blew bubbles at us while we were shimmied in and out of the machine.....how's that for child oriented?

My dear friend Stacy immediately drove over to be with me and to help me think things through (packing at Target House, parking, eating....all important things when you're frazzled!) and I am forever thankful for her dropping everything for me.

Carter's surgery went well. He now has a valve placed on the right side of his skull (new "bumpy") and tubing that runs down the right side of his neck and into his stomach to allow the brain fluid to drain. Dr. K. (our neurosurgeon) removed the old "bumpy" which was another type of fluid reservoir.

We won't know anything definite until Wednesday when the brain tumor board at St. Jude will convene. They will look at Carter's case and determine the next steps. Since the chemo is not working, they will not continue it (from my understanding today). This means that radiation is the only option. Since Carter is so little and radiation is not typically done on children under the age of 3 and rarely in the area where Carter's tumor is located (thalamus and hypothalamus), it is most likely that we'll be headed to Jacksonville, FL to seek proton beam radiation with a St. Jude affiliated institution. St. Jude is building a facility for a proton beam, but it won't be ready until 2013.......

Heavenly Father, my faith does not waiver. I am at your mercy and I know that you have great things in store for Carter. This is part of the journey that we must take. You will heal my little boy, I know it. I feel it. I believe it. We are an army of thousands praying for Carter and who believe in your power. Carter is an angel here on earth sending the message of your love to so many. Heal him dear Lord. Let those who do not believe or question you see the miracles that you can provide. I do not question you. I do not waiver. Hold my sweet Carter close to you, oh Lord. In Your Name, I pray. Amen.

12/30/11

P.S. -
Dear 2nd Floor Nurses and PCAs at St. Jude (yes, I know that
you're reading this!)

Please know that if we don't make it back to the 2nd floor that I will
never forget you all. You have been my sisters and family over the
past two months and I cannot express the gratitude that I feel. We
have laughed together, cried together, and commiserated
together. What more could I ask for? You have been patient, kind,
understanding.....but most of all, you have loved my little boy like
he was your own - a gift that is beyond priceless. I will never forget
you! We will visit soon when Carter is healthy once again......

LOVE YOU!
((HUGS!!))
S.

I will never be able to thank the nurses at St. Jude enough for caring for
Carter. And let's be honest, they took care of me, too! I can't write about
them without getting emotional. I was alone, and they knew it but they
wouldn't let me feel alone. They told me that I inspired them, when
really it was them who kept me grounded and strong. These ladies hold a
special place in my heart. I couldn't have made this journey without
them. They are an incredible sisterhood – the nurses of St. Jude.

12/31/11
Carter is sleeping peacefully. He had a CT scan at 6am that
showed the ventricles have returned to normal size and that the
brain fluid is draining well. PRAISE THE LORD! If all goes well, we
may be discharged this evening to Target House.

It dawned on me at some awful hour in the middle of the night of
what my sweet boy has been through in the past four months:
3 brain surgeries
2 rounds of chemo
6 MRIs
4 CT scans
6 (at least) blood transfusions
2 platelet transfusions
1 Hickman port placement
1 plane trip to Memphis
5 (at least) x-rays
Loss of beautiful blond hair (haircuts and chemo)

Who said that being 2.5 was easy? Poor little guy has been through more than many in their 50s and 60s!

((HUGS!!))

12/31/11
It's New Year's Eve and my baby boy is sleeping peacefully in our bed here at Target House. I am so thankful that we were discharged this evening. What a blessing for this holiday! It amazes me the changes a year makes.

I can't even remember last New Year's Eve or the one before - I think that I was in bed and asleep ......but I remember the year before, because I was pregnant with Carter and incredibly ill. I remember posting something about "worshiping the throne" to ring in New Year's 2009 on FB - and commenting that it didn't have anything to do with drinking! I had a horrible virus and was miserable. I think most of my night was spent on the bathroom floor and the next day I was in bed for the majority of the day. Of course, this was not my worst New Year's ever and tonight won't be either.

I am amazed that my little boy literally had brain surgery just over 24 hours ago and is now sleeping in the room beside me. What a blessing and miracle - thank you God for this gift. For me, it is priceless. Although we're not at home with family, we are together and we are in comfortable surroundings - it makes such a difference!

I've thought about resolutions for the New Year - and short of getting Carter better, there really aren't any to make. I will go wherever God guides us to make Carter well again. I am convinced that it will happen this year.

Isn't it funny how New Year's resolutions are made and typically they're all about making ourselves better? I remember that last year was my year to get in shape and focus on "me" - obviously God had other plans and I never had the chance to even glance at that resolution! I guess that I'm simply looking at resolutions from a different perspective this year. It's not about me. It's about my child and what I can do for him to make him better. And no, not everyone has a child battling an illness, but what if everyone were to reach out to someone else - a child, a parent, a friend, or even a stranger? What if everyone were to make a resolution about helping someone else? What if everyone reached out to someone who they hadn't spoken to in years? Or if everyone resolved to "pay it forward" on a daily basis? Maybe if we focused on other people this year - we might save the money on the gym membership that we're only going to use until January 19th.

And isn't it funny that we need a new year to make resolutions? Why can't we make them on a Tuesday or Wednesday in March or August? I have so many things to ponder this year. My life has been illuminated in ways that I never dreamed because of this journey and everything is different now.

Tonight I rejoice in having Carter sleep cuddled up next to me. I rejoice in God's love and guidance. I celebrate the challenges of last year and getting through them and I look forward to the challenges that this next year will bring. I am strong because of the strength that God gives me and the love and support of my family. As I have said before, I have God in front of me and my prayer warriors behind me - how can I go wrong?

Heavenly Father - thank you for this year of illumination, please continue to light the way. Thank you for bringing Carter and me back to Target House and for a successful brain surgery yesterday. Your healing hands made this happen. Father God, walk with me through 2012 and grace me with your presence every day. Tonight I celebrate Your Glory, dear Lord. Your mercy is great. Amen.

It still haunts me that this post mentions days in March and August specifically. I had no idea what was to come and it was a totally random thought. I had no idea what would happen in either March or August. I had no way of knowing.

1/2/11
Carter is taking a nap and I need to be cleaning/organizing/etc. - just in case we are sent to Jacksonville soon.

The tumor board will meet tomorrow afternoon to discuss Carter's case and the next options. I have contacted a top pediatric oncologist in Boston to see if there may an opportunity there for Carter. My biggest concern is that if the protocol here at St. Jude isn't working - what happens if the proton beam radiation doesn't completely rid Carter of the tumor? I have a lot of questions for our doctor tomorrow....I sure hope that he is prepared and has some answers! I told God at the very beginning of this that I would go where ever I needed in order to get Carter well ......and it may be Boston if St. Jude can't help him. Gotta think two steps ahead......

So many of you have commented on how strong I am and how strong my faith is......what other choice do I have? If you were in my shoes, you would do the same. I certainly have my moments and I cry from time to time (not as much as I used to), but I have to be strong for my little guy. I don't have immediate family here - so I do a lot of talking to God and I think a lot about God's plan for us. My job is to be the mommy and do everything I possibly can for my little boy - and God's job is to get me through it!

People who know me well know that I am typically quiet about my faith - I express it in written words to friends or with comments from time to time. I really use CaringBridge as my journal. Sometimes I even forget that others read it. I use this as a tool for me more than anything - writing has always allowed me to work through the hard times. Thanks for putting up with my random thoughts and comments!

((HUGS!!))

1/3/11
Right now we're just in a holding pattern until the tumor board meets. I spoke with the doctors this morning and they are still unsure about the proton beam radiation because it may cause problems for Carter later. One doctor said that we might just need to keep the tumor stable until Carter is three and then proceed with the radiation. The tumor is inoperable because it's located in the thalamus and hypothalamus near the pituitary gland and it's too risky - again, it could cause issues for Carter later. In the meantime, I'm trying to research and learn more.....

1/4/12
Dear Clemson Tigers -

Please win.

((HUGS!!))

Sadly, the Tigers lost that night.....don't know if I wore make-up or not....but it was a bad omen in my mind. I tried to push it out of my thoughts, but it didn't feel good for Carter. Call it silly, call it stupid, but when your son is fighting for his life.....you call it hope – and I needed it.

1/5/12
Love my Tigers anyway......just praying that it isn't a sign.....if so, we've got an ugly battle ahead of us!

Headed to the hospital soon. LOVE the fact that we have solid appointments from lunch through 4pm.......don't all 2.5 year old children take afternoon naps? I'm guessing that mine is the only one.

Praying for answers, to be patient and civil, and to see what God has in store for us next.
((HUGS!!))

1/6/12
In the midst of all the chaos, Carter and I learned yesterday that we can go home for a whole week! I'm SO EXCITED! We have an 8:30am doctors appointment and then I am hoping to get on the road soon after. There is so much to write about, but it will have to wait......basic gist - two more months of a different combination of chemo and then radiation if the chemo doesn't work.....trying to buy time.

PRAY!

I was so excited to head home and to see our new house that I didn't care that it was Country Cares Week at St. Jude. I didn't care about meeting country singers or having pictures taken with them. All I wanted was to see our new home, sleep in my own bed, and see my husband and Mason. It was a no brainer as far as I was concerned.

1/9/12
Just a quick update - Carter and I arrived home in Greenwood safely late Friday night. It's good to be home......but so different than Locust! We gave up size in our new home for land (about an acre now) and we have a view of several small connecting lakes from our backyard (or is it a series of ponds? jury is still out). I spent most of Saturday and Sunday cleaning and organizing the

kitchen......I'll be conquering a room a day it looks like....there are boxes everywhere still.

It was so nice to be able to take Mason to preschool this morning and meet his teachers, see his school, etc. So much to tell you all, but so little time.....I'll try and write more tonight after the boys have gone to sleep......right now I need to head out to Wal-Mart to get Mason's school supplies (that are a little over-due!)

Heavenly Father - thank you for the comforts of home and family. Thank you for the messes and temper tantrums. They are reminders of normality, dear Lord. They are blessings which you send to remind me to be thankful for normality. Father God, thank you for this gift of being with my family and seeing my new home for the first time. In Your Name, Amen.

1/10/12
I have a quick minute to update - the boys are still sleeping (???? it's almost 9am!) and so I have a minute.

Since Carter's tumor is still growing, he has been pulled from the SJYCO7 protocol of chemos and will be starting a new regimen. The new chemos include Avastin, Tepotecan, and Vorinostat. This is a random concoction of chemos that the doctors think might work to either stabilize and/or shrink the tumor. We are essentially trying to buy time. The closer to age three we can get Carter, the better.

After two months, we will do another MRI to see if the tumor has stabilized and/or shrunk. If it hasn't, we will immediately begin radiation therapy at St. Jude - not in Jacksonville. Due to the location of Carter's tumor, the radiologist thinks that traditional radiation (with some minor adjustments) will be the most effective (this is also based on the volume of Carter's tumor). We also discussed pencil point radiation at MD Anderson in Houston, but again, due to location and volume of the tumor - it seems that this form of radiation probably won't make a difference in the tumor.

Due to Carter's young age, he does not qualify for many of the studies and trials being conducted by doctors in the COG (Children's Oncology Group). These are the top pediatric oncologists in the states. What is so difficult about this situation is that Carter basically has a tumor that an adult would have - a high grade glioma. What makes the situation more difficult is the location of the tumor - pretty much in the center of his brain. If his tumor were located somewhere else, it could be radiated and/or removed - but because of the location, it cannot be removed and radiation is a risk because of his young age.

I need to run - Mason just woke up and is calling for me.....

1/15/12
Heavenly Father - Thank you for the past few weeks. Carter has felt well and been a typical little boy. We were able to go home and see Paul and Mason. Our travels home and back were safe and uneventful. Thank you for this respite. Father God, I know that this next part of our journey is critical for Carter. Please stabilize or shrink his tumor. Let these new chemo drugs work. Place your loving hand on Carter and heal him. You are the ultimate physician dear Lord. Please make my little boy all better. Amen.

It's interesting taking a 9.5 hour car ride with a 2.5 year old little boy. Carter did really well both to and from Greenwood. He slept a lot, but we had all sorts of random discussions and we were just plain silly. I think that Carter is probably the only child who will not watch a DVD in the car - just my luck! And really, it was my luck - because Carter and I got to chat about all sorts of things.

One such discussion was when Carter realized his "bumpy" on his head had moved from one side to the other. Carter had been feeling his stitches when I asked him, "do your stitches hurt?" He said, "No - but MOMMY! My bumpy MOVED!" Of course, I responded, "REALLY?! How did it do that?" and Carter said in a very serious voice, "my puppy moved it." When I asked, "how did puppy move it?" Carter simply responded, "I don't know!" Now, for those of you who don't know - "puppy" is Carter's favorite stuffed animal which was given to him by Amy and Brian (one set of his Godparents). It took everything I had to hold it together. He is convinced that his puppy had something to do with his shunt surgery.

Getting into the mind of a 2.5 year old is an interesting task. I did a lot of prying while we spoke. Carter at one point asked me, "Where's the Holy Spirit?" to which my response was, "He's in your heart." Carter then said, "The Holy Spirit is in my heart to make me feel better." Amen Carter!

Yesterday, after waking up from his nap, Carter looked at me (without prompting) and said, "pray for me to make me all better." Of course, I will baby boy - no question about it!

I sometimes wonder if Carter is an angel here on earth. He is so sweet and loving (most of the time!) and says the most profound things that I sometimes do a double-take. How can Carter only be 2.5? Hasn't he been here all of my life? How is it that he can make sense of the most complex things in such simple words? So many people have commented that Carter is an old soul - isn't that just another way of saying that he's an angel? And how is it that other people see it, too? For so long I was worried that it was just because I was Carter's momma......so it's reassuring that others see it as well. It simply baffles me that such a young child can be so wise.

This next week will bring a whole new journey for us to start. If this chemo goes well and if Carter does not have any adverse reactions, we may get to go back to Levine in Charlotte for outpatient treatment. I've been scared to say anything because would love for this to happen. I'm praying that if it is God's will, it will be done. It wouldn't be Locust, but it would be a lot closer.......and Mason and Paul could visit on the weekends. Our quality of life would be a lot better.

As for Carter, he just wants to be a little boy and do all the things a 2.5 year would do......

((HUGS!!))

1/17/12
I like roller coasters. Literally. However, I'm not a fan of them in the figurative sense. Unfortunately, I am riding one of the most unpredictable roller coasters known to mankind......and I have to learn how to like it so that it doesn't get the best of me.

I remember my first roller coaster ride. It was at Great America and it was called The Demon. My dad terrorized me as we stood in line for ninety minutes waiting for our turn (and if you know my dad, you know what I mean!). I was certain that I would die on the roller coaster, but oddly enough, I didn't and actually enjoyed the drops and upside down loops. I turned into a roller coaster junkie (like my dad).

This journey that I am on is not one that I'd ever stand in line for or would I want anyone ever to experience, but I'll get through it. It will not get the best of me. I envision one of those cameras at the top of the first drop on the coaster that takes your picture when you look the worst and there I am, smiling and looking perfectly wretched. And no, I don't typically buy the pictures they take on roller coasters either......but I promise you, it ain't pretty!

Today I thought that Carter's new chemo would start. And it was supposed to, until it got too late in the day and Carter was miserable because it was nap time and he wasn't taking a nap (for the second afternoon in a row!)......and then he had his stitches taken out of his head ......not a good afternoon. Needless to say, we (the doctors and me) realized that Carter was crying because he wanted to keep his stitches in his head......now try to explain why stitches cannot stay in your head to a two and a half year old who hasn't had a nap.......don't you envy me?
So - the chemo will start tomorrow.....which is a good thing.

The other dramatic change is that the doctors are predicting we can head to Charlotte soon......as in early next week soon! This came as a surprise to me because I was under the impression that we'd be here for at least the first week of chemo if not the first two weeks of chemo. Guess they changed their minds or I didn't understand.....needless to say, I'm thrilled to be heading closer to home.

Please know that we did have the option of doing the out-patient chemo in Greenville/Greenwood, SC - but because we have a relationship with the doctors at Levine and we have a place to stay, it was decided that this would be the best place for us. We've already been to four different hospitals in four months - the idea of learning a fifth hospital really didn't appeal to me......and it will be easier on Carter to be with doctors and nurses whom he has already met. We will also be able to see our friends in the Charlotte area when Carter is feeling well which is a plus, too! Paul and Mason will be able to come up to see us on the weekends when Carter is feeling alright and we're just hoping our quality of life is better overall. My dad will be driving out from Virginia to help me pack and move out of Target House. How is it that I arrived with only two suitcases and I need a 12 passenger van to move out? Geesh! So, once again, my dad gets to move me! (We have a moving relationship with one another - literally!)

On a totally separate note - many have asked why Carter's tumor is inoperable.......so here it goes - I need you to imagine a peach, plum, or avocado......a food with a pit in the center. Carter's tumor is the pit. In order to get to the pit, you have to cut through the outer layers to get to it and possibly damage those layers. I hope that this makes sense. Carter's tumor is literally in the center of his brain and it is extremely difficult to get to it without causing other issues.

And yet on another note - many of you have asked if we've considered the X Clinic in Texas. We have looked into it, however insurance does not pay for the treatment and as you can imagine, it is quite expensive. The other issue is that there is a two year commitment for us to be in Houston - which would not be good for our family at this time and quite frankly, we need results for Carter a lot faster than that with the flexibility to be able to go wherever we need to go at any given time. It is also known that this type of tumor typically only reacts to radiation - the chemo is typically used as a way to prevent it from coming back. Example - if Carter was an adult with this type of tumor, radiation would be started immediately and then chemo would be used once it was gone.

Really - we're just trying to buy time for Carter's little brain to develop so we can minimize the damage that the radiation will do to it.

Heavenly Father - Thank you for the roller coasters of life. Thank you for the twists and turns and loop-de-loops. They are all a part of your ultimate plan and once the roller coaster slows to a stop, I will look back and marvel at it. With you by my side, I am not scared of the roller coaster, for you have laid the track before me. In Your Name, I pray. Amen.

1/18/12
It's late. I should be sleeping. I need to be sleeping. I am praying to get some sleep soon.

Today Carter seemed to do well with the Avastin IV chemo. He wasn't real thrilled with the oral chemo that he had to take later in the day. I'm going to have to work on this......it could be a long fourteen days of oral chemo. Pray for me.

so far. so good. Thank you Jesus!

((HUGS!!))

1/19/12
My sweet friends -

Tonight I have something heavy weighing on my heart and I need to share.
I need you all to realize that even though St. Jude is the Disney of hospitals, and there are so many miraculous stories here - there are also stories that are heart wrenching and tear jerking. There are stories that will crush your spirit and cause you to ache. Please remember that there are so many here who really need your prayers. Please pray for all of the children of St. Jude.

One of our dear friends is fighting an awful battle right now. He is a buddy of Carter's and has been fighting for a long, long time. Chase has been such a fabulous friend to Carter and he needs our prayers. Chase is from SC and should be a freshman at Clemson. Please pray for Chase, he and his mom have been such bright spots during our stay here. Carter raids their candy bowl, invites himself into their room, and pretty much lives each day to see Chase. Today Chase had surgery. Please pray for his healing.

The longer we stay here, the more we hear of the sad stories that exist. St. Jude cures 80% of their patients, which is phenomenal. Unfortunately, there is another 20% who do not make it. It is agonizing to hear of these children who are fighting every day for their lives.

Please pray for these families. Pray for their comfort. Pray for their peace. Remember that for all of the beautiful St. Jude poster children, there are others who don't make it.

Heavenly Father, I beg of you to envelope your love around those St. Jude patients who need it most right now. Let them be at peace because they know you are near. Father God, let there be grace and dignity in the lives of these children who are fighting a battle that they should never had to have fought. Help these children fight dear Lord, show them your mercy. I lift my heart up to you, dear Lord. Amen.

1/21/12
I'm a little nervous. Actually, I'm a lot nervous. This chemo seems too easy. I'm baffled that Carter hasn't had more side effects yet. Not that I want side effects either.... I worry that this means the chemo isn't working. I am trying to wrap my head around the fact that the last chemo protocol made Carter so sick and didn't work, and this chemo round doesn't seem to be affecting him at all. Heavenly Father, grant me peace with this process.
I know that God is at work. Carter acts like a normal 2.5 year old. Well, actually - he doesn't ......he acts like a normal 3.5 or 4 year old. I'm not just saying this - other people are amazed that Carter isn't older than 2.5. He speaks clearly. He has an amazing memory (long-term memory is rather shocking!). If you were to see Carter in a store, you wouldn't know that he wasn't well ....unless you were to see his bald little head with all of its scars on it! I know that this is a gift from God. He wants me to relish in having my baby healthy through this process as much as possible. If you were to walk by our door at Target House, more than likely, you'd hear giggles. We are trying to celebrate the gift of normality - because it is a gift. I consider it a gift to give Carter his chemo instead of having to be in-patient. Each day I give Carter his medicine orally. He is pretty good about taking it. Tonight I gave it to him too quickly and he gagged, causing him to vomit. Bad mommy. I learned my lesson. He will take the one chemo orally for ten days and the other for fourteen days. On the fifteenth day Carter will receive another IV chemo - this time we will be out-patient in Charlotte for it.

Please pray that my dad gets here safely. He's driving from Northern Virginia to Cincinnati to Memphis. Last night he drove to Cincy and slid off the road when he hit an ice patch. Thank God he wasn't hurt and neither was the van. Seriously - I need to put the man in a bubble (LOVE YOU DADDY!)! Anyways - once he gets here, we will pack up and return to Greenwood. We will take a respite there and then drive to the condo in Cornelius to get things set up there. It is such a blessing that this condo is available for us to use. God had a reason for it. Needless to say, the condo is empty, so I will need to purchase a bed and sleeper sofa for it quickly. I think that we have most everything else .....it's kind of like arriving at Target House back in November.......only without furniture!

I have been packing our room here at Target House. It is almost surreal because I know that we'll be coming back to Memphis eventually for radiation. Today we created our canvas scrapbook page to "leave our mark" here on the second floor of Target House. It turned out so well and again, I'm so thankful for Stacy for helping me with it. I'll try to post a few pics later.

Today there was a Zumbathon in the town where we lived until December. Approximately $600 was raised in Carter's behalf. I'm am so humbled by this fundraiser - we don't even live in the Locust area and they're doing fundraisers for Carter! Even though St. Jude pays for almost everything here - we had over five figures in bills for the three weeks that Carter was in the hospital in Charlotte. I almost have to laugh at the bills sometimes. When we were home, one arrived for the Hickman port surgery. It claimed that it was for $3800 and that Blue Cross Blue Shield wasn't going to pay for it. REALLY? We were sure to raise issue on that one! I can't imagine NOT having a Hickman port for this journey.......duh! Also - just in case you didn't know - did you know if you call to pay your bill and ask if there is a discount for paying in full, most of the time the billing clerk will give you a 20% discount.....just for asking! I'm learning so much on this journey.

On a happy note, Carter has been adopted by a women's team at Rhodes College here in Memphis through the Friends of Jaclyn Foundation. Thank you for working so patiently and so tirelessly with me! I'm so excited that little man will have a whole new group of girlfriends! And these girls won't stick him with needles and give him nasty medicines!

I'm sure that there are a ton of other things to tell you, but it's late and I can't remember right now.......

Please keep praying. I cannot begin to tell you how much we need your prayers.

Heavenly Father, I beg of you. Hear our prayers. Heal my sweet Carter. Make him well again. Love him and hold him in your embrace. Grant me peace through this process, dear Lord. Please

God, take away this tumor. Just make it go away. I am faithful to you Father God, now and always. I lift up my heart - Amen.

1/23/11
St. Jude - Patron Saint of Hopeless Causes, hear my prayer. Please heal my little boy, Carter. Remove the tumor that ails him. In return, I will sing your praises by writing a fictional book about St. Jude and donate some of the monies to St. Jude Children's Hospital. I have heard that you listen to the prayers of those who will give back to the hospital and I promise you, I will give back as much as I possibly can if you will only heal my little boy and make him whole once again. I will tell the world of your greatness and mercy. Hear my prayer, Amen.

I need to note that I am Episcopalian, so praying to a saint isn't something that I typically do. The exception to this being St. Joseph as I buried him our yard - speaking of which, there are three St. Joseph statues in our yard in Locust - upside down. Maybe that's why our house sold in just four months??? However, that being said, I have heard time and time again on this journey that if you pray to St. Jude and offer him something in return, he will grant your prayer. So I am going to do it ......

(Disclaimer - pep talk to myself) - So I'm going to promise something big and radical. I know that I can write and I can write well. I know that my experience as a middle school teacher will aid in the writing of this book. I know that I can write a fictional book which highlights the fictional journeys of St. Jude patients and bring a heightened awareness to the world about pediatric cancer and the devastation that it brings. I know that I will be supported by friends and family. I know that I can do this for Carter. I have to do this for Carter.

OK - so now I've got to write this book and be accountable for it. And hope and pray that some publisher out there might want to print it.......but I'll figure that out later.....gotta write the book first.

Anyway - I spoke too soon about not seeing the side effects of the chemo this round. Carter has vomited a few more times (including once in the middle of Target), but he has gotten mean again. He was literally trying to bite the side of the chair at one point tonight because he knew that he couldn't/shouldn't bite me. And then within seconds he was laughing and riding his truck up and down

*the hallways with his buddy. The chemo causes a switch to flip -
one second he is my sweet little boy and then next he is just as
mean as possible. My poor baby.*

*Tomorrow Carter has a check-up at the hospital to see how his
counts are doing and to see if he'll need blood before we leave for
Charlotte. If all goes well, we'll drive back on Thursday. We're
waiting for my dad to arrive with the van (yet another fiasco
occurred today). We will drive to Greenwood for a brief stop (as in
a day) and then on to Charlotte.*

*I am eternally thankful for everyone here in Memphis - the phone
calls, the food, the gifts......you truly have helped make our visit
easier. I am so blessed for everything that you've done. And this
isn't good-bye, it's see you later.....because we will be back.*

*I need to head to bed. I haven't gotten to bed before midnight the
past two nights (nothing like a tornado warning to get the
adrenaline pumping at 10pm at night!) and I'm beyond
exhausted....I know this because my fingers twitch when I try to
relax!*

((HUGS!!))
S.

This journal entry in my mind haunts me. I thought that I would write a
fictional book. I thought that I would be able to share a story that wasn't
true, that wasn't personal, and that wasn't about my son. I was wrong.
This story is mine. It is Carter's. It is my love story. It is a story of love,
of perseverance, of hope, and of resilience. I am blessed that I can write
it. I realized that it my job as Carter's mommy to tell his story.

1/24/12
*Carter and I had a very serious discussion.....we talked about
what made him happy. Here's what he said......*

Happiness is:

My puppy and football

Riding in my truck with Mason

Bojangles

Meeting new friends: Belle, Bradlee, Aiden, Chase, Viola, Kohl, Noah, Kayla, and Luca

Hanging out with the nurses on the second floor (especially Beth, Robin, Katie, Sammi, Sara, Brittany, Heather, Teresa, Kristen, and Lacie)

Getting to go home

Getting Carter juice (blood drawn) by Candice in A/T

Playing in the hallway of Target House

The ladies of Target House: Teresa, Sara, JoAnne, Barbara, Kari and Cleo

Taking the trash to the trash chute

Going to do the laundry

Playing on the playground

Miss Trish and sitting on ducks (not literally - think about the sound!)

E-Clinic: Miss Liz, Miss Crystal, Miss Dori, Miss Vickie (i.e. Mickie), Miss Theresa, Dr. Ross, the other Dr. Ross, Dr. Giles, Miss Amy and Miss Jackie

The Pharmacy: Jackie Q.

Ms. Jennifer and her peppermints.

Bojangles

Ericka and Anthony

Macaroni and cheese

Chase's mommy's candy bowl

Biscuits

Bojangles

OH BUMPERS!

Putting my window down at McDonald's to say hi

Bubbles in the bubble bath and playing with Diego

Mickey Mouse

Putting water on my forehead and saying "Father, Son, and Holy Spir-wet"

Mattie, Lily, and Ms. Stacy

Trains

Pirates

Hats

Bojangles

Calling Daddy and Mason on mommy's cell phone

Tiger and Saks

Grandy's van

Ummmmm.........ummmmmmm........

And that's about the time the snoring began.......

Heavenly Father - thank you for allowing me to see things through the eyes of a child. Thank you for this time with Carter - although I don't like the circumstances, I love the giggles and the joy that he brings to my life. Thank you for showing me the innocence of love. My only wish is that everyone could be so lucky. I lift my heart up to you, dear Lord. Amen.

1/28/12
There's always so much to write about and there never seems to be enough time! The good news is after a VERY LONG

JOURNEY we have reached the condo in Cornelius, NC. It's just that, a condo.....without furniture, cable, etc. My version of camping!

Tonight I am humbled by a total miracle. At least, I consider it a miracle. Some of my former students (they are now sophomores in high school) have been hard at work selling parachute cord bracelets for $5. Today they sold them outside of the Sam's Club in Concord/Kannapolis in NC. These students chose to give up a Saturday (all day!) to help raise funds for Carter. They had 50 bracelets to sell at $5 each - which should have meant a total of $250. These students not only raised $250 - but they raised $1300+ !!!!!!!!

In a day and age when teenagers are chastised for being lazy, demanding, and self-centered, I think that it is important to recognize the incredible selflessness that these teenagers have exhibited. These are kids who put up with my high expectations and crazy antics for an entire school year - and yet are still willing to give up their Saturday to help out their former teacher. I am typing through tears as I write this because I feel so blessed to know these amazing young adults. And to think, I had the joy of teaching them for an entire year!

Please don't misunderstand, I am forever and eternally grateful for every fundraiser and donation that is given in honor of Carter. I just think that it is so admirable that teenagers (and former students of mine at that!) would be willing to help raise money and give so much of themselves for my little boy.

One of these students also made it her mission to make sure that Carter had an incredible Christmas. Just before Christmas she and her parents drove to Spartanburg, SC to meet with Paul on his way to Memphis. They delivered Christmas presents to the boys. However, one of these presents was priceless because it was for me. The young lady took almost every photo of Carter and Mason from my Facebook account and had them printed. She then created an amazing collage of my two boys for me. I am having it dry-mounted and framed so that I will be able to share it with everyone who visits us in Greenwood.

Today, when the students delivered the money to us here in Cornelius, I was made aware that a woman was ugly with the students. The students explained that Carter was being treated by St. Jude. Her response was something along the lines of St. Jude paying for everything. I wish that I could have been present. I wish that I could have looked her in the eyes and told her how ignorant she was being.

St. Jude pays for the expenses that are incurred while at the hospital or while under treatment. However, Carter encountered over six figures for the first two weeks of treatment here in Charlotte. That means we're responsible for 20% of the bills. St. Jude does not pick these bills up. St. Jude does not pay for travel that is not medically necessary. So when we returned home a few weeks ago, St. Jude did not pay for it. They have paid for us to return to CLT for outpatient chemo. They do give us an allowance for food each week at Kroger, but they do not pay for the McDonalds and Dominos that Carter craves because his taste buds have changed (due to the chemo). They do give us housing at Target House, however, it is essentially an apartment with minimal sundries. I personally purchased additional cleaning materials, towels, sheets, and kitchen supplies. Please do not take this incorrectly - I am forever grateful for St. Jude and what they benevolently supply .....however, I want to clear up the misconception that St. Jude is an all-inclusive destination. We still have significant expenses. No one pays for the gas to and from Levine, no one pays for the furniture we need to furnish this condo where we will be living, no one pays for all of the extras that St. Jude doesn't provide. We don't qualify for Social Security Insurance or Medicaid. So seriously, lady at Sam's Club, get. a. clue.

Sorry - I'm off of my soapbox now.

It means so much to me to know that students that I once taught are fighting for my Carter. It makes me feel like I did something right. I may not have been the Teacher of the Year, but at least I touched a few hearts. I'm so thankful that we're here in Cornelius and that we already have been able to see friends. My spirit has returned. I can feel the love around me even though I have yet to see so many of our friends. I am so glad to be home, even if it isn't Locust. At least we are closer. At least I know the area. At least we are home.

Father God, thank you for the beautiful blessings of this life. Thank you for the young people who shine with your glory. Praise you, dear Lord, for bringing us closer to home to help heal our wounds and rejuvenate our fighting spirit. In Your Name, Amen.

1/31/11
Just a quick update - lots of unpacking and organizing to do! Good news is that we got the cable connected and Disney Jr. is included in the standard package.......it's the little things!

I swear that angels hang out in Target. I had Mason with me on Sunday and he was being good - just not as good as I needed him to be right then. A young woman stopped and said something to the effect of, "what's the worse that he's going to do? Run into some little old lady?" (which is a thought that mortifies me!) I very nicely responded, "you're right, but I'm a little stressed out right now - my other child at home is fighting a brain tumor and I'm more high strung than usual." She just smiled and said something like "Oh wow. Sorry." and walked on. The man however next to me in the cleaning aisle literally stopped in his tracks and asked me my child's name (in a very thick Long Island accent). I told him Carter and he immediately raised his arms to praise our Lord and said a prayer for Carter. And of course, I started to cry. He very simply said, "You need to remember that God has a plan. If it's God's plan for Carter to be here, then so it will be. If it isn't God's plan for Carter to be here, it just means that the world isn't ready for your little guy yet." Then this total stranger embraced me in the middle of Target and promised to continue to pray for my little guy. How incredible is that?

Last night two young men arrived at our condo door, supposedly selling magazine subscriptions. I'm not sure if they were legit or not, but once they caught sight of Carter running around naked in his diaper, their spiel totally changed. They obviously had a moment of some kind or another because they told me that they would remember Carter and that they would be praying for him. They even said that they felt bad for even asking me for a magazine subscription.

Maybe I can use this tactic on telemarketers, too? It won't be nearly as effective as Carter running around in his diaper, but maybe they won't pester us at dinner time if I explain that my son has a brain tumor? Just a thought.

Another happy note is that Carter will be receiving a wish from the Make A Wish Foundation. We'll find out more soon! So excited for my little guy!

Today is day 14 of Carter's chemo. Tomorrow we will go to Levine to see Dr. Chad and for Carter's Avastin infusion. On a bright note, the side effects have been minimal this round. He had some minor vomiting for a few days and then it subsided. Other than a runny nose, he's been a trooper! Of course, this makes me worry that the chemo isn't working........I've determined I'm going to worry regardless.......so be it.

Need to run and capitalize on Carter's naptime........it's just easier to get things accomplished when the little man is sleeping.

Heavenly Father, thank you for the everyday angels in our lives. Thank you for the blessing of a home in the Charlotte area - even if it doesn't have furniture. Father God, thank you for the adventures in our lives. They make it memorable. I lift up my heart. Amen.

2/3/12
How can it be Friday already? Paul and Mason will be here shortly. It has been a fast week. We've been attempting to get settled (key word - attempting). Carter has been in good spirits for the most part. I will write more early next week when my mind isn't so muddled with everything else that needs to be done!

((HUGS!!))
S.

2/4/12
Dear God -

It's me, Sarah. Can we chat again? Actually, if you don't mind, I'll do the chatting and you do the listening......and then I'll listen for your response via whisper......if that's your will.

So let's recap - you've purposely put me through trials and tribulations in my life to make me strong and to make me faithful. I get it. I didn't always like it, but I get it.

And now, we've got this Carter situation - which I'm convinced we'll win with your help. Even though I feel like I've been beaten up and spit out. It's OK - I can handle it. You're here with me. I'm good.

But here's my question.....I'm at my lowest, I'm exhausted (even my friends tell me that I look exhausted so you know that isn't good!), and I live in a total state of chaos (which city do I live in now? what day is it?). Yet you ARE STILL GIVING ME MORE ....REALLY? Do you think that I am THAT STRONG?

What was the point of moving into a condo without furniture and five years of dirt (which I thought would be our only issues!) only to have a dryer that wasn't working (and I am sorry that Dad had to remove the bird's nest from the dryer vent in order to make it work). What is the purpose of a dishwasher that won't work? And I totally understand why you made me endure cold baths at St. Jude because this water heater barely allows me to get my hair washed before it's frigid! I haven't been able to get to the grocery store for ample supplies because I'm too worried about buying furniture and cleaning. Poor dad hasn't stopped working since he's been here and he'll have to leave soon. What's really bad - is that I know you have a purpose to all of this chaos.....you've got a plan and I'm just not seeing it yet. But honestly, the stress is driving me nuts and I can't sleep because of it - even when I do take sleep meds, they don't work!

Heavenly Father - why are you still making things difficult? I still have faith in you. I still don't waiver......believe me cold showers, dryers that don't work, and no furniture really don't phase me......but would you please grant me something EASY in my life? Something that doesn't take effort? Is it there and I'm not seeing it? I am so blessed with so many wonderful friends and family and they have made this journey so much more bearable. They help me be strong, as do You. But I just need some simplicity in my life.....on SOME LEVEL. Please Father God, help me hear you. Am I doing something wrong? If so, please whisper in my ear and tell me what to do right......and you know that I will.

Thank you Heavenly Father, King of Kings, for the fact that Carter has felt well this past week. It DOES make life easier. Maybe this is the answer to my prayer about the side effects. When Carter feels good it allows me to get more done and to get the condo together. Thank you for the beautiful sunsets that you've granted me this week. I know that they are a message from you and they calm my heart. I once said that when I am close to the water, I am calm and I am at my best. Perhaps that is why you brought me here. Perhaps once I get through these initial hurdles there will be peace. I pray that Carter learns to love the boats and the sunsets and the serenity of the water, just as I have over the years. Now, if I could just jump aboard as rail-meat in a regatta, total bliss might be found.

There isn't a day that goes by that I don't wonder about the lessons that need to be learned, the lessons that I need to teach, and the lessons that need to be heard by the masses. Am I supposed to start teaching now? Am I supposed to find my voice now? Father God, if you want me to be loud and obnoxious about pediatric cancer, just let me know and you know that I'll get started! By the way, I've got the book outlined......just need to find some time to type!

Father God - thank you for your love. Thank you for the trials and tribulations, even if I don't always understand them. I lift my heart up to you. Amen.

((HUGS!!)

S.

P.S. And God, just remember, when I sign my posts ((HUGS!!)), I'm sending them to you, too........and it's amazing when I feel them come right back at me from you!

2/6/13
Thank you Heavenly Father for today. Carter was happy and joyful - tickling me, giggling with me, and telling me that he was my baby. Best of all dear Lord, you showed me that Carter's hair is REALLY growing back......and it's still angel white. Father God, thank you for helping today be a productive day and for the strength that you give me daily to fight for my little guy. I can feel

your arms around me giving me the hug I need to move forward. In Your Name, Amen.

Today was a dumb day in many ways. The bedroom now looks like a bedroom and most of the boxes and stuff have been put away. We're making progress in the kitchen and the piles of laundry are slowly diminishing. Miraculously, you can even see the family room floor now! It's the little things.

Even though today was more unpacking and more cleaning, Carter was such a joy. It amazes me that he is so happy when he is enduring so much. He is so loving and so kind. It makes it hard to say, "no" to his requests for Bojangles biscuits (which he had again today - but only 1x versus 3x ....progress!). He has been a big helper in so many ways. Today he was hooked on the fact that he is my baby. Time and time again, he asked, "I'm your baby? Mason's your baby? Daddy's your baby?" To which I would respond, "Yes, baby. Am I YOUR baby?" And of course, he would smile that big smile and get that twinkle in his eye - and then hug me in only the way that Carter can hug me......

Thank you God. I hear you, loud and clear. Sweet dreams.

((HUGS!!))
S.

2/9/12
Heavenly Father - I know that you are in my life. I know that you surround me by angels. When I least expect it, angels are there. They come in all different forms, they honor Carter in all different ways, but they are there......and for that, I am eternally grateful and forever indebted to you. Thank you for understanding my love story, dear Lord. Others may not understand it, but I know that You do. In Your Name, Amen.

I remember that one summer I went on a date with a guy from Bible study and we started talking about our Christian faith. I remember how he told me that God had saved his life intentionally and purposely - and how I agreed that I thought that God had done the same for me. This young man put me on the spot and asked me how......and at that point in time, I couldn't exactly articulate it. I couldn't tell him about the time the brakes went out on my truck while going downhill and I had enough sense to get into the left-hand lane and swerve into the grass versus swerving into the right-hand lane and going into the flood level creek......or how the only car that stopped to help me had a man with a beard that emulated Jesus. I couldn't help him understand that when you're mauled by a dog when you're seven years old that your only dream is to be pretty - or to even by liked by boys due to the scar on your face (even if it's only seen by you) that you believe God has something to do with it. I couldn't get the words out .....so many experiences, but no voice to utter the words.

You see - what those who know me will tell you (most probably) is that I'm an outgoing and outspoken person.....which really is only half of the story. I am outgoing and outspoken - when I'm comfortable.......and most of the time, I'm more comfortable writing than I am speaking. You see - my dad can tell a great story.....he has mastered the art of oral story-telling.....I, on-the-other-hand, will write a story and work out whatever it is I have to tell through words. If you know me REALLY well, you know that if I'm nervous or overwhelmed, I will do nothing but giggle and smile because I don't know what to say.....which may seem inappropriate at times, to say the least.....

When I posted the other day - I must have sounded pretty overwhelmed and pretty desperate.......I know this now because angels have answered, once again. Bed Bath and Beyond Coupons have arrived in droves, gift cards to BB&B and Target have arrived, and so have messages of hope. A friend from high school will be walking for Carter in a St. Jude walk/marathon, a sister friend and her husband will be honoring Carter through a St. Baldrick's fundraiser, and yet another sister friend and family has created a tournament to honor Carter and other families in need. Some of these projects have been in the works for months and only now are being told to me. Heavenly Father - when I am at my lowest, You lift me up.

The best news is that Carter has been happy the past few days and felt well. He is such a charmer and loves anyone who pays him attention. Today he was asking for Elise (a nurse) before we got to the hospital - and as we walked onto the elevator ....there she was! He talks incessantly and today was literally running down the halls of the Hematology/Oncology Clinic. Not only that - but he tells his favorite nurse, Jessica, what she needs to do in order to flush his lines and get "Carter Juice." His line of the day, "you put Heparin in my line?" I swear that he is enduring the youngest nursing school/pre-med school available!

Today, Carter's counts came back fabulous. All is well. I am praying that tomorrow we'll be able to drive to Greenwood to see the "new house" and to see Paul and Mason. What a fabulous treat it will be if we can go ....

Heavenly Father - you hear my prayers. You lead me, you guide me, you give me strength. Thank you for the angels that surround me - those known and unknown. Thank you for the good days - for Carter's charming ways and for the fact that this round of chemo has had limited side effects.......I am forever indebted to you dear Lord. I lift my heart up to you. Amen.

2/12/12
There is so much to write about, but never enough time. This weekend (and days leading up to it) has been fabulous. There are so many stories to tell and memories to write about......

We will be returning to Cornelius/Charlotte tomorrow. Grandy will be leaving the condo - he has a head cold and asked us to stay in Greenwood an extra day so that he wouldn't come in contact with Carter. He will leave in the morning and we'll arrive in the afternoon. From what I understand - the dishwasher is now working.....REJOICE!

I will write more once we return and once our lives have settled again .....are we ever settled anymore?

Can't wait to share the stories over the past few days - so many happy memories that have been made!

2/15/12
To quote a wise man, "Life is what happens, AFTER you plan it." I've been trying to write and get caught up here for a week and there hasn't been a moment. This is a long one - get comfy!

You see, last Wednesday Carter and I ventured to Locust to run some errands. I needed to go to the bank and clear out the safety deposit box as well as see some friends. Carter was on his best behavior all day and was such a joy.

We went to Bank of Stanly where he raided the lollipops and peppermints (and then declared to Mr. Mike that they were "disgusting!"). Carter also managed to convince Mr. Mike into giving him one of his miniature clock airplanes (which now sits on our dresser). There were lots of hugs from all of the "nice ladies" there, too! Mommy got the paperwork that she needed and Carter blew kisses as we headed out the door.

Since it was lunchtime, it was deemed necessary to drive-thru Bojangles and see our extended family there! Two biscuits, a sweet tea, and small season fry later......Carter saw all of his friends and, of course, I had to roll down the window so he could tell them all about his adventures. It was so nice to drive through a Bojangles and actually KNOW the staff. Mr. Gregory, Ms. Karen, and Ms. Nicole were all there to serve - PERFECT! OH! and Carter swears that the Bojangles in Locust is the best!

Carter munched on his lunch as I drove across town (all of five minutes!) to Locust Child Development Center to see his old teachers. We stayed outside and they were able to come out, one-by-one, to see little man and hear his stories (have I mentioned that Carter likes to talk and tell stories?). It was so good to see the women who were second-moms to my little guy. It did both of our hearts good to see everyone there.

We did a quick drive-by of Locust Valley for a hug from Miss Candice. It was heart-wrenching to see our old house for the first time. I'll keep my commentary to myself.

After our hug, it was on to Charlie's Hardware to see Mr. Charlie and give him a BIG HUG, too! Not only did Carter get a hat, but he found more ways for Grandy to spend his money (yes, Carter wants the little wheelbarrow for his birthday Grandy!). It was so much fun to see Carter explore the hardware store and talk to Charlie - I think Carter would have stayed all day if he could have ....it was a playground to him!

We then made a quick stop at Wells Fargo/Wachovia to clear out the safety deposit box where we ran into an old student of mine from the college and Miss Amy and Hadley. Did I mention that Carter is a celebrity? Can't go anywhere without being recognized! In fact, I think that Amy was actually driving by and saw us in the parking lot! It was wonderful to see them all as well and I wish that we'd had more time to chat and catch up.

We then met up with Ms. Deidra for a quick cupcake (because you can't go to Locust without a cupcake!) and then we headed over to see Ms. Bernice at Tiger Lily (I was in desperate need of my favorite Tyler candle and some aromatherapy!). And, of course, Carter told stories through it all (and I think that he would have bought just about everything in the store there, too!)and we LOVED every minute of it.......just wish that there had been more time to see more people!

phew! And that was just Wednesday!

Thursday we headed to Levine for lab work which was perfect! This meant that we were able to head to Greenwood for the weekend! Carter and I arrived in Greenwood on Friday afternoon. It was a whirlwind weekend, but we were able to see a good many of our Greenwood friends when they came over for an impromptu cookout on Saturday night. It was nice to be in Greenwood and to be surrounded by friends......especially considering I got lost driving to the little market down the street (literally less than a mile from the house!). It's hard feeling like a stranger in your own house and the town where you live, but I'm slowly meeting people and learning my way around. And yes, I'm still trying to figure out where the things are in my own kitchen......ask any of the guests who were in attendance!

I have been blessed to have found two church families in Greenwood. The first is where Mason goes to preschool and where I am blessed to know that my little guy is in such good hands. They have been so amazing to us and we are so thankful for them. It is apparent that Mason is in good hands because he is learning all sorts of new things and gaining a solid Christian foundation. I cannot articulate how much this means to me. The second is our new Episcopal church. Both have reached out to me and our family and it is so reassuring. It's hard enough moving to a new town under the best of circumstances, but it makes it so much easier when your family is being embraced by two different churches in two different ways.

I was able to go to church on Sunday. This was a blessing to me because it has been since Christmas since I attended. At the end of the church service on Sunday, it dawned on me that the lady sitting in the pew next to me had fraternal twins. Coincidentally, this same woman sent me an email several weeks ago welcoming me to the neighborhood and the community and offering me help in a variety of ways. We never met or spoke on the phone prior to Sunday, but she had told me in her email that she had fraternal twins. I truly believe that God led me to sit in that pew on Sunday so that we could finally meet face-to-face. She immediately hugged me and introduced me to several people. I was led into the parish hall and immediately welcomed - what an amazing feeling! I feel so blessed for finding this new church family in so many ways.

Sunday afternoon I was able to do all sorts of menial tasks around the house - the kind of things that I rejoice in now......

Need to run......I'll write more about this week tomorrow.....unless life happens again!

((HUGS!!))
S.

2/17/12
Today has been awful. I couldn't sleep last night and Carter started vomiting at 4am and didn't stop until lunch time. He wouldn't take his anti-nausea meds and I didn't have the strength or will to fight him. Even a trip to Bojangles (he insisted) resulted in Carter vomiting in the parking lot.

We did, however, manage a three hour nap - the highlight of the day.

At least we were able to have a picnic on the balcony of the condo for dinner........maybe that was the highlight of the day.

I have felt so alone today. It's the eve of my birthday and typically I would be excited and anticipating something (even if it didn't happen). Today, I honestly could care less. I now understand people who consider birthdays to be just like any other day. In years past, it has always been my one day (although less and less over the years). This year - who cares? My baby is sick. I'm exhausted and trying to recoup from being sick earlier in the week. I keep listening for God.....and I just can't seem to hear him today.

122

Please pray that Carter has a better day tomorrow. We both need it.

((HUGS!!))

2/17/12
Dear Lord -
I hear you. I am so sorry for throwing myself a pity party. Please embrace my dear friend Marisa and her son, Sebastian (who is also 2). She just got word that after 6 months of chemo her son's tumor has doubled in size and he may only have 4-6 months to live. My heart is breaking. I feel guilty for thinking today was an awful day.....I cannot imagine what she's going through. Please provide peace for her and a miracle.

Hugs,
Sarah

2/18/12
What started as a perfectly awful birthday weekend, turned out to be pretty wonderful. Thank you God for this blessing. I know that you heard my words, thank you for such a fabulous gift.

Thank you all for the birthday wishes - they definitely helped! Your love and support gives me strength.

Mason and Paul arrived on Friday night. It's always so good when they walk through the door. It feels like the puzzle is complete instantly.

Saturday I was able to get away for some retail therapy and some mommy-time. This may sound selfish, but it was definitely needed. Paul napped with the boys while I was gone and then took them to the park to enjoy the beautiful weather.

The best gift was that we were able to be a normal family for a brief moment, once again. It is a gift that I no longer take for granted.

This afternoon Mason and Paul returned to Greenwood and Carter and I had visitors. It was so wonderful to see friends from Locust. Our friends brought dinner from The Fresh House (chicken and dumplings and cobbler, too!). It was marvelous to see them and I think that Carter enjoyed having people other than just me around (I'm boring after a while, you know!).

Mom arrived early evening and will be here for the next ten days or so. She and Dad traded places. She is such a big help and I'm glad to have the support.

Carter did much better taking his chemo tonight - he still doesn't like it, but at least it didn't take an hour and a half to get him to take it! I've mixed the chemo with cherry juice (from the cherry jar). Please pray that he'll continue to make progress with taking the oral chemo.

Today is Day 5 - that means we are half-way through one of the oral chemos and a third of the way through the other oral chemo. We'll go back to Levine on Feb. 29th for the second IV infusion of Avastin and complete this second round.

I have to admit - there are so many moments when I question whether or not this chemo protocol is working. Since the side effects are minimal, does it mean that the chemo is working? Or that it isn't working? I wish that I knew the answer......and it's hard waiting until March 13th to find out the answer. I would love to be able to make plans after our trip to St. Jude and the MRI, but I can't - everything is tentative and everything is based off of whether or not the tumor is growing or whether it has stabilized. As a planner, this is the hardest part of this journey - God is the ultimate planner, not me......

I replay December 30th in my head over and over again. The phone call saying to head to recovery because they didn't do the spinal tap......the knowing in my gut that something was wrong, but not knowing what......the feeling that I was experiencing October 6th over again......but not knowing why until later. I remember showing up to E-Clinic in tears and the sweet ladies at the front desk whisking me to the back.......and watching the doctor walk in with red eyes and knowing that he had been crying.

My prayer is that March 13th is unlike any of this......I don't know if I can do this scenario again for a third time......

I am thankful that we'll be headed to Disney the week prior to Carter's MRI. It will be a much needed distraction and I know that the boys will be in total awe. This is the same trip that we had planned to take the week after Thanksgiving - but were unable to due to Carter's diagnosis and chemo. This year has been a year in the making now........never will I postpone a trip again for any reason (it was originally going to be in May, then got moved to November, etc. etc.). God, you have shown me to seize the day.....

Heavenly Father, thank you for the gift of life. Thank you for the gifts that surround me every day - not just on my birthday. Praise you, Father God, for the tantrums and fits because they make me appreciate the good times so much more. Thank you for the love of friends and family, for the support and nurturing that they provide. Lord God, thank you for each moment that you give me with Carter. I cherish them, for they are truly a gift. In Your Name, Amen.

2/20/12
It was brought to my attention today that perhaps I sound too positive about Carter's tumor......that I am not being realistic enough about his diagnosis......that I am too hopeful.

I have to admit, I'm almost dumbfounded by this scenario.....perhaps I haven't written about the gross realities of a brain tumor diagnosis, perhaps I sugar coat my writing, perhaps I just refuse to quit on my son.

You see, if you take the time to research high-grade anaplastic (malignant) Astrocytoma gliomas in children, you'll find that it isn't always a happy ending. In fact, since Carter's Astrocytoma is inoperable, the reality looks pretty glum. If Carter was an adult or even an older child, the doctors wouldn't even do chemotherapy initially. They would remove the tumor (if it were operable) and then do radiation.....and then possibly do chemo depending on testing, scans, etc. Radiation will possibly cause cognitive impairment and hormonal issues - especially since Carter's tumor is so close to the pituitary gland. And, depending on who you ask or what you read, living beyond 3-5 years after treatment of an Astrocytoma is rare. The reality isn't like a Sweet Valley High romance novel.

So - all of that being said, I know that God has a plan. I don't know what it is, I don't know where it will take us, I don't know how this story will end. I do, however, know this.....God is good. God is a healer. God will show us the path that we need to take. God has a plan for Carter......and if you look closely - I think that you can already see God at work rallying the Prayer Warriors, giving people hope, and helping people understand what it's like at St. Jude.

I have always believed that God created doctors (or any profession for that matter) because He wanted them here on Earth to complete a task. The way medicine is changing, what's to say that Carter will not be a part of a doctor's task? Cancer medicine is changing on a regular basis. There are weekly, if not daily, news articles about cancer treatments being developed. When I speak to doctors, they tell me about the developments that are being made but which aren't yet approved to be used on patients.....what's to say that one of these treatments won't help Carter? How can I not be hopeful.....

And besides, Carter has a multitude of angels looking out for him - both earthly and heavenly......

So why do I not sound more realistic or cut-throat about Carter's diagnosis? Because I have faith........it's that simple. Maybe Carter is the child who will defy the odds, maybe he is the child that will help lead a doctor to a new treatment, maybe Carter is the one who will teach us all something.

Only God knows.

((HUGS!!))

I believed this with every depth of my being. I believed that there was going to be some type of treatment or something to help my sweet boy. It wasn't denial, it was hope. It was faith. It was knowing that my God heals. I still remember the message that my friend sent. She didn't know. She wasn't trying to be mean. She just wanted to prepare me for the worst. The truth is, you can never be prepared for the worst. You can try, you can pretend, but you can't escape it.

2/21/12
My dearest Carter,

By now, you must realize what an amazing Mommy you have. What a gift to spend all day everyday with her! Running errands, getting "Carter juice", and best of all, going to Bojangles (just to name a few). She is there when you wake up in the morning and even when it is time for bed. Mommy is there, whether 'there' is Memphis, Charlotte, Greenwood, Locust (.....did I miss one) and always overflowing with endless love for "Her baby!" Yup, you have a wonderful Mommy. She has built an ARMY OF PRAYER WARRIORS, and it continues to grow through her unwavering love for you. Our support structure has grown exponentially due to her relentless pursuit of developing new contacts and cultivating her strong existing network. Her boundless devotion began the day you were born and can be clearly seen today in her daily routine (playing, eating, laughing, crying with you, giving you "CC's" that are more like YUCK, YUCK's, changing 'Buddy's' dressing, etc.). Never did she want to become a nurse, but has now had more training than the average Mommy and possesses a natural talent in her bedside manner. She takes the aches, crying, vomiting, trips to the hospital, etc. in stride (most of the time!)

While these various activities are happening, Mommy still has the strength to communicate the most recent events for all the PRAYER WARRIORS on this site!

Gracious and Merciful Father,
Thank you for blessing Carter, and Mason, with such an incredible Mommy. She only thinks about what is best for the boys, and myself. Thank you for her dedication to this family and granting her more patience than she ever thought she had. Her words continue to be an inspiration to us all and I am humbled to call her my wife.

In Jesus name,

Amen

2/22/12
As of today, we have one week left of this round of chemo.....I don't know whether to celebrate or cry......my baby who used to

take medicine like a champ fights me now with every ounce of fight he has in him (and believe me, he's strong!). Giving oral chemo - even flavored with cherry juice is cruel and unusual punishment to a 2.5 year old.

We'll make it.....we have to make it.......

Yesterday I didn't post because Paul surprised me by posting instead. He is such a wonderful father. It made a really hard day so much easier by reading his words.

Yesterday morning Carter awoke at 5:30am......not good for Carter, and not good for me! He started complaining that his neck hurt, head hurt, and tummy hurt - all on the side where his shunt is located. I gave him some sweet tea to try to "make it all better," but he started vomiting instead. In fact, he vomited seven times in two hours. This meant that we were headed to the hospital.

Too illustrate just how frazzled I was (and exhausted from only having 5 hours of sleep) - a sweet little girl ran up to me and I immediately called her "Stella" and I then proceeded to call her mother "Mandy".......for whatever reason my brain thought that the only friends we knew at Levine were from Locust. In fact, it was our dear friends Kelley and Belle from St. Jude! Thank goodness that Kelley was so understanding.....I was mortified! We actually got to see Stella and Mandy the previous week - which was wonderful, too!

Anyways - yesterday morning included an x-ray series of Carter's shunt (head, neck, tummy), lab work, and a CT scan. You see, Carter said all of the "red flag" words that make the doctors go nuts and then he coupled it with the vomiting......at first the doctors were convinced he had the Norovirus, but in fact, I think that he was just extremely constipated (sorry if it's too much info!). This is a side effect of the chemo. This morning, I am glad to say - Carter is all better. Although grumpy and tired, he only vomited after gagging on the chemo.....

It's funny, when you have children you get accustomed to dirty diapers, wiping bums, vomit, etc. When you have a child with cancer - you get used to a whole new realm of bodily fluids.

I have to say that Carter was an absolute ROCK STAR for the CT scan. This was his sixth CT scan in five months. I essentially laid on top of Carter while we rode in and out of the CT scanner.....I honestly think that he could have done it by himself without me. He even told the radiologist tech that "Bald Guys are Hot!" I think that we made his day since the man didn't have any hair either!

Today has been an easier day in so many different ways - still difficult, but easier.

As we enter this Lenten Season, I am still trying to determine what to give up this year. I don't listen to the radio anymore because I appreciate the quiet time in the car. Facebook/CaringBridge/the computer are my ways of communicating with so many people about Carter and his situation. I have given up so much in the past few months, there isn't a whole lot left! I'll keep thinking...However, for Lent I usually try and do something good, too. So I'm going to try and be good about posting here each day - regardless of how good or bad it was, regardless of how tired I am, regardless of what there is to report (so please bear with me!).

Heavenly Father, as we enter this season of Lent, help us remember that you gave your only son for us. You gave up so much more because you so loved us. Father God, cleanse my heart during the next forty days and help me to worthily magnify Your name. Please give me strength, courage, and grace to deal with everything that comes my way. I lift my heart up to you. Amen.

2/23/12
So it occurred to me today that I should help everyone understand the chaos in my life by documenting my daily schedule.....maybe it will help illustrate why I don't pick up the phone to chat with anyone (and I sometimes go several days without talking to Paul). I don't exactly sit around watching soap operas and eating bon bons all day!

6-7am - Carter wakes Mommy up, and yes - we sleep in the same bed because that way I can take care of him immediately during the night should he need me. His vomiting can come on suddenly and leave him unable to call out for me. Depending on the chemo day depends on whether or not we start the day with vomiting or not.

7-9am - Try to convince Carter to eat something (although Gimi hit a gold mine by making him Egg Beaters this morning!). Mommy attempts to get a quiet shower, but Carter is never less than five feet away - usually whining, crying, screaming about something.....

9am-noon - This is the part of the day that is always changing and is never dull. We either a) go to the hospital for blood work/check ups/infusions or b) run errands that need to be run with Carter in tow or c) have visitors

Noon-1pm - lunch time.....try to figure out what Carter might actually eat other than Bojangles....and then usually give in and drive to Bojangles for food since he hasn't had anything to eat and that's just not good.

1-3pm - nap time for Carter.....this is either a) errand time for Mommy (today it was Urgent Care for a random heat rash) b) work on my Facebook store or c) do laundry/dishes/trash/etc.

3-5pm Try to keep Carter happy and content with walks if the weather is good, running a quick errand (it has to be an easy one or life is miserable), or playing with toys, etc.

5pm - attempt to give Carter his chemo and pray that it won't take long (today's attempt with applesauce went fairly well). Usually this is at least an hour long process and it gets pretty ugly.

6pm - try to determine what Carter wants to eat again.....

7pm - Bath time.
7:45 ish - Bedtime.

8pm until midnight - laundry, return emails/FB, process orders for the store, write Caring Bridge, research, and anything else that might need to be done.

Midnight - bedtime.....and no, I would much rather be in bed by 9pm. It might explain why I am exhausted and just a little stressed.

So - although this is a comedic routine, hopefully it helps illustrate a lot. Nothing frustrates me more than someone saying, "but you never call me!" Ummmm - sorry? I'm about two months behind in returning phone calls and writing thank you notes. Hopefully I will catch up eventually. Seriously - the best way to get in touch with me is to either email or text. I know that sounds awful, but that's just the nature of the beast these days.

I hope that I don't sound ungrateful or bitter - because I'm not. I'm simply trying to cast a light on the chaos that reigns in my life. Carter is 2.5 (almost 2.75!) and if he were a healthy child, life would be challenging ......now add being on chemo, being exhausted, etc. etc.

My daily prayer is to simply get through the day with grace and ease. Sometimes I am blessed with an easier day, but many days I am not. And when I have a break, I just want to be quiet and enjoy being alone and peaceful. I want to do mindless things like watch a TV show or work on Pinterest. I don't want to read. I don't want to talk. I just want to be. I'm sure that sounds selfish, sorry.

Most merciful Father, help there to be calm in our lives. Help Carter feel well and be able to be a happy 2.5 year old. Watch over him, Father God, and help him understand that Mommy wants to help make it all better. Lord, hear my prayer. Amen.

2/24/12
It just dawned on me that a week from tomorrow we'll be heading toward Walt Disney World......this has put me into a frenzy - You would think that I'd be micromanaging this trip, but no.....In fact, now I'm realizing just how many outfits I need to pack for the boys.....and if you know me, that isn't an easy task. When you own a clothing store for children - well, let's just say that I'm picky! (and proud of it!)

We had a quiet morning for a change - my gift to myself because I was so exhausted I could barely get the day started at 6:30am.....Carter was whiny and so we just took it easy. Such a nice change! My post last night made me realize that the errands will wait until tomorrow (I know, I know - this contrasts my earlier post about not putting things off .....but really? I can buy a shoe organizer tomorrow and it won't be a big deal - the shoes have been on the floor for this long - what is one more day?).

I was able to speak with Rev.Cox from our church back in NC - she's fabulous and always makes me feel sane. She has been with us on this journey from the very beginning. I will never forget walking into the "family room" at Levine on the PICU floor and seeing her there. She prayed with us that day - anointed Carter with oil - and made sure that we knew she was there for us. And she has been, every step of the way.

My dad has often talked about the relationships he has had with the priests of the churches we've attended over the years (and prior to my being born). You know, although I acknowledged them and I appreciated his stories. I never really understood how important it was to have a relationship with someone in the church.

Years ago, I remember speaking with some teenage boys in our neighborhood about going to church and somehow we got on the topic of shaking the priest/pastors hand at the end of the service. They told me that they had never even met their pastor/priest. That their church was too big. I continued to ask them about whether they knew any of the clergy/elders in their church, and they couldn't think of one. They didn't even know their youth group leaders names.

My prayer is that they eventually met someone to help become their mentors in the church.

As a young child, I remember the children's sermon at the front of the church the rector telling us marvelous stories and helping us to understand Christianity.......I still remember him pulling things out of a box from time to time.

As a teenager, it was my youth group leaders - Bob and Kim. They were second parents to me and helped me through pitfalls when I couldn't or didn't want to go to my parents. Even today, I know that they are there for me if I need them.

During college it was the rector at my college - and even though I didn't always talk to her about issues, I knew that she was always there for me and would help solve them just by speaking to her (even if it was in a group setting). She even came to St. Alban's in DC and married Paul and me almost ten years ago.

Of course, there were the Bible study leaders in college. One of them knew my heart in ways that I couldn't express, moving me to tears with his prayers and discussions. Every once and a while I can still hear him say, "Say-ruh!"

After college, I had Hut and Denise - who even with their own children managed to adopt me and make sure that I stayed on a Christian path. I will never forget Bible studies at the yacht club that I managed and studying Philippians. And I was so blessed that their children accepted me - poor Robin came home from college and suddenly had an older sister......

I guess what I'm trying to say is that I've been blessed by people throughout my life who have built relationships with me around our Christian beliefs. How can I not be thankful for such fabulous relationships? In fact, some of my closest girlfriends are the ones that I went to Bible study with during college. I cannot imagine being on this journey without them. And I certainly couldn't be on this journey without all of the friends from my church from high school in Virginia - they were my extended family then, and even though the "old" church family has gone separate ways.....the families are still close to my heart.

My prayer is that everyone could be so fortunate as to have strong relationships within their own church. I cannot imagine going on this journey without these people in my life. These relationships make me accountable and strong. What an amazing gift from God. I only wish that everyone could be so fortunate.....

On a different note -

We had a wonderful evening with friends from Locust tonight. They actually ended up giving Carter his chemo meds (applesauce with peppermint sprinkles and cinnamon was the magic concoction). And yes, it took a good hour to get him to eat all of the applesauce!

My computer battery is going to die now, so I need to wrap up.....

Father God, thank you for the relationships that I've been able to cultivate in the church environment over the years. They make me strong. I pray that everyone could be so fortunate and feel so loved. Heavenly Father, thank you for the gift of friendship and for the gifts bestowed upon us. We are so blessed on this journey. We have You, our friends, and the love of both. I lift my heart up to you. Amen.

2/25/12
Today I was reminded about courage. You see, courage is not something that is easy. It takes gumption. It takes determination. It takes love.

You know, one of the best lessons my parents ever instilled in me was never to quit. I remember so many times wanting to quit dance lessons, science fair projects, or relationships. Quitting was just the underlying message that they taught me, really it was all about having courage and determination to fight through it. I guess that's why I'm so hurt when people quit on me - in whatever form or fashion. It's the fact that they aren't willing to fight. They aren't willing to conjure up the courage to fight through the battle.

I saw a quote today in Barnes and Noble on a magnet, it said "If you're walking through Hell, keep walking!" AMEN! Seriously, why would I want to stop walking and end up stuck in Hell? Duh.

This journey with Carter takes an awful lot of courage. It takes an awful lot of determination. Most importantly, it resonates that I am not going to quit on my son. I've got gumption. I've got determination. I've got love. I've got Courage.

When I think of courage, I think of the tender-hearted lion in The Wizard of Oz who so wanted courage and didn't realize that he had it. He was so convinced that he didn't have courage, that he didn't realize that it already existed within himself.

You see, I guess you could call me the cowardly lion. I never thought that I would be writing a journal for the world to read. Complete strangers read my journal and Heaven only knows what they think of me! Courage makes you vulnerable. It makes you susceptible to criticism. It makes you strong. I've realized that I have more courage than I ever knew......

I haven't always had courage. I've quit on relationships that I probably should have pursued. I've backed out on opportunities that I should have gone after. I've let down people because I just didn't have the courage to go on with some things. Courage isn't always easy.

With Carter, my sense of courage seems to be instilled. He vomits, I don't flinch. I change his dressing and do it as fast as possible. I have to give him shots, and I cry. I have to give him oral chemo and I get creative. I hold him as he asks me why there is a tumor in his head - and I explain that I don't know but that I'm going to make sure I make it all better. I don't even shed a tear....at least now anyways.

I know that everyone has courage and they exhibit it in other ways. I am reminded of a friend who had the courage to come to me and tell me that she had an eating disorder and didn't know what to do. She showed me where her skin had rubbed off into sores because she didn't have the fat to buffer her legs when she rode horses. She was asking for help. That takes courage. I remember sitting at my dad's bedside in the pre-op room, knowing that he was going to have open heart surgery. But somehow he still managed a smile - that takes courage. When my mom had to bring her parents and brother back to Virginia with her because they could no longer operate their antiques business due to health issues, that takes courage.

Courage surrounds us, embraces us, and pushes us forward. It isn't something that we do intentionally - it just happens. God makes it happen when we need it the most.

I can honestly tell you that it may take courage to write what I do - to open up my heart and mind to total strangers and critics, but it doesn't phase me. I write what is in my heart and God conveys the courage for me to do so.

I promise to live the rest of my life courageously. I will act when I need to and not think twice about it. I will say what needs to be said in hopes to help others. I will not quit on anyone or anything. I will live to be courageous.

Most importantly, when you plan on winning a battle, it takes courage. I'm a fighter. I have God on my side. I will win this battle in one way or another. Bring.It.On.

Sarah Bucciero

It's funny - during my fourth year of teaching, the assistant principal degraded me in front of my peers in a meeting. I remember telling him those exact words - bring.it.on. He reprimanded me for using them, even though he had used those exact words in more than one conversation about overbearing and inept parents. I remember thinking - this man has courage when he is alone or when he is with people he thinks he can trust, but he doesn't have courage when faced with the crowd.

I'll never forget my first year at that school - the culminating portfolio event for my students was to read at a "coffee house" in the school media center. It was an event to help develop their courage. For whatever reason, none of my co-workers were there. None of the administration was there. It wasn't a big deal in my life - I knew that I could handle it.....or at least I thought that I could handle it until the microphone somehow malfunctioned.

Picture this: Approximately 125 seventh grade students and their parents in a standing room only event and the microphone stops working. A microphone that I had no idea how to work. So, instead of keeping my students quiet as they stood in line awaiting their turn to read their best piece of writing from the year (and so thankful for the moms that were trying), I held the microphone wire as best I could to ensure contact - so the students could be heard.

I remember thinking that I had the situation under control and that the microphone was sounding pretty good. That was until I heard a male voice with a New York accent boom from somewhere in the crowd - and although I don't remember exactly what the man said, I remember it was not nice and it wasn't something that other parents wanted their children to hear. From somewhere deep inside of me, the words came, "I'm doing the best I can." And I simply moved on to the next child - hoping to give them the courage to read their work. That wasn't me. That was God. You see, every ounce of me wanted to go head to head with the man. God, on the other hand, granted me grace (which was recognized in many emails the following days by parents of the other students).

Courage isn't always fighting. It's having the grace and dignity to handle a situation as best as possible.

Please don't interpret my words as me being a totally courageous - because I'm not. Sometimes it takes every ounce of my being to be courageous - especially when it comes to Carter. Seriously - how could I move to Memphis with him, leave Paul and Mason behind, and seek treatment at St. Jude for him? Courage.

Heavenly Father - Please continue to grant me courage. Give me the strength and dignity to fight this battle for Carter. May the courage you give me act as a testament to your love, your name, and your grace. Most merciful Father, I humbly ask for you to embrace all of those who know and love Carter and give them courage, too. In Your Name, Amen.

2/26/12
I'm one tired Momma. I need sleep. This journey is exhausting on a good day. Last night was a LONG night. Please say a prayer that both Carter and I get some much needed sleep. It makes it so much easier when we're both well rested.

I'm sorry that I'm not posting more tonight, but I honestly don't think I can write without my falling asleep at the computer.

OH! I put Carter's chemo in sweet tea tonight and he drank it all within minutes! SCORE! Just two more days of the second chemo......and then an IV infusion of Avastin on Wednesday. THEN WE'RE FINISHED WITH THIS ROUND! Praise the Lord! These past two months have flown by in comparison to the first two rounds at St. Jude.......so much easier on so many levels. Praying for good news on March 12/13.

((HUGS!!))

2/27/12
So I have been awful about writing thank you notes to everyone for everything that you've done for our family - so I'm hoping that this long list of items encompasses all of them.......and if I've forgotten your item, please know that I'm sorry - I'm missing a piece of paper that got misplaced in the move......so I'm going from memory!

- *The meals....oh the wonderful meals - Locust, Memphis, Cornelius. Thank you for making sure that we eat and for easing the stress of the day!*
- *For all of our Prayer Warriors praying for Carter and this journey that we're on together......*
- *American flags flown over Afghanistan during a combat mission (one for Mason and one for Carter!) with certificates in a B-1 Bomber (and yes, I cried and cried over this one!)*
- *The TOYS! Oh.my.goodness! we have just as many as FAO Schwartz and Toys R Us (not complaining - just saying that my children have been blessed!)*
- *The Domino's gift cards - enough to buy three months of pizza at least once a week for Carter (just used the last one!)*
- *The "grown up" food gift cards: Panera, Carraba's, Olive Garden, and Chili's - variety is good and take out is wonderful when the fridge is empty!*
- *The town of Locust - you know who you are and what you have done for us......and STILL do for us! ((HUGS!!))*
- *The Bed Bath and Beyond gift cards and coupons (bought just about everything the other day for a total of $25 thanks to you all and the coupons!)*
- *For Mouse Tales Travel - not every travel agent would re-book a WDW trip so many times and still want to talk to me!*
- *The Target gift cards - SO HELPFUL in so many ways*
- *For all of the financial contributions to Carter's fund - this has helped us out so much ....the bills are crazy, regardless that we're at St. Jude.*
- *The fundraisers - God bless each of you who have taken your time to do this for us......I know how much a time commitment it has been and I am forever grateful....*
- *Our St. Jude family and friends - nurses, doctors, Target House buddies, and those who have embraced Carter and me as friends.*
- *The cards from friends, family, strangers, students, preschools - it's always a bright spot to find one in our mailbox*
- *The prayer shawls - they are beautiful and give us peace when draped or wrapped around us.*
- *The additional help - thank you to the men's group at our new church who helped Paul clear out three years of yard debris at the new house last weekend......six men, three hours .....saved Paul (and me!) a lot of time and money!*
- *The emails - the articles, the support, the love, the friendship*

- *The support of my online store - this is such a huge help because it takes a huge amount of time, yet is my income right now.*
- *The CaringBridge tributes - they have doubled in the past week....WOW!*
- *Those that are running/walking/training for St. Jude or other marathons/walks to honor Carter*
- *For those who are honoring Carter through a fundraiser*
- *For the support and love of our family*
- *For the support and love of perfect strangers*
- *For adding Carter to prayer lists around the country and abroad*
- *The books - fun, devotional, and helpful*
- *For all of the wonderful hats that Carter has received - they are so fun and he loves trying new ones!*
- *The prayer beads, the healing water, the healing oil - all of which I have used.*
- *The sweet and loving notes*
- *For the Sigma Chi brothers who have helped us*
- *For Calvary Church Memphis who adopted me and had someone call each week to ensure that I didn't need anything....and for allowing me to cry throughout the entire Christmas Eve service*
- *The love offerings from Mason's preschool, Union Grove Primitive Baptist church, and from friends both known and unknown.*
- *the treats and goodies that have helped bribe Carter to take his medicine or to eat!*
- *How can I not forget my college family - sisters, mentors, and friends? Couldn't do this without you all.*

I am certain that I am forgetting someone or something - and please forgive me.....I've so tried to keep a running list of all the love you've sent our way....I am eternally grateful for each and every gift......they touch my heart, they help me remember that I'm not in this alone, and they remind me of all of the good in this world. I never, ever would have thought that my family was so loved - but it is so reassuring to know that we have an army of Prayer Warriors behind us ....pushing us forward and helping us fight!

God bless you all for being here for us. We can't do this alone.

((HUGS!!))
S

2/28/12
I am literally bawling my eyes out right now......God is so good!

Today was a pretty awful day. Nope - it was a no good, perfectly horrible, day......until the angels started to descend around me.

Carter woke up well and happy - wanted to call his "aunt" and talk to her about all sorts of silly things. He was telling some pretty good stories! I figured that since Carter felt well we'd run over to Concord Mills quickly for a swimming suit for me and a pair of shoes for him.
I should have known that Carter wasn't feeling well when he didn't want to try on shoes.....the kid LOVES his shoes and he didn't want anything to do with a new pair. I sat in the aisle at the Stride Rite outlet and rocked him until he felt well enough to get back into the stroller.

We zipped across the mall (literally a couple of stores down) for me to run into a store and get a swimsuit - there was ONE that I liked and a pair of shorts to try on too .....not like it would take a lot of time. We should have been in and out within ten minutes. Mom walked Carter around and then he started screaming. She came back to the dressing room area to talk to me and Carter started vomiting everywhere......or at least all over himself - we were able to avoid messing up the dressing room.....of course, that was the same moment that I tried on the swimming suit in the dressing room. So, here I am, desperately trying to get the suit off, my clothes on, instruct my mom what to do (use the coat to catch it!), and figure out why Carter was vomiting ......Yes, I belong in a bad sitcom!

Anyways - the woman working was fabulous, didn't have a problem with it....provided extra bags for dirty clothes, paper towels, words of encouragement.....I, however, was mortified. This is now the second time that Carter has felt fine and then vomited during errands. Lesson learned - stay home, order online.

Carter fell asleep in the car and didn't wake up for another three hours.......(we went straight to the condo and put him in the bed).

I went out to run errands and returned to find several amazing emails.....a definite positive to such an awful day.

It is mind-boggling to me how much good there is in this world and how it is so often overlooked and so often chastised.

However, today I saw EXACTLY how God wanted to put two families in my life. Yesterday I was supposed to have a small loveseat delivered to the condo from The Rooms to Go Outlet. I picked it out last Wednesday - the first delivery day was Monday....it was a splurge at $250, but I was tired of sitting on the floor and we can use it in the new house (all the furniture here has to be new because of potential germs, etc.).

Anyways - RTG told me that I had to stay at home all day yesterday to wait for the delivery. At 2pm they called to tell me that their truck had broken down and that it couldn't be delivered until NEXT Monday.......I was not a happy camper and just told them (very nicely) that I would be out of town (the truth). They arranged for one of their freelance drivers to deliver the sofa today.

Two very nice men arrived around 4pm (as they said they would!). They didn't know the story about the delivery incident yesterday and I told them how thankful I was that they were able to deliver it today. Carter was awake and talking and I simply explained what why we were in the condo. We paid the delivery charge and the men left.

Within five minutes, the doorbell rang and the owner of the company, Andrei, was at my door returning the delivery charge. He said that he couldn't take it because it wouldn't be right and that maybe the blessing would be returned to him if he was good to us. My heart simply melted. It wasn't a lot of money, but it was the fact that this man was so genuine and sincere......and what an angel to me!

The night went on - Carter wouldn't take his antibiotic, wouldn't drink the sweet tea with chemo, wouldn't take a bath......you get the picture. He went to bed about 7:30pm - Mom was wiped from our long day and went to bed shortly after.

At about 8:30, there was a knock on the door......now, I'm a city girl and when there's a knock on the door at 8:30 and a man is standing outside, I get suspicious. I knew that I recognized him, but I couldn't remember where from......until he started talking.

It was one of the men who delivered the sofa. He explained that he had tried to call, but that I hadn't answered (the phone is on silent once Carter goes to bed). He continued that he had just gotten off of work and wanted to come back. Then he said that his family was here and that they had some things for Carter. He walked downstairs to get them and I put on my robe (and tried to determine if I was totally insane).

I walked outside to the overlook and he brought his wife and young son up - carrying a remote control car and a Play-doh. The company owner, Andrei, then pulled up and came up with his two boys and wife, too. I have to admit, I was a little baffled as to what was going on, but I didn't feel scared or threatened. I knew that these were good people - I could just feel it. God surrounded me with peace.
Andrei started to explain how he had told his wife the week earlier that he wanted to do something to help a child and that he didn't know who or how to do it, but that God would show him the way. He then proceeded to hand me a very thick envelope and explained that his business card was inside and they were here to help us.

Tears. Tears. and more tears poured down my cheeks as I spoke with these families. I wasn't even certain if I should accept the envelope, but they insisted. I invited them in - told them Carter's whole story, shared my faith, and prayed with them. And continuously, they reassured me that they would be here for us and that they would help in any way that they could. Total strangers. Total angels.

You see, it dawned on me just as they were leaving that God had sent these families into our life. The Rooms to Go truck didn't "just" break down yesterday - that was God......he sent Andrei to us.

Literally, when they left (with all of my contact info) - I fell to my knees and prayed and sobbed.......I am so blessed - to be able to share my story with others, to be able to be surrounded by angels, and to be loved. It is overwhelming.

I am continually amazed by God. Tonight God showed me in a very clear way that He does everything for a reason. It was obvious in every way to me - God sent these families into my life and I am forever and eternally grateful for these new friends.

Heavenly Father - You are the best at helping me see the clear picture when things seem to be the darkest. You lift me up when I am crumbling. You open my eyes when they are blind. You fill my heart when it is empty. You, dear Lord, are good. I pray that everyone is able to see just how awesome you are in their lives, Father God. Thank you for all of my angels - those that I know personally and those that I do not. Thank you Lord for the blessings of this life and the angels that you surround me with every day. Father God, I lift my heart up to you. Amen.

((HUGS!!))
Sarah

I still cannot read the previous entry without crying. It was one of the most beautiful acts of kindness that I have been blessed with in my life. I remember it frequently and I will never forget the love that was shown to us. God was there.

2/29/12
Today was a really long day - but fabulous in so many ways.

Today was Day 15 of the round. This means that Carter has had four rounds of chemo (albeit of two different protocols). It also means that March 12/13 will show us the effectiveness of this latest protocol.

When Carter goes to Levine for an infusion, we don't simply walk into the infusion room and get started. He must be seen by the doctor, have lab work done, and provide a urine sample. Little man took his own sweet time with that this morning....... Once we got the labs back, it was apparent that Carter needed platelets. I thought that he looked pale yesterday, but I still second guess myself. I'm so accustomed to having lab work done at St. Jude every other day. I've never claimed to be a nurse....and never wanted to be one either!

While waiting for the platelets and chemo, we got lunch and tried to keep Carter happy. We even had a visit from our beloved

Locust Child Development Center owner, Debbie and her mom! We had arrived at 9:45 am and by lunch time, the poor kiddo was tired and ready to go.

Shortly after lunch, Carter and I cuddled up in the reclining chair in the IV room and nodded off to sleep - all while his platelets and then later chemo were dripping. This was such a blessing - it's much easier on Carter to take a nap during an infusion than to be chained to an IV pole ....Carter likes to GO!

Anyways - it was 3:45 before we got out of the infusion room and then almost 4:30 before we got back to the condo (guess who wanted Bojangles?).

It was a LONG day, but it was a GOOD day because it was the LAST DAY OF CHEMO for two weeks!!! (can you see me doing the happy dance?)

Dear Lord - thank you for parting the clouds on the darkest of days and shining Your light down on me. Praise you dear Lord for getting Carter through four rounds of chemo. Your mercy is great, Father God. In Your Holy Name, Amen.

3/1/12
I wish that I had something profound and meaningful to write tonight, but I don't. Today was just a dumb day. I didn't want to take Carter out today because I'm not sure of his counts and don't want to risk him getting sick this close to our trip. So we napped.....a lot......which wasn't a part of the schedule, but obviously we both needed it.

If you think that it's hard packing for a vacation, consider this.....try having two different parents pack for four different people in two different locations.....and add to that a laundry list of medical supplies, medicines, etc. ...it is really quite humorous.....so I'm just packing it all! And, what we don't have, we'll buy!

Tomorrow morning Carter will have labs drawn to make sure that his counts are good. Please pray that we get a good report! It will make life so much easier if he has a good report!

I cannot wait to see my little guys light up when they see "Mickey's House".......Carter keeps telling everyone that we're "going to Mickey's House and we're going to sleep there!"

I must get some more rest - Disney is hard enough when you're well-rested.....can't imagine what it would be like for a tired momma!

((HUGS!!))
S.

3/3/12
Sorry that I didn't post last night - I fell asleep with Carter when I put him to bed.

Yesterday was a rough day, but I'm hoping that it has passed and Carter will be fine for the following days.

We're both so excited - we will head to Greenwood today! Can't wait to see Daddy and Mason!
Please continue to pray for Carter's health and for safe travels.

((HUGS!!))

3/3/12
We are here in Greenwood. Tomorrow we will drive to Disney. It feels so good to be home and in our home with Mason and Paul. I am filled with peace when we are all together. Mason is quite smitten with our "nanny" Sarah who will be making the trip with us. So thankful for an extra set if hands! Please pray for an easy trip for us tomorrow - we need it!

Things change really quickly in the world of cancer. One moment we were headed to Disney and experiencing the magic and the next Carter was sick and we were headed to the hospital.

3/7/12
Update from Sarah. Carter was vomiting excessively while at Disney World. Sarah took him to the Orlando hospital this morning. Unfortunately after a CT scan it revealed that his tumor has grown. Please, please pray for Carter. Sarah is meeting with the doctors now.

3/7/12
Update from Sarah- "Being flown by ambulance plane to Memphis." Sarah and Carter will be flying out soon. Prayers needed from every prayer warrior possible.

3/8/12
Update from Sarah this morning: They are still in ICU in Orlando Hospital awaiting for transport.

3/8/12
Update from Sarah: Scheduled to leave (not sure the hospital or the airport) at 3:00 this afternoon....will be in-patient at St Jude.... Sarah's father and brother will arrive in Memphis separately tomorrow evening.

Sarah had to cancel the first airline company because they would have had to use a jet at substantially more expense and the company was not authorized by BC/BS...They charged me $500 for cancelling!!!!....

It's important to note that the first air ambulance company did not charge me for cancelling. My mom made the mistake of mentioning this situation to someone and they took it to Facebook. The company was bombarded with phone calls, negative posts, you name it. Another person called a local TV station in Orlando. I was just trying to get to Memphis. Looking back, the whole situation saddens me. My mom was blindsided and was so upset that she had said anything. It was drama and the one thing I didn't need was drama. I was living it.

3/8/12
UPDATE- Sarah and Carter made it safely to Memphis. They are headed to St Jude's ICU.

3/9/12
Sarah says that it was a long night. Carter is having a MRI at 1 so that means Carter can't eat anything. He, of course, is grumpy.

3/9/12
Dear God -
I am not ready to lose Carter and I am not going to give up fighting for his life..... My prayer is that you won't either. Please give us more time dear Lord.......

Love always and forever,
Sarah

3/9/12
While Mark, our chaplain here at St. Jude, was visiting, Carter announced that Jesus was going to take his brain tumor away and make him all better. Then Carter continued by saying he was going to WIN!

Thank you God for sending these words to me. I know that you used Carter to send me strength and encouragement.

I am so thankful for all of the prayers going up for us. It makes it easier knowing that Carter is so loved and so supported.

((HUGS!!))

3/9/12
UPDATE: PRAYERS NEEDED
Sarah and Carter are being transferred to Lebonheur Children's Hospital ICU for emergency shunt surgery again. Our sweet boy's tumor has grown. I will update as soon as I hear something. Please do not call Sarah because she is with him right now. Please God keep watch over Carter during his surgery.

3/10/12
Carter's surgery to put the second shunt in to relieve the pressure in his head was a success this morning. He was happy afterwards and eating like a champ. If everything continues to go well they might be able to head back to St Jude tomorrow. Once we have the next step, Sarah will update. Please continue your prayers and thank you all for the beautiful messages.

3/11/12
Sarah and Carter are being transferred back to St Jude to the 2nd floor.

3/11/12
Carter is having small absence seizures and shunt doesn't seem to be helping. He needs everyone's prayers right this very moment.

3/11/12
Dear God -
Today has been a dark day, but I have felt you with me. I know that you are here holding my hand and embracing me with love and warmth.

I don't know what your plan is for Carter. I do know that whatever happens was meant to be and that Carter was brought here for a reason. He is an angel of yours, dear Lord. I know it.
I hear you whispering to me today through the tears. I think that I know what you're trying to tell me. I hope that I'm hearing you right.

I am not giving up hope. I am not going to quit fighting. I am not going to stop having faith in you. Carter will win this battle - whether it is here on earth or with you dear Lord. It's a win-win situation. I am at peace with that.

I hope that you hear my prayers, dear Lord. Can you hear me now? We are an army fighting this battle and you are leading the way. We have brought new believers to you. We have brought those who have lost faith in you back. We have strengthened the faith of loyal followers. We have shown the world the power of prayer and the love that you have for your children.

I will not ask you for a miracle, Father God. That is for you to decide. Not me. It is in your hands Heavenly Father. I'm not giving up on Carter. I am giving it up to you.

((HUGS!!))
Sarah

Let me explain. We were having a great time at Disney World. Carter befriended everyone he met….cast members, people in lines, everyone. About two days into the trip, he started vomiting. I thought he was dehydrated. The desk supervisor at the Wilderness Lodge, a gentleman by the name of Bennett, had told me that if we needed anything to ask for him. So after a long night of Carter tossing and turning, and then vomiting multiple times, I did. I called the front desk and asked Bennett where I should take Carter. I had no idea what the closest hospital was and I had never expected to need it. He encouraged me to take Carter to

Arnold Palmer's Children's Hospital. It was not the visit I ever expected to have on our trip.

You see, the pediatric oncologist knew our doctor at St. Jude and was in contact with him. They decided to do a CT scan, just in case.

Carter and I waited in the ER, and then the social worker and chaplain came in our room.

You know that things aren't good when a hospital sends the chaplain and the social worker into your room. I ignored their ominous visit. Carter was talking and chatting away. He was telling them about Jesus and about the boo-boo in his head. I was convinced that everything was fine.

But it wasn't. The tumor had grown exponentially. It was a beast and was everywhere. There was necrosis. Our doctor at St. Jude later said that he didn't even know what he was looking at.....it was that bad. What was so odd though was that Carter seemed fine until after the surgery. It wasn't until then that things got scary.

I didn't think that Carter was going to live 48 hours. I don't know if the nurses did either.

I cried. I prayed.

Remember Trish? She was on duty. She stood by my side while I cradled Carter and cried with me. She listened to my prayers. She heard my fears. She knew my heart and my wishes for my son.

I will never forget Dr. Giles asking me what I wanted to do. He asked me if I wanted to go home with Carter on hospice or if I wanted to do radiation. I looked him straight in the eye and told him that I wasn't done fighting and that I wanted to do radiation. I wasn't going to give up on my son.

Dr. Giles is my hero. He looked me straight in the eye and told me that's what we were going to do then. He was willing to try if I was willing to take the risk. At any other hospital, we wouldn't have been given a choice. Carter would have been sent home to die.

3/12/12
Today was a better day in some ways. We kept Carter medicated and he has rested a good bit of the day. He had an EEG this

morning (that he didn't like at all) and a radiation simulation this afternoon, which he was sedated for (and he will be sedated for all of the radiation treatments).When he was awake, he was lucid and ate well. The absence seizures seem better (he started Keppra today for them even without the results of the EEG). It's easier for me when Carter has a good day.

I have come to terms with the fact that Carter is an angel of God and that he was sent here for a reason, and I am fortunate enough to be his mommy. I'm not certain what Carter's mission was exactly - but I do know that he is loved by every person that meets him. He has changed so many lives. Carter is creating miracles every day that he spends on this earth.

My dad once told me that this journal was my "love story" - the love of a mother to her son. This is true in so many ways, but there is more to it than that......this is the story of how the gift of a child brought love to others......and to God. One little boy. One incredible smile. One angel of a child.
I am so humbled by the prayers of complete strangers, friends, and family. God is at work my friends. I feel it. I know it. I am overwhelmed by it. It is a miracle in so many ways.

Tonight I need to get some rest - the days to come will be hard and I need to be my best for my little guy.

((HUGS!!))
S.

3/13/12
Carter is in recovery after first radiation treatment - please pray that all went all.

3/13/12
Carter is back in his room and eating pancakes!!! He also had his first stinky diaper in 6 days! YEAH!

3/14/12
Thank you everyone for your love, prayers, and support. I would not be as strong on this journey if I didn't have them.

Memphis friends and prayer warriors have been asking about helping out. Once we know what our housing scenario with be, I will be sending out requests - don't worry, I will utilize your offers! : Carter had a good day yesterday, but a long night. He didn't sleep well and needed potassium. Since he needed potassium, he didn't get to go to radiation first thing this morning and now he's asking for pancakes and syrup. Poor baby - he has been through so much.

The good news is that his eyes aren't dilated as much (3s vs. 5s) - the pressure in his brain was causing the eye dilation, so I'm praying that this means some of the pressure is being relieved.

Carter checked "poopy diaper" off his list yesterday - never been so glad to see poop! This means that his digestive system is working properly and that the signal from his brain is reaching his stomach/intestine.

Today I pray that we'll be able to get him up and walk a bit. He hasn't walked since a week ago Tuesday and we need to get his little legs moving again!

Please continue to pray for comfort for our baby boy. I just want to know that he isn't uncomfortable.

((HUGS!!))
S.

3/15/12
Today I was once again delivered a small miracle. Carter was discharged from being in-patient at St. Jude! A week ago today we arrived by Learjet (medical) and were admitted to the ICU. A week ago tomorrow I was given the option to stop treatment and go home with Carter. A week ago Sunday, I thought my son was going to leave his earthly home. Today - my baby smiled and smiled all day long. He walked for the first time in over a week, he ate Bojangles (shipped overnight from corporate!), and he was discharged from the hospital. God is good!!!

We are now back at Target House ....wow. What a difference a week makes!

Thank you Lord for being so good! I rejoice in the little things that you give us. I even smelled the flowers today and it made my spirit soar! You are merciful. You are miraculous. You are good. And for that, I am thankful to be one of your children. Heavenly Father.
I need to get to bed with the little man. He keeps calling out for me.

((HUGS!!))

There is so much to tell about this week of chaos and miracles.
There was the Learjet flight back to St. Jude. The Angel Flight didn't budge during the worst lightning storm I had ever experienced in a plane. The man who watched over Carter was a Mason. I noticed his ring. My grandfather and great-grandfather were Masons, both with the organization and their surname.....and hence Carter's older brother, Mason.

When we arrived at St. Jude via ambulance, they wouldn't let us in to the campus. We were in an ambulance at 10pm at night.....finally, they let us in and delivered Carter and I to the PICU. The St. Jude PICU at that time was super small and wasn't a place that you ever wanted to experience.....but I was so thankful for the nurses there. They were wonderful.

3/16/12
Today was the most amazing day.......it's hard to say that when a week ago I expected the darkest of days to be in my near future......

Today we had blood drawn, radiation, and a neuro-oncology visit. But that was the boring stuff.

Late this morning friends descended upon Target House to deliver the most incredible gifts. I need to mention that one friend flew in for the day and two others drove five hours each way to be here for the afternoon.......have I mentioned that I have the most incredible friends?

So it turns out that my good friends planned quite the event for Mason and Carter - today they had a 1/2 birthday party and an "almost" birthday party.......complete with gifts from friends from afar (and a stash that rivaled Christmas!).

Not only did Rachel (from a salon in Germantown) arrive to do my hair and make-up, my dear friends drove up to take photos, and another flew in (for the day!) to set up the party decorations. And of course, Aunt Stacy helped coordinate it all! I've got such fabulous friends!

The boys were dressed beautifully, the decorations were divine, the presents abundant, and I even felt human again! Most importantly, it was fabulous to be surrounded by friends and to laugh......especially when my "perfect" family acted not-so-perfectly.

Later in the afternoon, our dear friend Leslee brought dinner. She can be seen in the picture of Carter with his chef outfit on at the St. Jude gingerbread decorating event. Dinner was amazing and was a perfect way to finish the day!

Carter is exhausted after all of these fabulous events today. It does my heart good to have him doing happy things. We are making forever memories together.

I don't know how much time that I may have left with my little boy, but I promise you this......I will cherish each moment good, bad, or ugly. I will continue to shower him with the love only a mother can give. And I will rejoice in the Lord who blessed me with such an amazing gift of a son.

((HUGS!!))
S.

So here is what I didn't say…....I was so exhausted. I was so stressed out. It was awful timing….but I was thankful. When you're just starting to bounce back from the most horrific days of your life, anything and everything is a blessing. Carter wasn't happy for a good bit of the day, and quite frankly, neither was I. But when you're given blessings - it is best to accept them.

3/16/12
ACK! My brain is obviously MUSH! I forgot to thank Annie for making cupcakes and for helping out with everything! She has been such an amazing help on this journey, too! SO SORRY that I forgot to include you (I'm multitasking and that just isn't a good

thing to do when the brain is mush!)........and she got Rachel (from the salon) to come see me!

((HUGS!!))

3/19/12
I cannot begin to explain the emotions that this journey evokes. One moment I'm on top of the world, the next I am planning funeral arrangements for my little boy.

A week ago yesterday (Sunday), I was convinced that I would lose my little boy before radiation would have a chance to begin. Paul and I had discussions that no parent would ever want to have about their child and I certainly never dreamed of having with my husband.

Today - Carter, albeit grumpy and whiny - completed his first complete week of radiation. It's a miracle in my mind. Last week I told God that I was ready to give my child up to Him. I told God that I understood that Carter was an angel of His and here to complete some sort of task. I told God that I was alright with Carter going home to Him.

God has not taken my son. He lives. He smiles. He is grumpy. He is tired. He is a 2.5 year old on steroids and radiation. But, Carter is still here and still mine. I rejoice in this simple pleasure.
I re-read the journal and it seems that I've left out a lot of details. It was a crazy time and I wasn't always able to think, write, post here. So I will now.

While we were at Disney, Carter was doing pretty well. We arrived on Sunday night, and Monday morning he vomited once. I figured it was from the chemo a week earlier. No big deal. He was tired throughout the day, but that would be typical. On Tuesday, Carter was fine. We saw "Finding Nemo" and met the cast (thanks Paul and Lucretia) and all seemed well. On Wednesday morning, Carter woke up in the middle of the night hungry. He slept with Paul, so I knew he was up - but didn't tend to him. Between 7am and 9am, Carter vomited at least four times. I knew that something was wrong and his eyes were dilated. I figured that he was dehydrated.....certainly I hadn't been a good mommy and tracked his input/output.

I have to mention that Carter had already captured the hearts of the management team at the Wilderness Lodge. I am so thankful for Bennett and his comrades for all of their help and support. When we realized that Carter was ill and needed medical assistance, we notified Bennett first and then called 911. Bennett was there within minutes. I am so thankful for his love and support of our little guy. I know that he was an angel because he mentioned that Arnold Palmer Children's Hospital was in Orlando to me. This was an incredible gift because I stupidly didn't even know the hospitals that were in Orlando......I was naive enough to think that we could get through the week without incident.

Once at Arnold Palmer (via ambulance), Carter was given both a shunt series and a CT scan. Have I mentioned how fabulous this hospital is??? If not, let me do so now - THEY ARE FABULOUS! The ER doc told me the membrane between the cerebrum and the cerebellum looked herniated due to tumor growth and had Dr. Smith on the way down (pediatric oncologist). Our nurses were amazing and took care of us throughout the day. They even cried with me when I got ready to leave (and Paul came to spend the night). I was on the phone with Dr. Giles at St. Jude almost before the ER doc was out of the room.....and I can't forget Audra and Bentley - the social worker and chaplain who came to see me and spent most of the day with me. I couldn't have gotten through the day without them.

Before I knew it, an air ambulance was being arranged and transport to St. Jude was being determined.

So, Paul spent the night with Carter while I went back to the Wilderness Resort (Did I mention that Denny is fabulous there, too? He made sure that I got dinner that night!). I packed and said my goodbyes before catching an early cab to the hospital the next morning. OH! and the management team let me buy a bag in the gift shop before it opened because I had too much stuff to carry! GOD BLESS THEM!

Thursday afternoon we flew to Memphis via air ambulance (aka Learjet). It was raining. It was lightening. We didn't feel a thing!

Upon arriving at St. Jude (aka Fort Knox), they would not let us in because the security guard didn't think the ambulance was valid??? I called Dr. Giles' cell and said, "Do you think you could pull some strings and get us admitted?" It was humorous at best. It's pouring down rain. We're in an ambulance. I have a seriously ill child in the back - who has a medical record number, a room number in the ICU, a parent accompanying them, and WE ARE IN AN AMBULANCE......and it STILL took 15 minutes to get through the front gate.......

Fort Knox. Promise.

Anyway - once here at St. Jude it was a non-stop. We were in the ICU on Thursday night and then the MRI was on Friday morning. After the MRI I was given the option to stop treatment for Carter. You see, the tumor is now HUGE. It is everywhere in Carter's brain. The tumor has also changed composition from a solid tumor to a sponge-like tumor (which could be necrosis or the tumor changing to a Glioblastoma Malforme - GBM tumor). We don't know. We do know that the Avastin didn't work .....nor did the other chemos. Since the tumor was blocking the right ventricle it was highly recommended that if we were going to pursue treatment that we'd have a shunt put in immediately. So, we were suddenly on our way to the ICU at LeBonheur (where the St. Jude neurosurgeons operate).
Saturday morning - Carter had a shunt placed .....it ties in with the first one that he had placed on Dec. 30.

On Sunday morning we were transported back to St. Jude.....

And that's when the bottom seemed to fall beneath me.....

Carter started having absence seizures. He had Tourette's like outbursts. He would stop chewing when being fed. He was distant. He wasn't Carter. He was going downhill fast and the nurses acknowledged this......I even spoke to our doctor via cellphone because I was so concerned. This was the darkest day that I've experienced on this journey. It was worse than the day that Carter was diagnosed. It was worse than the emergency surgeries. It was just awful.

I told God that if He wanted to take Carter, He could. But, He didn't...and I am thankful.

Mark - our chaplain at St. Jude said to me earlier in the week that he came to terms early in his career at St. Jude that "a complete life doesn't necessarily have to be a long life." This is so true and something that resonates with me. I have always felt that Carter is an angel of God, here to complete a mission of some sort. In a way - this is saying the same thing that Mark said to me. Carter has completed more in his "almost" three years than many complete in 70, 80, or 90. He is a special little boy and has touched so many lives in so many ways in such a short time.

So - as we begin week number 2 of radiation, I pray that Carter continues to be stable on steroids (did I say that?)........and I continue to pray that the tumor is being obliterated pieced by piece.

Tonight I leave you with Carter's prayer -
Dear Jesus -
Please take my tumor away and make me all better.
AHHH-MENNN!

((HUGS!!))
Sarah

3/20/12
The love and support that we are seeing from friends, family, and perfect strangers is absolutely overwhelming. We are so thankful and so humbled.

My dad and I stood in awe at the five packages that arrived today for Carter. And then, Stacy arrived with more that had been sent to her home.......

Carter now has his own website (yes, my son has his own URL now!) - this site is being utilized for a silent auction for Carter........I'm having a hard time wrapping my head around this one. WOW! Please visit and see what an amazing job they have done with the site and see all of the goodies that they are auctioning! Or, if you have something to donate, you can do so on this site, too!

And a "Day in the Park for Carter" is being planned in Locust, NC on April 14th!

I cannot begin to express my gratitude and thanks to everyone.....it is overwhelming to think that you all would do so many fabulous fundraisers for us. I cannot tell you how much I appreciate them.

Thank you also for all of the kind messages, words, cards, and posts. I read every single one of them and try to get back to each one, but it is hard to keep up at this point! Please know that I am reading each one and thankful for them!

Today is laundry day. Laundry (unfortunately) doesn't stop when you have a child with cancer. Neither do the dishes......and I still haven't finished unpacking.....the Target House does provide bathroom cleaning service once a week (PRAISE THE LORD!).....so at least I'm good on that one! All this being said, I need to run and do my cleaning while Carter sleeps.

BTW - little man had a relatively good day. We had a lot of appointments at the hospital, but he was a trooper (albeit grumpy!). We're starting to wean him from the steroids (very slowly!). Tomorrow we start 5ml vs. 6ml. Please pray that Carter responds positively!

((HUGS!!))

3/23/12
It has been a day. It has been a week. It has been a month. It has been a LONG journey.

There are things on this journey that I forget to add here. Things others are seeing for the first time and mentioning to me. I take it for granted that so many kids are bald, tiny, and ride in red wagons around the hospital. I take it for granted that we say hi to so many people in the hallways and people stop us for hugs and updates (or that I do the same to others). I take it for granted that the radiation nurses know that Carter wants a warm blankie and pillow when we arrive and brown crackers with (graham crackers), peanut butter, and a sippy when he awakes from sedation each day. I take it for granted that the nurses love on my sweet boy and get a koala bear hug. So many things to be thankful for here at St. Jude.

*The hard part about St. Jude is getting to know so many families -
and loving their children as your own. You hope for them, you pray
for them....they become extended family. So when things go
REALLY well for a member of your extended family, you rejoice.
And when things go horribly wrong, you cry with them.*

*Today I found out that our dear friend Sebastian passed away last
night. He was two years old, just like Carter. He was here for six
months doing chemo and did so well for the first four months, but
something went horribly wrong during the last two months and the
tumor took over. The doctors gave him 4-6 months when he went
home less than 30 days ago.......*

*My heart is breaking for my sweet friend Marisa who was such a
good momma to her little boy. Sebastian passed away in her arms
last night. I cannot imagine what she is going through today - my
heart is breaking.*

*St. Jude has an 80% cure rate - which is amazing.....but
sometimes I have to wonder where this percentage comes from.
Sometimes it feels like death surrounds me.....surrounds us.
Sometimes I wonder if we just got the wrong type of tumor. It is so
hard to hear about friend's children who have developed lung
tumors or have endured long treatments only to pass away. And
that's when I realize that these are the children that are teaching
the doctors, they are the ones that are the angels here on earth
leading the way to new cures, they are the ones that are impacting
lives around the world.*

*You see, even Carter's doctor is baffled. Carter is asymptomatic
and atypical. He is not your average patient. Carter is so articulate
and so smart - he understands things at a level which is beyond
his years. So Carter has been teaching the medical staff from the
beginning.*

*A good friend today told me that there was something special
about Carter, something different. I have to totally agree, but I'm
his mommy! I think that Carter is going to fight this battle and then
he is going to teach the world something about brain cancer. I
don't know what - but I feel it.*

*The good news is that Carter is being weaned some more off of
the steroids - this is superb news for me since I am really tired of*

grumpy Carter and would much rather have happy Carter around on a full time basis. I am also praying that Carter doesn't go through the 2 pound bag of animal crackers before he is weaned off of the steroids! The child is eating hamburger buns and animal crackers with an appetite that cannot be suppressed! CHUNK IS BACK!

I am praying for a quiet and uneventful weekend. We're going to have some pictures done by a foundation tomorrow and then we'll go to Sesame Street LIVE! I'm praying that this goes better than our trip to Disney......

Heavenly Father, please hold the children of St. Jude close. Wrap your loving arms around their parents and loved ones. Kiss each and every one of their foreheads with strength and courage. Bless them dear Lord, for they are our future. Amen.

((HUGS!!))
S.

3/24/12
Best.Day.Ever.

Last night we actually got some sleep! Carter only woke up one time at 3am and was easily satisfied with some sweet tea (PTL!). He awoke at 7am happy and joyful - he even got out of bed himself (first time in two weeks!). Today was a serious testament to Carter feeling much better and being well-rested. He didn't eat nearly as much because we're weaning him off the steroids and was even up to some visitors this afternoon!

I was even able to get all the laundry done this morning - MAJOR FEAT!

We went to McDonald's this afternoon for lunch and Carter ate chicken McBites - this is the first time he has had any sort of chicken in two weeks, too! WOO HOO!!!!

It was such a joy have my "old" Carter back. I so pray that this becomes the norm vs. the oddity.

Father God - thank you for the good days. Thank you for the smiles and the giggles. Thank you for the hugs and the kisses.

Praise you dear Lord for high fives, knuckles, and elbows. Oh - and I can't be remiss and forget the muscles! Father God, please know that I appreciate each and every day.....but that I especially love the good days. They bring such happy memories and give me such hope for Carter's future. I lift my heart up to you, Amen.

3/28/17
Carter was SO happy today. It made me joyful. He is slowly coming off of the steroids (1ml 3x a day now). He is a little chunk compared to what he was just three weeks ago! It is hard to believe that this week marks our halfway point of radiation. We know that our last session will be April 12 - I'm not 100% clear as to what will happen after that with appointments. However I do know that we'll be going home to Greenwood shortly after the last radiation treatment.

When we go home, we will be finished with all treatment. There is nothing else that they can do for Carter since the chemo hasn't worked in the past. Please pray that the radiation will work and the tumor will disappear. We know that Astrocytomas respond positively to radiation - but there are no guarantees.

Many of you have written about the Clinic. I wrote about it a few months ago. This clinic is not an option for us. It is totally out-of-pocket and the costs are astronomical. It also would require a two year commitment "IF" Carter is accepted - and would require us moving to yet another state....which is also not an option. The Clinic publishes how many people the have helped - but never states how many lives have been lost through this practice. I know that many children who were treated at his clinic end up at St. Jude when it is too late. And, ethically - I cannot come to terms with putting my 2.5 year old child on an "unknown" protocol which is not FDA approved. While I appreciate everyone's help trying to research and find answers. This is not one that we're going to pursue.

I am so thankful that Kim has been here the past few days to help out. She is so good with Carter and he has truly loved having her here. They enjoying playing trucks together! Kim was my youth group leader in high school and has always been a second mom to me.

Carter was so sweet tonight - he looked at me when we were getting him ready for bed and said, "I am so happy that I'm here." I told him, "I am so happy that you're here, too. Do you want to stay a while?" And he smiled his big grin and melted my heart by saying, "Yes!" This conversation was odd to me because he had just been crying earlier about going home to Daddy and Mason in Greenwood. So, of course, I probably read too much into Carter's words. I'd like to think that they were his way of saying, "I am going to keep fighting Mommy - I don't want to leave you." Or maybe God was trying to send me a message.

I am treasuring every smile. Every giggle. Every cuddle. It's so nice to have Carter almost off of steroids. My little boy is back.

Please keep two of our St. Jude friends in your thoughts and prayers. Two young ladies - Deana and Viola are both fighting for their lives tonight. They were both put on life support today (separate cases and incidences). Viola was our neighbor on the second floor when we were here the first time. She turned 18 in January right before we left. She is such a sweetheart. Please pray for them and for their families.

Thank you to everyone who has sent gifts recently – our favorite store on Etsy sent Carter a beautiful Easter train wreath which is the envy of Target House! and it makes it feel a little more like Easter here. Many have sent meals through a casserole company and they have been SO yummy! It is a good thing that I have to walk so much at St. Jude - going to need to diet after this journey anyways! The front desk staff now jokes as to how many packages Carter is going to receive each day. It's such a blessing to be loved! Thank you!

I need to head to bed - tomorrow radiation is at 7:15am again......this means that Carter will get his brown crackers (graham crackers) earlier! He so loves the radiation nurses and doctors.......it makes it all easier!

Heavenly Father, please watch out for our dear friends who are fighting to stay with us, but grant us peace if they move on to live with you. We know that they will be healed and whole again if it is your will that they be with you. Thank you for each and every smile that Carter sends our way. They are reminders of your love and greatness. Every day he is here is a blessing and I treasure

the gift that you sent me almost three years ago. I lift my heart up to you. Amen.
 ((HUGS!!))

3/31/12
There are so many times during the day that I think, "I need to write about that" and then I don't......I forget, I get distracted, etc.

On the darkest day of this journey, the Sunday we had returned to St. Jude from LeBonheur, there was one tiny bright spot that I keep forgetting to share.

When everything was so bad, I remember turning to one of our nurses and asking if another nurse, Trish, was working. It turned out that she was working that weekend. This was a blessing to me.

You see, Trish is a line nurse. This means that she trains parents how to change dressings that cover ports and how to flush them. This is a process that every parent must be checked-off on after they first arrive at St. Jude.

I am fairly certain that my training took longer than most. In fact, I know it. Have I mentioned that I never wanted to be a nurse?

So on this terrible day when I was praying that my little boy would make it a few days to start radiation - Trish arrived at my bedside. I knew that Carter's dressing needed to be changed, but he was so irritable and unstable I didn't think that I could do it. When Trish arrived, Carter was sleeping - so we decided to pass on the dressing change. I was in bed holding Carter while he slept, so Trish and I talked quietly about everything that was going on and I just cried and cried.....and then cried some more. Trish is used to me crying .....this was nothing unusual for her to see. In fact, when we first arrived at St. Jude, I could make it through the entire day and not cry .....and then we'd go to Trish and I would become a blubbering baby. Carter was so unpredictable during those training sessions. One second he'd be fine and laughing, the next he'd be screaming and crying......it was daunting, especially since I never wanted to be a nurse!

In the middle of all my tears, Trish thanked me for nominating her for the Daisy Award. This is an award given to nurses at St. Jude for excellence in nursing. Several nurses are given this award and recognized each quarter. I never told Trish that I had nominated her because I didn't know if my entry would even be considered.

This is what I wrote for the nomination:

Being a single mom with an active toddler at St. Jude is not an easy task. In fact, it is overwhelming, stressful, and daunting. From the very first day I met Trish, I knew that my little boy was receiving the best care possible and that helped relieve some of my stress. Trish was always compassionate to both my little guy and to me - nurturing us both with the guidance and wisdom necessary to prepare for the marathon we were preparing to run.

Attempting to teach a single mom how to flush lines and change dressings while a two year old is chatting incessantly and itching to move is a skill that Trish has mastered. She immediately became best friends with my son and skillfully managed to teach both of us about dressing changes and flushing. Not an easy task. She was a constant cheerleader and a relentless advocate for my son and for me.

When mentioning Trish's name to other nurses, immediately they say, "I know Trish! She's great!" or something to the effect. They know her enthusiasm, professionalism, and love of her job.

I cannot imagine St. Jude without Trish. I think that the memory of my son, Carter, running down the hall with his arms wide-open for a hug from Trish pretty much exemplifies why I'm nominating Trish for the Daisy Award. In my mind, if a two year old loves a line nurse THAT much - she must be doing something pretty spectacular.......and indeed, she does.

So, on that dark day, the bright spot was that Trish told me that she'd won the award because of what I had written.

There are so many excellent nurses and staff members at St. Jude - they love my little guy like their own. But there were so many days when we first arrived here that I seriously considered packing my bags and heading back to Charlotte. Carter's love for

Trish was one of the reasons I stayed. I had never seen a nurse care for a patient with such love. It was magical to see.

And if Carter ever tells you that he "sat on a duck" and laughs hysterically - blame Trish!

((HUGS!!))
S.

4/2/12
It is hard to believe that ten days from today we will be getting ready to leave Target House and St. Jude. We will return for scans and brief visits, but after the radiation there will be no further treatment.

It's a scary thought - but I know that God is in control and that Carter is working miracles here on earth. I know it, I feel it.

This means that Carter and I will return to Greenwood. It means that Paul, Mason, Carter, and I will be able to be a family again. It means that we will hopefully begin to have a greater sense of normalcy in our lives.

It means that I can finally unpack all the boxes in the new house. A house where I have spent less than two weeks total time. A house where I have no idea where to find anything. A house where we can create some new memories.

Today Carter was in rare form. He was happy (for the most part), he refused to take a nap, and he would not stop talking! It was wild. He says the most profound things for a 2.75 year old. Sometimes I wonder if it is the tumor, God, or just Carter......it's hard to know.

This morning we had radiation at 7:45 and Carter was once again a champ. He has figured out that radiation isn't bad as long as he can get back to the sedation room. Once he's there he knows that the graham crackers are arriving soon!

For whatever reason, Carter was not interested in napping today. He was extremely excited that "Mr. Frank" and the Moped to Memphis crew arrived at Target House this afternoon. Carter managed to give the tour himself - showing the group the highlights of both Target House 1, 2, and the playground.

If you haven't already heard about the Moped to Memphis group - let me enlighten you. Frank is a teacher at Clover High School in Clover, SC (coincidentally the same school district and high school where I was a substitute when I was a grad student at Winthrop). Anyways - Frank strives to raise $1million for St. Jude each year and if he doesn't, he rides his moped to Memphis! He has been doing this since 2008. From what I understand, fundraisers include a "womanless" beauty pageant and a second chance prom. He is an amazing guy and Clover should be proud of his efforts! I am eternally grateful for this crew and all of their hard work. It meant so much to have a group "from home" visit today. They are more angels who have touched our lives.

Heavenly Father, you send angels my way in the most unlikely ways, and for that I am thankful. They come on mopeds, they deliver sofas, and they pray with me in Target. Only You dear Lord would send angels so indiscreetly. Hebrews 13:2 is never far from my heart: Do not forget to entertain strangers, for by so doing some people have entertained angels without knowing it. Thank you for this constant reminder dear Lord. There is so much good in the world and I am so grateful that I am able to see it. I pray that others look for the angels in their own lives. I lift my heart up to you. Amen

((HUGS!!))
S.

4/3/12
No update tonight. This momma is grumpy! Carter hasn't napped in two days and hasn't slept through the night (except for one!) since we returned to St. Jude. With no extra help here, I'm feeling overwhelmed and exhausted. Please say a prayer that I get some rest tonight and that I can feel God's light in the morning. I need it!

((HUGS!!))
S.

4/4/12
I've been meaning to write about Carter's "chances" of survival for a long time. So many people ask, "What are his chances?" Honestly, I don't know what his chances are and I never asked the doctors....and I won't.

As a teacher, I never looked at my students files prior to them entering my classroom. Yes, I met with the resource teachers, nurses, etc. prior to the first day of school, but I really tried not to form an opinion of a child prior to that first day. You see, a child is not the paperwork in their file folder. After the first two weeks, I would have a general sense of the child, their attitude, and their abilities......and then I would look at the file.

In a very odd sense, this is what helped me during my second year of teaching when I had a child with paranoid schizophrenia in my class. I think that there were many days that he didn't take his medication and we certainly had conversations about his behavior. However, I will never forget having to write him up at the end of the year. He told the principal that "Mrs. Bucciero always writes me up." To which the principal responded, "Son, Mrs. Bucciero has never written you up and we can look at your file to confirm it." It wasn't always easy and I can confirm that I had my fair share of wine that year, but I tried so hard to let the child be successful in my classroom. He wasn't a percentage, a number, a problem....he was a child who wanted to be accepted.

This is the same attitude that I've tried to take with Carter on this journey. I don't know what the percentage of survival is and I don't know that the doctors even really know an accurate percentage. And really - what's a percentage? A number for me to cling to with hope? And, what if that percentage is low? I would hate to think that would in some way change my attitude towards God, Carter, etc. Or what if it is high? Would I be more relaxed about treatments, procedures, and meds?

So no, I do not know the percentage of children that survive inoperable Astocytomas and I really don't care. Carter isn't a number or a percentage. What I care about is doing everything I humanly can as a mommy and letting the rest be done by God.

Carter continues to be atypical and asymptomatic. Today he played catch with the security guard in the lobby of Target House and laughed hysterically. The sound of his belly laugh echoed throughout the first floor - it was the sound of joy. It wasn't the sound of cancer.

Dear God - Help us to look at situations for what they are and not for what others want to make them. Help guide us with our hearts and open our eyes to your glory. I lift my heart up to you. Amen.

4/5/12
Sometimes writing makes you vulnerable - it helps sort through emotions, clarify questions, and embrace thoughts that race through your mind.

As a third year teacher I was charged with teaching writing to seventh grade students. It became my challenge, it became my passion, it became my pride. I didn't have a book (or not a good one) or a curriculum to follow. I just had to figure out what the state test required and then somehow create lesson plans that would work towards the goal of my students passing.

God was with me a A LOT that year......and I was frustrated and cried at night.....and sometimes didn't leave the school until the janitors kicked me out because they wanted to go home.

So, I had students create a book over the course of their seventh grade year. It started on the first day of school with an essay (All About Me) and didn't end until the last week of school.

My students hated me. Promise. Of course, the ones that listened to directions and got good grades tolerated me a little bit more than the others. Most of them would tell you I was strict, but funny (or maybe just a little crazy). Every once in a while I will get a thank you note from a student who has just gotten a good grade on a college paper - and those notes are the ones that make it all worthwhile.

Anyways - my favorite part of the school year was when I got to teach poetry. I didn't teach the traditional poetry that they learned about year after year, but random forms that made it fun to write. I had parents question me about senryu poems and I think that some of them thought I had lost my mind. I wasn't teaching sonnets, ballads, or iambic pentameter - I was teaching seventh grade students how to put their feelings down on paper.

So - here are some of the poems that I've written about this journey using the formats that I used to teach my seventh graders. This is just something fun that I did to relax .....nothing too serious.

Chemo

Chemo tastes like the metal that lingers in your mouth
It sounds like the hum of machines in the hospital room, dripping
the poison into your veins
It smells like vomit
It looks like a bald head
Chemo feels like slime creeping through my body

St. Jude Momma

Don't mess with me, I'm a St. Jude Momma.
I can change the dressing on a Hickman Port, carry fluids in a
backpack, and catch vomit before it hits the floor.
Don't mess with me, I'm a St. Jude Momma.
I can walk three miles around the hospital pulling a red wagon with
my child in it, attend six medical appointments in a day, skip
breakfast while my child is NPO and still have a smile on my face.
Don't mess with me, I'm a St. Jude Momma
I know the names of the children, the staff, the doctors, the nurses
even if I haven't slept in seven months and can barely put my
makeup on it the morning.
Don't mess with me, I'm a St. Jude Momma
I can sob tears of sadness at the loss of a child and pull myself
together in an instant when my baby asks, "Why are you crying,
Mommy?"
Don't mess with me, I'm a St. Jude Momma
What I did back home doesn't dictate who I am here, it doesn't
matter if I was popular, hated, rich, poor, educated or not
Don't mess with me, I'm a St. Jude Momma.
And I will fight this battle with God as my Commander in Chief and
an army of prayer warriors behind me for my baby
Because I'm a St. Jude Momma.

Cancer

Cancer really stinks
It forever changes you
Praying for a cure

Heavenly Father, please help those who need to find peace do so.
Help them find a way to get their emotions out, to make
themselves vulnerable, to work through the hurt that they are
enduring. Father God, wrap them in your loving embrace and

carrying them through the dark days that are ahead. Help them find some way to make this journey positive and to see your glory. In your name, I pray. Amen.

((HUGS!!))
Sarah

4/6/12
Please pray for our friend Viola's family here at Target House. She became an angel this afternoon. I just talked to her daddy yesterday and she was doing a little better......I'm crushed. Every time a child dies here it is senseless. The last time I saw Viola was the day before her 18th birthday in January......she was happy and healthy and smiling at Carter and his friends racing cars in the hallway........

((HUGS!!))
S.

The pendulum continuously swings at Target House and St. Jude. It isn't easy. It isn't anything. It is just how it happens. Parents learn to accept the roller coaster of emotions and the tumultuous paradigm of life. We keep on moving forward.....

It was during this timeframe that Carter was referred to the Quality of Life Department at St. Jude. They wanted me to speak with our local hospice group in Greenwood, just in case. I told them that I wasn't going to because Carter wasn't going to need hospice. While I didn't spend a whole lot of time in this part of St. Jude, I am thankful that they exist for those who need it.

4/8/12
What a blessed Easter it has been! Carter felt well and we made a last minute trip to the Peabody to see the ducks in the water fountain......he got to see Anthony, the Duck Master, and received a special duck pin from him. Then it was on to the gift shop where the ladies doted on him the entire time......Have I mentioned that Carter collects girlfriends everywhere he goes?

We then came back for a nap and got up only because it was time for the Easter egg hunt here at Target House. I am so glad that I didn't purchase any candy for Easter! Carter was given a small basket here and literally filled it up and then filled the seat of the stroller up, too! I swear it is the largest average per child Easter egg allotment that I've ever seen......many other children were in the same predicament asking, "Where do I put all of my eggs?!"

We then came back to the room and sorted out the loot and returned to the playground for a few minutes before dinner.

It was a blessed Easter.

Tomorrow begins the countdown of our radiation treatments. We will have radiation Monday through Thursday of this week. My dad will arrive on Wednesday to help us pack (have I mentioned how difficult it is to pack with a 2.5 year old on steroids?)......and then we'll head to Charlotte.

If you haven't already heard, there is a fundraiser event in Locust, NC for Carter - ((HUGS!!)) for Carter Day. I know that our friends have gone above and beyond for this special day and we can't wait to see everyone. Please pray that all goes well and that we can be there!

I'm going to head to bed early again tonight. I'm worn out. I know this because I took a nap with Carter again this afternoon.......not good when I need to pack and clean so we can get out of here!

((HUGS!!))
S.

4/9/12
Today was one of those incredible and crazy days......a day when things go so well, but nothing really goes right......I wish that I could put an oxymoron tag on it, but nothing comes to mind. Carter started his final week of radiation appointments. It is nerve wracking to know that this is the last week because it will be the last radiation that he'll be able to have. ever.

I can tell you that in my layman's opinion, I don't think that the tumor is in the language part of Carter's brain. I say this because he has been talking non-stop. He says the funniest things and tells stories that contain facts from months or a year ago (if I hear the story of the helicopter at the Easter egg hunt at Lazy 5 Ranch again one more time.....). He is the epitome of an entertainer and we can barely get through the Target House lobby without him gathering a crowd. It makes my heart joyful though - knowing how bad he was just a few weeks ago and seeing him now.....my "old" Carter is back.

A noticeable difference is that Carter is watching television again. He had stopped watching it for a while and I didn't know if it was from boredom, attention, or sight. I think now that he was having vision issues due to the pressure on his brain. Carter is playing again - REALLY playing. He rode a tricycle so quickly on Sunday that he fell over a few times. I think that he was simply overjoyed that he could ride the bike! Each time, he picked himself up and just kept going - no tears. He is coloring again, reading (or pretending to), and running through the halls. All things that I have missed desperately.

It's so hard not to get my hopes up that the radiation is eliminating the tumor. I try not to think about it because I thought that the chemo was doing the job before and it didn't. It's all in God's hands now.

Our day started at 3:30am this morning......I love Carter being on steroids....really. It's fun. Nothing like having a 2.5 year old go from 3:30 am until 8:30pm non-stop (minus the sedation for radiation - and no, I don't get to nap during that time because that's when I get to eat breakfast).

Anyways - it's becoming difficult to write due to the fact that I am using one hand to prop one eye open......and who knows what I'm writing at this point ....

Dear God -
Sleep would be a good thing......could you pull some strings for me? Thanks.
Love,
Sarah

4/10/12
Just found out that Carter is going to be the honorary Duckmaster at the Peabody Hotel tomorrow at 5pm! WOO HOO!!!! Memphis friends, please come out and see Carter!

4/10/12
It's 10:45pm and I'm just starting to write .....why? Well, let's see....

Radiation was at 7:30 and we showed up on time. All went well. We then had our radiation consult immediately following which ran late due to a doctor being out. And then, somewhere in the middle of the consult the substitute doc said something to the effect of "well, your radiation ends on Saturday." WHAT!!! STOP THE PRESSES??!!!?? I tried diligently to maintain my cool, but I about lost it. In my most diplomatic tone and manner I asked when this had been changed and why I hadn't been informed and a laundry list of other questions.

I was seriously close to a panic attack ......I kept thinking about having to tell everyone that Carter wouldn't be at ((HUGS!!)) for Carter Day and a multitude of other things I would have to take care of due to the schedule change.

At 9pm tonight the doctor called and explained that the radiation would end on Thursday as planned. It was a good thing I was in the middle of packing.

So - tomorrow I have to figure out why they have scheduled an MRI for MONDAY when we won't be here........yes, I'm a little frustrated! I'm thrilled that they want to do an MRI to see what's going on with the tumor (however they told me they wouldn't do one until May?).....but REALLY? MONDAY? Everyone knows that we need to be back in Locust for SATURDAY!!!

I'm so ready to be home and to be with Paul and Mason. I'd like to unpack the multitude of boxes from the move to Greenwood. Perhaps I'll even figure out where the utensils are hiding in my kitchen. And, if I'm really lucky, I'll have a chance to decorate in some way shape or form.

Would someone please buy me an energy drink? Coke Classic isn't cutting it anymore!

The good news is that Carter is going to be the Honorary Duckmaster at the Peabody Hotel tomorrow at 5pm.......cannot wait! What a treat!

Thank you to everyone who has sent packages, gifts, food, gift cards, and financial contributions to Carter's fund. You have no idea how helpful they are - and we are forever thankful for them.

Father God - I know that you're in control. I know that it is YOUR plan and not mine. Please help me be patient. Please help me be kind. Please don't let my exhaustion get the best of me. Please help me get home so our family can be united once again. I lift my heart up to you. Amen.

4/11/12
Schedule update (because things are never dull around here!):

Wednesday: 5pm Peabody Hotel - Carter will be the honorary DuckMaster

Thursday: Radiation 7:45am

Friday: MRI 8:30am (more details later)

Immediately following the MRI and results, we will drive to NC so we can attend ((HUGS!!)) for Carter Day in Locust, NC. Hope to see you there!

((HUGS!!))
S.

4/12/12
Sarah just informed me of yet another change in plans.

THE MRI IS HAPPENING NOW! NEED ALL PRAYER WARRIORS SUMMONED!!! THANK YOU!

LOVE

PAUL

4/12/12
REJOICE!
The tumor has already responded to the radiation and is 20-25% smaller!!!! Please continue to pray for the tumor to shrink and be eliminated from Carter's body over the coming weeks. The radiation will remain in his body for at least 6-8 weeks. YOUR PRAYERS ARE WORKING!!!!!

THANK YOU!!! PRAISE TO YOU LORD CHRIST!

I will write more after Carter goes to sleep tonight - so many thoughts to share!

BIG ((HUGS!!))
Sarah

4/12/12
I know that I said I would write tonight after Carter went to sleep.....but I've been packing and trying to get ready to head out. We will leave for NC first thing in the morning. I am exhausted. What an incredible day......so this is what it feels like to get good news from an MRI scan. PRAISE THE LORD!

Heavenly Father - You are the ultimate healer. You know the plans you have made for Carter. You and you alone are the Commander in Chief of this journey. And YOU, dear Lord are lighting the path before us. Father God, we rejoice in you and humbly thank you for listening to our prayers. I continue to pray dear Lord that the tumor will be dissolved in Carter's head and that he will be healed and whole once again. I lift my heart up to you. Amen

((HUGS!!))
Sarah

4/13/12
Operation Going Home is about ready to commence! Signing off! ((HUGS!!))

Part Three

~

Home

4/17/12
Sorry that I haven't posted - I will as soon as I recover from the twelve hour drive to Charlotte, ((HUGS!!)) For Carter Day, packing the condo, moving everything back to Greenwood, unpacking the boxes from both Memphis and the condo, and sleeping with both boys the first night back.

Yes - I'm overwhelmed. Yes - I'm exhausted. Yes - I'm frustrated and unhappy. No - I don't have any help (although our nanny Nancy is a Godsend and does help a lot!). Carter and I are headed to Cleveland this weekend to visit a healing doctor. I will eventually get caught up with all of the posts that I need to make. Need time. Lots and lots of time.

((HUGS!!))

4/19/12
Has it been a week already? Where has time gone? It has been an incredible week: incredibly exciting, incredibly exhausting, and an incredible roller coaster!

Here's a quick recap (or maybe not so quick?

Wednesday - Carter was the Honorary Duckmaster at the Peabody Hotel in Memphis. It was so much fun. He was in a big hurry when we arrived and wanted to take the ducks up to the rooftop immediately ....so much so that he threw a small fit in the hotel lobby. I can blame this on the steroids, right?

Anyways - once Carter figured out that it was time to get the ducks to walk the red carpet and into the elevator, he walked behind them holding my hand. He was all smiles as we entered the elevator, declaring "these are good ducks!"
Priceless.

We took the ducks up the their rooftop penthouse where their dinner awaited and Carter told them all sorts of stories.

Thursday: Our schedule totally changed in the sedation room at St. Jude due to our FABULOUS nurses. I'm SO thankful that they were able to change the MRI for us. Hindsight is 20/20 and I don't know if we'd have been able to make it for Carter Day if they hadn't changed it for us. To me, it was an act of God that they were able to do it. One of our sweet nurses even got reprimanded for it by another nurse and when I said something to her about it - she said it was the right thing to do and she didn't care. God love her for taking a hit for Carter! Carter is still talking about our sedation nurses, warm blankies and pillows, drawing pictures, and graham crackers. He loved all of these amazing nurses and these things made radiation so much easier on us both!

I'm still in disbelief that the tumor has shrunk 25% and that Carter is a happy and active little boy these days! This is also an act of God and a miracle in my eyes. I was planning a funeral in March and now my little boy is riding in his motorized truck with his big brother and telling everyone about his new scooter! PRAISE THE LORD!

Last Friday we drove twelve hours (usually a ten hour drive but my dad was driving the mega van which is slow going in the mountains and Carter needed some longer breaks to run around). We arrived at the condo where Mason and Paul were waiting for us. It was past midnight. We were exhausted, but we were so excited to be together again as a family.

We got up early Saturday morning and headed to Locust for ((HUGS!!)) for Carter Day at the Locust Town Center. The day deserves its own post (which I have been composing all week!) - but the highlights include the ever fabulous West Stanly Fire Department (brought out the BIGGEST fire truck with the BIGGEST ladder raised outside of city hall - complete with American flag waving proudly!), event planner extraordinaire Holly, a fourteen year old auctioneer whiz kid, Joey Logano's super-fast (per Carter!) race car, Carter's favorite Moped to Memphis (brought him a wagon that he pulled all.day.long!) and the amazing Carson Hill, and so very much more......I tried so hard to see all of the vendors and tried to thank them all personally......but somehow I ran out of time. We were there from 10am-5pm.......and THANK YOU to everyone who came out to support us and to love on Carter (and all of us!).

As I have said before, Locust truly is a "City with a Soul"......and before I start crying, I will promise to highlight this superlative of a day soon......

Which brings me to Sunday......we drove to our new home in Greenwood, SC.......it just felt good to have our family under one roof and to know that Carter and I wouldn't be leaving for a long trip any time soon.....(please note that I said LONG trip - because there are several SHORT trips.....). Monday started a roller coaster of another sort......I'm a stranger in my own home. I don't know where anything is or where to find it. I can't drive anywhere in town without getting lost. I was late picking up Mason from gymnastics and broke down crying in front of the instructor because I felt like an idiot. I end up calling Paul several times a day because I can't find something, I'm lost, or I'm ticked off that something was done (or in most cases wasn't done!).......and I know that he is seriously questioning why he wanted us home so badly at this point!

I told our nanny, Nancy (who again is a Godsend!), today that I felt like a stranger in a foreign land. After thinking about it - I feel like I don't speak the language, haven't packed the right clothes, and don't have a map! This IS NOT in reference to the people of Greenwood/Abbeville- because they HAVE BEEN MY SAVING GRACE! We have been welcomed with open arms into the community and it does make life so much easier. It's just hard having a new house where you've barely spent two weeks on top of everything else that is going on.....I feel blessed to be a part of such a wonderful new community - they help with Mason, they help with food, they have helped with financial contributions, they have even helped with yard work!!! I feel so fortunate to be welcomed with such love.

So - today Carter and I got back in the car and headed to the condo. We're headed to Virginia tomorrow and then on to Cleveland to visit a doctor. He is a practicing physician who has been known to pray with/over his patients and heal them. We have a dear family friend who was cured from Lupus this way. I figure, why not? Whom am I to judge whether or not this man has healing powers, especially since we know someone who has experienced a miracle from him!

We will drive back to Virginia on Sunday/Monday and then back to Greenwood by Tuesday.....*phew!*

Have I mentioned that I am exhausted?

Sarah Bucciero

Father God - Hold me close right now. Help me to feel your mercy and your grace. Thank you Heavenly Father for the gift of family and for the love that you provide. Help me to be patient. I am nothing without you dear Lord. I know that. Thank you for the gift of friends, the gift of life, and the gift of love. I feel these gifts each and every day - no matter how bad they may get. Thank you for GPS systems, but I know that only you are the map and hold the directions I need. I lift my heart up to you, Amen.

4/24/12
I can remember only four days that rank "perfect" in my life.

The first would be the day I married Paul. It was everything I ever imagined.

The second would be the day that Mason was born. He was the most beautiful thing I had ever seen and I was in awe for weeks that something so perfect and beautiful was a direct result of me.

The third would be the day that Carter was born. Despite his fast appearance and despite the first few seconds of his life were in question, he was perfect and it was an incredible day.

The fourth day would have to be ((HUGS!!)) for Carter Day in Locust on April 14th.

It's hard to describe what made it perfect. Was it that the weather was the perfect temperature with a little breeze in the morning? Was it that Carter managed to go all day long without a nap? Was it that we were able to see so many friends meet so many new ones? I can't put my finger on it, because it was all so perfect.

We actually arrived after the day started - many were up all night and at the crack of dawn for a yard sale. Others walked 2.2 miles through Locust to the Town Center. Still others were up and moving to Zumba outside on the Town Center lawn, getting their "Shakira" on for my little guy! TNT sent tumblers to flip and soar through the air......all before we ever arrived at 10am!

Our family arrived at 10am and we were greeted by the West Stanly Fire Department and many friends whom we have missed dearly. Shortly after we were introduced to the crowds and presented with two, custom, Carter-blue fire helmets which are simply breathtaking. These helmets symbolize so much to me. They are my past, they are my friends, they are Locust. I know that I should let the boys play with them, but I think that I'll just look at them for a while......they are too perfect.

Immediately after an auction of items started. The auctioneer was a 14 year old boy who probably could have given an adult a run for his money! He knew how to work the crowd and auctioned all sorts of donated items. He made me want to get in on the bidding!

Of course, it was convenient that the Bojangles tent was close to the stage and the auction! Our dear Locust Bojangles sold food and supplied Carter with his heart's desire.......and when he started to have a tantrum and Karen handed him a Bojangles box, the tantrum stopped and never returned! The Bojangles staff in Locust has been a supporter of Carter's from the beginning because it was what he craved while on steroids after being discharged from the hospital......and now it's just what he craves because he loves it so much! Our family is so grateful to Gregory and his staff - they are family to us at this point. No trip to Locust is complete without a trip through the drive-thru!

There were so many vendors and local businesses that participated to help our family. I tried my best to thank each and every one, but I know that I didn't get to personally visit with each - I'm sorry! It literally took me all day just to get around the circle! It was amazing!

I am so thankful for Kristy and her beautiful photography. She did an AMAZING job capturing the event. Joe Gibbs' Racing sent out Joey Logano's Dollar General car (which Carter LOVED), there were inflatable bounce houses (which both the boys LOVED), and I certainly can't forget our beloved dentist (Dr. Jason) who contributed the "Dunk the Dentist" booth. There were so many others including Thirty-one, Body by Vi, and Scentsy. Cabarrus Family (Dr. Maggie and Carmen!) handed out all sorts of goodies and Locust Child Development Center sold hot dogs and treats. I cannot forget to mention our dear friends from Clover, SC - the Moped to Memphis crew. Not only did they bring out the famous moped (Carter still calls it the motorcycle), they also brought Carter a wagon which he pulled around all.day.long.

I cannot forget the fabulous music that played throughout the day. The beautiful Carson Hill touched our hearts with her incredible music. Bands kept our toes tapping throughout the day. It was amazing feeling to know that these musicians gave up their Saturday to sing for us.....and it was fabulous music!

I would be remiss if I failed to mention the efforts of Steve, Holly, and James. These individuals made this day PERFECT for our family. We are so thankful for all of their work and efforts.

We were so touched by those who came out to meet Carter and see him. It was extra-special that so many from Cabarrus Pediatrics attended. The nurses and the doctors all came to help celebrate Carter's life. They have loved Carter since his first visit at two days old. They have supported me through ear infections, croup, colic/acid reflux, phantom fevers, and now this......I couldn't ask for a better group of nurses and doctors. They have been with us every step of the way.

Locust is truly a "City with a Soul" and it is a soul that is compassionate. I feel so blessed to have lived there. Each tear that I cried, each smile that crossed my face, and each laugh that escaped my mouth on ((HUGS!!)) for Carter Day was a direct result of that compassion and love. When you're going through a journey like ours, you don't know how much you need love and support until it's there.....and then you relish it with tears of joy. Locust is forever in my heart, and forever in my soul.

Thank you for loving our little boy. You will never truly understand how you've touched our hearts. ((HUGS!!)) for Carter Day was perfect......absolutely. Perfect.

((HUGS!!))

5/1/12
I'm so sorry that I haven't posted. The past two weeks have been totally overwhelming. There is so much going on and I feel like I can barely keep my head above water.

Carter and I drove to Charlotte a week ago Thursday to head towards Cleveland. On Friday, we drove to my parent's home in Virginia where we spent the night and picked up my dad. We were able to stop at my alma mater on our way up and Carter met the ladies in the Alumnae Association and Development Office. He had a grand time and even managed to swipe a large pink beach ball from Miss Melissa (and yes, the ball went to Cleveland with us!). On Saturday, the three of us drove to Cleveland for the healing service.

Sunday afternoon we attended the healing service. It was very peaceful and there was nothing flamboyant about the service. It was held in a ballroom at the Holiday Inn Express near Cleveland. At the front of the room, there was a small poster of Jesus on the wall. There were probably 100-150 chairs that made up the rows and most of them were full. The first hour or so, the doctor was introduced and spoke a little about his beliefs and thoughts. It was not a sermon of any sort. He then spent most of the time answering questions that the attendees had for him.

I didn't realize that the doctor had been on the Dr. Oz show - that came as a surprise. There are clips from the show on You Tube if you're interested in viewing them.

The small children were seen first and Carter, my dad, and myself were the second group prayed over. The doctor came out and prayed over the first group which included a little girl in a stroller. When the doctor prayed over the girl's mother, she fell backwards and there were some gentlemen there to catch her. This kind of shocked me because a man had told me that he would catch me prior to the doctor starting. I told him that I was used to holding Carter and that I probably wouldn't fall - which I didn't, but I was determined not to after that!

I don't know if Carter felt anything when the doctor prayed over him or not. I do know that Carter became very quiet and still as he laid his head on my shoulder. I noticed that my own breathing became slower when he prayed over me. I didn't feel anything really, but I wasn't the one there to be healed either.

It was a good service and the doctor's message is so true - the love of God is the ultimate healer. Carter's healing is in God's hands.

Our next scans will be June 19th in Memphis - please continue to pray for the reduction in size of the tumor. Please continue to pray for Carter's healing.

These days you would never know that Carter is sick - except he has a bald head with two shunts on the right side. Of course, his hair is growing back and looks similar to a mohawk right now. Poor kid - probably the only time in his life that his momma will let him have a mohawk!

We are learning to be a family again.....and healing together. It is something that we haven't had a chance to do on a regular basis since November.

I will do my best to post again tomorrow. I'm trying to keep my head above water. So many things going on and to write about .....

Heavenly Father - thank you for bringing Carter and I back to Mason and Paul. Thank you for putting us under one roof again and for allowing us to have time together. Father God, embrace our family during this time and help us to revel in it. Cast fear away from our minds as we know that You dear God will heal Carter in your way and in your time. I lift my heart up to you, oh Lord. Amen.

((HUGS!!))
Sarah

5/4/12
Where was I? Ah yes, Cleveland.....So after the healing service Dad, Carter, and I got dinner in the hotel and headed to bed for the night.

It was WAY too cold to go outside.....did I mention that it SNOWED on our way home??? Yup, gotta love wearing capri pants and a cotton shirt through the mountains of PA .....and having to stop at one of the many lovely plazas on the Pennsylvania Turnpike......froze.my.bum.off!

Anyways - we drove back to Virginia on Monday and spent the night there with Mom and Dad (and dropped Dad off). Carter and I then drove to Charlotte on Tuesday and spent the night at the condo. Wednesday we drove back to Greenwood.
Carter gets a gold star for being such an amazing car traveler........

On Wednesday afternoon our Make A Wish volunteer visited with us to find out Carter's wish. He has been enamored with a photo from his "Aunt". This photo is of the Disney Dream and all of the Disney characters (signed for Carter, too!). So - since the picture has arrived, Carter has repeatedly said, "I want to go on that boat!" Which is usually followed by Mason saying, "Carter - you CAN'T go on that boat!" Oh.Boy. Poor Mason is going to be eating his words soon!

So, on Thursday I spent THE.ENTIRE.DAY. getting the paperwork ready to expedite the passports for the boys (note - if your children don't have passports - get them now when you don't need them....it's cheaper!). And GOD was looking out for me because I mentioned to the postal worker that I couldn't be at the appointment (because I was headed out of town) and he promptly gave me forms to fill out with directions to City Hall and the notary.

Have I mentioned that our lives are chaotic?

So - I got all of the papers together, gave Paul LOTS of instructions, and prepared to head to my alma mater for the Alumnae Board meetings.

Pop-Pop and Aunt Janet arrived on Thursday night and Mason and Carter were totally distracted by all of the love and attention. God bless Aunt Janet - Mason was attached to her hip the entire weekend. He slept with her, ate with her, loved on her.....used her Nook to play games all weekend. Predictably, Mason had Aunt Janet withdrawals when she left!

Friday morning I left for my alma mater and drove straight there, in time for my meetings. *phew!*

I cannot tell you how hard it was to be away from Carter - I haven't been away from him since October and he is truly my wing-man. Fortunately - board meetings are busy and there was a lot going on, so I was distracted, too.

There were so many sweet moments over the weekend. When I walked into dinner in the dining hall, I could barely get through the crowd without someone hugging me or talking to me. It was an amazing feeling knowing that so many in my college's community are following Carter's story.

One of the most meaningful encounters was when the president stopped me and told me that she was keeping up with Carter's story. Now, I don't know how other colleges and universities operate but I was shocked that she even knew who I was let alone that she knew of Carter's journey and was following it.

Another amazing moment was when I walked into the Alumnae Board session and was greeted with a HOLLA! HOLLA! song, blue bows on the tables, and Prayers for Carter posters. I couldn't quite make sense of it at first......me? HOLLA! HOLLA! for me? Really? Oh - and I failed to mention that the majority of the board had on ((HUGS!!)) for Carter t-shirts......not typical board attire!

And I certainly cannot forget the senior who found me after the dinner to tell me that she was an ALL survivor and wants to study pediatric oncology........OH.THE.TEARS!!! Even better that her picture showed up in my mailbox today for the annual fund with the message "And because of you I can....." YES! YOU CAN! ... and yes, I have made my annual fund pledge.

I am so blessed to be a part of this community. It was all a part of God's plan for me to attend there. I cannot imagine my life if I hadn't been a student there. I cannot imagine where I would be today without these amazing people in my life.
HOLLA! HOLLA!

So - Sunday I headed back to Greenwood and back to my guys....

Somehow - today is Friday.....and I'm really not even sure how I got here and managed to survive this week.

Chaos reigns here.

In the midst of trying to unpack the house, sell my store inventory, remember preschool drop-offs and pick-ups, groceries, home repairs, and heaven only knows what else - I was working with Make-a-Wish to figure out Carter's wish.

Fortunately, the expedited passports arrived today and I was able to scan and send them to the head office in Charleston. This meant that they were able to book our cruise!

We will be headed on our MAW trip on May 20th - this is a little crazy because we'll be in Virginia for the Not So Silent Auction and my 15th reunion on May 18-19. Just a little hectic.

We will cruise May 20-24 and return to Charlotte. We will then stay in Charlotte to celebrate Carter's birthday and return back to Greenwood on May 27.

It's a good thing that I got my hair highlighted today - surely I will be totally gray by the end of these ten days!

Dear God - From You all blessings flow. You have brought such joy and happiness to our family. Praise to You, Lord for carrying us through this journey and for surrounding us with such amazing people. Father God, I am so thankful for everything, even the chaos - for chaos means that we are busy and we are able! I lift my heart up to you, Amen.

((HUGS!!))
Sarah

5/8/12
So many people have told me recently that I'm an inspiration and that I'm so strong. Honestly, I'm not - I'm just a normal mom fighting for her little boy. I hate being elevated to some "Super Mom" status - because I'm not. I have wretched days just like everybody else, and I've had a lot of them recently.

It isn't easy to move into a new home. Couple that with not having been at home when the move took place, and it becomes even more difficult. Add trips, scheduling a birthday party, unpacking, and a dash of chaos (or a couple of dashes) and life ends up being a perfect mess trying to stay on top of anything and everything. There are so many times that I wish I could afford a staff of twenty or so because I could probably keep them all busy and then some!

Now, remove the safety and security of the St. Jude bubble. If your child is sick, the doctors and nurses are less than a mile or two away at most. If there is a problem, you can address it immediately. There is a daily schedule and routine to adhere to -

so every day is somewhat predictable. There is love and support from other families, staff, nurses, doctors everywhere.
I've upset a lot of people because I don't write emails back or communicate on a daily basis, and for that, I'm sorry. But honestly, some days it takes everything I have just to get through the day, and I promise, you don't want to talk to me. I have nothing to say other than tell you how crazy life is these days.

So it's hard to write that everything is happy and uplifting when I'm struggling each day. My constant prayer is that the tumor is shrinking. I can't look at Carter without saying a prayer. I know that my little boy is doing better because he is running, jumping, playing, and watching TV - but the not knowing of what will happen on June 19th is scary. I know that this is all in God's hands, but I also know that I'm merely the gift holder of my precious baby boy.

Heavenly Father - Please give me strength. Please wrap your loving arms around me and cradle me when I am at my lowest. Help me to remember that I can only do so much and that I'm not "Super Mom". Father God, please take my fear and worry away. I lift my heart up to you. Amen.

((HUGS!!))
Sarah

5/11/12
I had a dream last night that I couldn't find our house (I'm getting better at finding my way around, fortunately!). It was awful - until I realized that I couldn't find our house because all of the houses had blue ribbons on the mailboxes. Our blue ribbon on the mailbox has been a beacon to me. It symbolizes Carter. It symbolizes unity. It symbolizes home.

Needless to say, I woke up with a start and didn't know where I was ....it's nice to not be a nomad these days.

I've been working on unpacking the boxes and getting the house settled. The downstairs is looking pretty good. The upstairs, not so much. Yesterday we had the windows and gutters cleaned, and the house power washed. It is amazing how much light shines into this house now! I might not have to repaint the rooms a lighter color after all! The house is starting to look good from the street, too - no more pine needles hanging from the gutters and the white trim actually looks white! We've got plans to tackle the yard next.

A week from today we'll be at my alma mater celebrating my 15th college reunion and preparing for the Not So Silent Auction (if you haven't bid on something yet, you're missing out!). My college classmates have gone to extraordinary lengths to create an incredible auction to help us and we are forever indebted to them. I haven't seen some of these ladies in fifteen years and they are giving their time and talent to help my little guy. It's an amazing feeling to know that we are so loved.

Carter has a lot of "moms" out there looking out for him. Some are friends, some are nurses, some are ladies we haven't even met. Some have children and some don't, but he is the luckiest little boy to have so many "moms" sending love and prayers his way. It isn't unusual for Carter to meet a new lady friend and melt her heart within moments. I know - he melted my heart the first time I laid eyes on him, too.

So, thank you to all of the "moms" out there pulling for Carter and helping fight this battle with us. I'm the luckiest one of all because I'm surrounded by amazing women who are fighting for Carter like he is their own son. I couldn't ask for more.

You know - I don't even remember Mother's Day last year. I know that I got some cards and probably some flowers, but I don't remember any moment of the day. This year, I'm going to remember plenty of moments so that I can cherish them forever. I need to.....

Father God - Thanks for helping me feel like I'm not so lost. Thank you for blessing me with amazing women in my life whom have helped me be strong for Carter. Please bless these "moms" in Carter's life with a wonderful weekend and joy in their hearts. Praise you, Lord Christ, for all of the beautiful moments that will be cherished in the coming days. I lift my heart up to you, Amen.

((HUGS!!))

5/14/12

Right now, both boys are outside playing with our nanny who comes each afternoon. I love to listen to them play. They giggle, they yell, they conspire as only brothers can......if Carter had a full head of hair, you might think that everything was normal in our household!

I am busy packing for our Make a Wish trip on the Disney Dream next week and for my 15th college reunion. Two sets of luggage (one for each trip) will hopefully ensure that we have clean clothes and everything is packed for each one.

The boys each have two outfits a day - one of which is a Disney themed outfit. I know. I have a problem. God knew what He was doing when He didn't send girls our way. I've called it "God's economy plan" since Carter was in-utero.....although it hasn't really been an economy plan the way I thought it would be.....

Tomorrow our Make a Wish volunteers will come to present Carter with his wish. The boys have told everyone that we are taking an airplane to the boat and the boat to the beach......which has caused for some discussion in Mason's preschool class from what I understand. The students are learning that there are other ways to the beach other than a car. God bless Miss Beth for having to sort out that discussion!

We will leave on Thursday for the condo in Charlotte where we will spend the night. On Friday morning we will get up and drive to Virginia for reunion. We will be there Friday night and Saturday until after the auction. Speaking of which, if you haven't checked out the Not So Silent Auction (because the women I went to college with aren't exactly "silent") - There literally is something for everyone. It is an amazing fundraiser for Carter. There will be a live auction after the Not So Silent Auction ends and you don't have to be there to participate! You can fill out a proxy on the website, too! They have thought of EVERYTHING!

I don't know how much more I'll be able to write this week, but I hope to write this weekend and while we're on our MAW cruise. I know that there will be LOTS to report!

Please continue to pray for Carter. I am so nervous about having this trip being similar to the last. The good news is that this time

190

Carter is not vomiting, he's watching TV (eyesight not compromised by pressure in brain), and he's running all over the place (BIG DEAL!).

Heavenly Father, please grant us peace throughout the next two weeks. Please let these trips be wonderful and filled with as little stress as possible. Hold us close as we attempt to bring joy to our little boy's life and let us revel in it. Father God, help us to forget for just a brief moment. I lift my heart up to you, dear Lord. Amen.

((HUGS!!))
Sarah

5/27/12
Dear God –
Thank you for blessing us with this glorious day! I am in awe. I remember the miracle you blessed me with three years ago today and today I rejoice in yet another. Carter is three and acting like a typical little boy. Thank God for this gift. I rejoice in You and your glory!

((HUGS!!))
Sarah

It was Carter's last birthday here on earth. While I didn't know that at the time, I wanted it to be amazing in every sense of the way. We had a party for him at Great Wolf Lodge. Carter and his friends had so much fun. It was a reunion of friends. It was a celebration of life. It was a celebration of love.

6/2/12
WARNING: This is a long one!
I feel like it has been forever since I've written. So much has happened since we left on our ten day journey!

First, our journey took us to the condo in Charlotte where we dropped off a set of luggage, picked up our beloved babysitter (Sarah), and spent the night. We then headed to Virginia for the Not So Silent Auction and my fifteenth reunion. It is always amazing to be on campus. There is such a sense of home when I drive through the gates. I was so excited to see everyone, to have Paul and the boys on campus with me, and to show Sarah the campus!

It was a pretty humbling experience to be on campus. At registration, Lucretia was telling everyone about the Not So Silent Auction and sporting her ((HUGS!!)) t-shirt. She made sure that everyone had a photo sticker of Carter on their name tag and that they knew where and when the auction would be held. She is an amazing PR person! I think everyone knew Carter's story before they left the registration tables!

We then headed to our dorm and unloaded into our quad. We weren't there long before we ran into all of Carter's "aunts" and we got to catch up.

I headed to the Development Office to figure out our Reunion Giving numbers. We evaluated the giving sheets, figured out numbers, and determined how many contacts we needed in order to not only set a record for participation, but also a record for the Young Alumnae Giving Participation.

There is something about the college I attended and food. It is almost always amazing. Couple the food with your besties from college, a beautiful evening in the quad, and a mission to contact each classmate who hadn't given a gift to the annual fund and a good time was had by all. I don't remember the last time I have laughed so hard. Impromptu phon-a-thons in the quad are hard to beat!

It was great seeing Carter play in the quad with all of the other children. He laughed, he ran, and he played. It wasn't until he took his hat off that many realized he was "the" Carter. Such a miracle.

After the sun went down, we ventured to the conference center to put together the Not So Silent Auction. Let me rephrase that, I stood in awe as everyone else worked their behinds off. Although I tried to help, I did very little other than talk to everyone! These ladies were absolutely amazing and the auction looked phenomenal. Each item was beautifully and professionally displayed. It rivaled the best of Junior League or charity auctions and these ladies only had a few hours to set everything up!

I have to thank Catering for providing their famous cookies fresh from the oven for us.....what a treat and pick-me-up!

My classmates were up and going before the crack of dawn. They were posting signs around campus, blowing up massive balloons (seriously have never seen balloons so big!), putting out the bid sheets, and perfecting the last minute details.

Then we headed to the reunion luncheon to hear about the efforts of our classes and to see both the Outstanding Alumna and Distinguished Alumna presentations. It was hard not to get caught up in all of the excitement!

I am happy to report that all of the hard work paid off - not only did our class receive the Young Alumnae Participation record, but we set a class giving record, too! HOLLA! HOLLA!!

I feel awful because when I stood to present the giving totals, I totally forgot to have my incredible classmates stand to thank them for all of their efforts. I got so excited about the participation awards and so nervous about remembering everything, that I totally forgot to have them stand. EPIC. FAIL. on my part. I hope that they know how much I love them and how sorry I am to have forgotten to have them stand! You would think that I would know by now to make notes of what I need to do when I need to speak......Public speaking lesson number one! GRRR.

It was then on to the auction event where there were so many alumnae who participated. They were eager to hear Carter's story, to help support us, and to offer their love and prayers. I was really proud of myself for not crying .....at least until the end. Lucretia unveiled the picture of Carter by Jamie (our long-time photographer and friend). At which point, I lost it. Jamie's contribution to the event was this portrait (beautifully framed). The item was then "reversed auctioned" for me - meaning Lucretia read all of the donations made towards the photograph for our family. You wanna make a girl cry.......that's the way to do it! I literally bawled as each donation was read out - a total of $2300 for just the photograph! I think that it goes in my "miracle" category.

Probably the most meaningful and touching moment of the entire event was when Lucretia led us in prayer after the auction. She makes my prayers look elementary! It is one thing to be with your classmates and to have their support and love. It's a totally other thing to have them lift you up in prayer after such a wonderful event. I know that God was with us, I could feel Him embracing us together, touching each of our hearts.

It wasn't long after that the Bucciero clan had to get in the car and head back to the condo in Charlotte. Our flight was Sunday morning for Carter's Make A Wish trip and we needed to get back!

After the four hour drive, we met our dear friend (and Carter's God-mommy), Amy. You see, in our packing we managed to forget the double stroller. The only Toys R Us that had a cheap double stroller was closer to Pineville - far enough away that we wouldn't make it there in time before closing. God bless Amy for getting it for us (the airport trip would have been a disaster without it!) and then meeting us in Concord.

We finally made it to the condo, put the boys to bed, and then proceeded to re-pack and reorganize the few things that needed to be included on the Make a Wish trip. Paul and I were up until midnight and up by 6am to ensure that everything was ready.

Both Mason and Carter were incredible at the airport and on the plane. These boys love to fly! Once we arrived in Orlando, we made our way to the Disney Cruise desk, checked-in, and got on a bus for Port Canaveral. Disney makes it so easy to travel with them.

The boys were overwhelmed with excitement just seeing the ship. We boarded easily and then started to discover the ship. Mason and Carter were eager to check out Nemo's Reef (splash park) and the Mickey Pool, so they had some pool time before we ever left port.

We were fortunate to have the 5:45 dining, so we cut the swimming early and got ready for dinner. The first night we dined at the Royal Palace (and it was fabulous!). After dinner, Paul took the boys to the room to get ready for bed and I set off to get them registered for the Ocean Club. What I didn't realize was that I had already registered the boys and didn't even remember (have I mentioned that Disney makes things easy?). I also discovered the interactive detective game, the shopping, and some other things.....but I did not nearly discover the entire ship!

The first day we docked in Nassau and spent the day on the ship. OK - I did get off during nap time to check out the shopping. We took the boys to the Ocean Club to see if they would like it, and neither one of them even looked back at us once they were inside. I didn't know if I should be proud of my kids for being independent or heart-broken that they didn't think twice about me! Mason did really well and constantly wanted to go to the Ocean Club and Ocean Lab while we were on the cruise. Carter would do well for a short amount of time and then wanted us. How did we know? The counselors would either text or call on a wave phone (provided by Disney) to let us know that Carter wanted to leave.

That night we dined in the Animator's Palate restaurant which was really neat because Crush (the turtle from Nemo) talks to the diners throughout the meal. Mason and Carter had great fun watching the animated sharks, Dory, and Nemo swim around us.

The second day was at sea and the captain dropped anchor somewhere in the middle of nowhere - which was perfectly breathtaking. We took pictures with the princesses. We explored the ship. The boys solved the case of the lost puppies and went to the club. That night dinner was at The Enchanted Garden. So much to do, so little time!

The third day at Castaway Cay (key) we got up early and we were some of the first off of the boat. After pictures outside the ship, we made our way to the second of the beaches, Pelican Point (I think). The boys loved riding the tram out to the beach and were over-the-moon when we arrived at the beach. I tried not to have a heart attack while worrying about sunscreen protection for Carter or worry about sand getting into his Hickman Port. I pretty much bubble-wrapped the boy to ensure it wouldn't be a disaster of a day. We spent about an hour and a half on the beach and then headed back. It was an overcast day and very windy making it very chilly at times. We had a late breakfast and then hit the nearly deserted pools and splash park. Dinner was at the Enchanted Garden once again that evening.

Paul and I have decided that when we do another Disney cruise (because we will - we're hooked!). It will have to be a seven day cruise because there simply isn't enough time to do everything in just three days! We never made it to the movie theater (showing current Disney movies), or the D Lounge, or the adult only restaurants, or the excursions, and I could go on and on.....That being said, it will be a long time before we can actually afford a Disney cruise again (and we only had to provide spending money this time around!).

I forgot to mention that there was a special gathering of the Make A Wish families on the last day (there were twelve families). We gathered for cookies and milk in the Cabanas restaurant where Captain Mickey made a special appearance. Mickey loved on Carter and we got some great photos. I will try to post them later.

phew! I just typed through naptime! The boys are awake now, so I need to run.

AND PRAISE THE LORD! Carter felt fabulous the entire time we were on the ship! He played like every other child and did everything that a "normal" child would do - HOW IS THAT FOR A MIRACLE!?!

Father God - I know that you hear our prayers, because you are answering them. I see the miracles that you bless us with daily. I hear your whispers when I see Carter running and keeping up with Mason. I sense your presence around me every day - no matter how good, or how bad - You are there. Thank you Lord for the miracles you've provided us with - I am at your mercy. My heart is yours. My life is yours. My love is yours. I lift my heart up to you. Amen.

((HUGS!!))
S.

6/10/12
A week from today, Carter and I will head to Charlotte.

A week from tomorrow, we will board a plan to Memphis.

A week from Tuesday, we will know what is going on with Carter's tumor. I will either laugh and rejoice, or I will crumble to my knees .....or maybe a combination of both.

Carter seems to be alright - he laughs, he plays, he runs, he fights with his brother......all the things that he should be doing for a newly turned three year old. The problem is that he has always done these things - so I don't know what to think.

My heart wants to believe that all is well - that Carter is healed and that life will begin to resume normal.....but my mind doesn't want to set me up for another downfall. I am at war within myself - my heart vs. my mind.

It is in these moments that I call out to God. I talk to him incessantly at times pleading with him to save Carter. I tell St. Jude, over and over, I will write a book that will benefit St. Jude - if only you will spare Carter. And then I remind myself that God has been good to me and to Carter, and that there are whispers echoing .....no matter what, Carter will be fine. No matter what happens, no matter how bad it gets, everything will be alright. It may be here on earth and it may be in heaven, but regardless of where Carter is - God will cradle him in His arms and take care of my little boy.

Please keep us in your prayers. Please put Carter on your church prayer list and ask a friend to put him on theirs. I know that God hears the prayers as we lift up Carter's name to Him. If I could put Carter's name on every church prayer list across America, I would.

Father God, I rejoice in the blessing that you have given me. I rejoice in the everyday chaos and mayhem. I am blessed with the runny noses, the fighting over toys, and the potty training. I thank you for the mundane that so many take for granted. I ask that you grant us more of the mundane and more time for it. Heavenly Father, Carter is an angel of yours sent here to spread your word and touch lives. I have seen him in action and I know that You have as well. Please heal Carter and grant him a healthy life. Let this be a stumbling block or a hiccup - one which we never have to look back on again. Please keep moving me forward, one step at a time with You holding my hand. Praise to you, Lord Christ who fills us with your mercy and grace. I lift my heart up to you, Father God. In Your Name, Amen.

((HUGS!!))
Sarah

6/12/12
Exactly a week from now I will have answers. God has this in His hands and everything will be fine, regardless of the answers we hear. The hardest part is the not knowing ....
((HUGS!!))

6/17/12
Carter and I will have some lunch and then head to the condo in Charlotte tonight. We will fly to Memphis tomorrow.

Please continue to pray for Carter's complete healing. Paul and I will celebrate our 10th anniversary later this week and my prayer is that our gift will be Carter's health and well-being. It would be the best gift ever to know that our little guy is whole once again.

I know that God is with me. I feel His presence. I hear His whispers. I see the gifts that He has granted us. There are signs of God everywhere and I am blessed and thankful.

Thank you for continuing to prayer for Carter and our family - it gives us strength and courage to know that we have an army of prayer warriors behind us.

WINNING IS THE ONLY OPTION!!!

((HUGS!!))
Sarah

6/18/12
We are back in Memphis. It's almost like coming home. Isn't it odd that a hospital feels like home? That's the power of St. Jude.

The flight was a little bumpy, but Carter did pretty well. We were picked up at the airport, dropped off at Grizzlie House, and then we went to check in at the hospital.

St. Jude is beautiful in the spring.....but it's gorgeous right now. So many beautiful flowers! They've been busy since we've been gone. The A/T registration lobby has been updated with a new mural and virtual paintings that change scenes and has movement sensors.....almost like Disney!

Our St. Jude chaplain, Mark, happened to be in registration when we arrived and it was great to see him (maybe a good sign?!). He was so excited to see Carter and to see how well Carter is doing.

As soon as we registered, one of Carter's favorite nurses (Candice) appeared with a big hug! I almost wanted to cry! It was so good to see her and to have someone welcome us back. And, of course, Carter was immediately given lots of love and attention.

We headed to the cafeteria for something to drink and there was another favorite nurse (Lacie)! It was perfect timing and we got to sit with her (in front of the bulldozer window - Carter's favorite) for a few minutes to catch up.

Then we headed up to the second floor with Lacie to see a few of our other favorites. We got to see Rory and Kristen along with a few others. Carter immediately raided the toy room grabbing the toy guitars, fire trucks, and a toaster.......He also wanted his blood pressure taken and to go into a room. Poor kid has been in the hospital WAY to much obviously!

Carter got his labs, height, and weight taken in A/T and was a rock star. Seriously, the child doesn't mind having blood taken from his Hickman port. It doesn't phase him. Of course, he wouldn't sit still long enough for the blood pressure machine to work.......

We headed over to Target House for dinner and surprised some of our buddies over there and met up with a few friends that knew we would be there. It was so good to see everyone. I keep thinking of the "Cheers" theme song......"Sometimes you want to go where everybody knows your name." That's what it felt like being at Target House and St. Jude today......I could actually feel myself relax a bit for the first time in weeks. Everybody gets it here. Everybody knows us. Everybody is family.

Aunt Stacy met us at Target House and drove us back to Grizzlie House where we ate Corky's BBQ and just got caught up on random stuff. Such a treat for me!

I need to head to bed. It has been a very long day. Carter is sound asleep beside me. We need to be at the hospital at 7:15 am tomorrow morning for sedation. It will be another long day. I will keep you posted as the day progresses. Please keep us in your prayers. Please hold us close to your heart tomorrow. It will finally bring answers.

Lord, I lift my heart up to you. This is in your hands. I know that you are in control. I know that whatever the outcome, You have a plan. Amen.

((HUGS!!))
S.

6/19/12
Tonight I am curled up in bed with Carter beside me, fast asleep. The poor kid had such a hard day, but was an incredible trooper.

Our day started at the hospital at 7:15am. It was determined immediately that Carter hadn't had a "clearance" visit for the MRI (scheduling error), so we had to head over to E Clinic for a quick visit with our favorite fellow, Dr. Ross.

Once Carter was given "clearance" we headed back over to the Chili's Care Center where we were taken back to MRI.

Unfortunately, Carter missed his MRI spot and we had to wait for another to open. It was 9:40am before he was totally sedated and taken back. Thank goodness for good meds that calm little guys down when they are hungry and agitated!

When Carter was in MRI I had this incredible sense of peace. I thought that I would be a nervous wreck, but I wasn't. When a moment of anxiety tried to sneak in, I simply told myself that God was taking care of Carter and it was in His hands. It really helped. I know that God was taking care of me today because I didn't cry once!

Carter had a harder time coming out of recovery today than he has in the past. He was seriously drunk on the meds - and not a nice drunk either!

We met with Quality of Life quickly, headed to the cafeteria for some food to munch on in our next appointment, and then headed to E Clinic.

The MRI results show that the tumor is now 2.86cm - which is smaller than it was in October when Carter was diagnosed and 1/3 the size of the tumor in March when we were airlifted back to St. Jude from Disney. PRAISE THE LORD!

We will come back in August to do another scan and to see if the tumor is smaller or stable. At that time, we will possibly discuss some experimental treatments. These treatments have not been mentioned prior to this point by the doctor. He did not go into detail today, since we will need to see the status of the tumor in August. However, the fact that there may be another option is HUGE in my mind ......I am willing to do anything to help my little boy survive.

I am surrounded by amazing prayer warriors, both known and unknown to me, whom have taken the time to pray for my little Carter. For this, I am eternally grateful for it is because of YOU that Carter is doing so well. God hears our prayers. He is listening and healing Carter in such a merciful way. ALL GLORY BE TO GOD for such an amazing gift!

On March 9th, I prayed to God to give me some more time. I told God that I wasn't ready to give up on Carter yet and I wouldn't stop fighting for his life. I know that God heard my prayer. I know that He isn't giving up on Carter either. I know that God is in my corner, fighting beside me.

I am so blessed.

Father God, tonight I rejoice in your glory and sing your praises. I give you thanks and revel in your love. Thank you for blessing us with this gift of shrinking Carter's tumor more. Thank you for the gift of time. Thank you for the gift of your love. Most importantly, thank you for sweet Carter. I lift my heart up to you, Amen.

((HUGS!!))
Sarah

6/20/12
What a great day.....my heart is lighter, my smile is brighter, my hugs are bigger. I am so thankful for this wonderful place that has taken care of my little boy, and me for that matter. The friendships, the support, and the love are all testament to this wonderful place.

Today I was greeted with smiles.....everyone had heard Carter's news. It isn't unlike a high school or a small college campus. News travels like wildfire, good or bad.

There were several times today when I literally heard my name being called out .....people literally were stopping me to give me a hug, to share in my joy, and to love on Carter. It's an amazing feeling. You see, these are the same people who cried with me in March and comforted me. Now, they rejoice with me.

Hope is the best present ever.

((HUGS!!))

6/25/12
Thank you everyone for your love, prayers, and support. I cannot begin to express my thanks. I know that it is because of Carter's Prayer Warriors that he is still here with us today.
Please continue to pray for the tumor to shrink .....please pray for it to be GONE! Please pray for normality in our lives.

Many of you have asked about Mason and his well-being. We're desperately trying to keep life "normal" for him. It's hard since he does not have a lot of friends here. Last week was such a treat for him because he got to go to the pool with Sarah and McKinley (something that he cannot do with Carter). We have enrolled Mason in gymnastics and in tennis lessons with hopes to get him out more. We're trying to figure out swimming lessons, too. It's so hard because there are so many things that Carter "can't" do at this point due to his Hickman port or due to germs. I'm trying to find a balance for Mason. He is such a good sport about everything and so loving towards his little brother.

I need to run. Time to change Carter's dressing again. I can't remember if I mentioned it or not last week, but Carter is now off of ALL meds ....including his weekly antibiotic regimen. This is good and bad. Good because it is one less thing to worry about. Bad because the antibiotic isn't fighting germs!

((HUGS!!))
S.

6/30/12

It seems like every little thing frustrates me to no end these days. I feel like I have to capitalize on each moment. I have no idea what the future holds and I want to be fully prepared for it when it is here.

Don't get me wrong - Carter is doing great and is a joy.....but the events in March reminded me that God is in control and that life isn't normal. I mean, we were at Disney World of all places and were put on a plane to St. Jude where they told me I could stop treatment for my son.....if that isn't a reality check, I don't know what is.....

So I feel like I'm racing against the clock trying to get the house together, trying to get it cleaned and sanitized for Carter, trying to make it a home. I am trying to liquidate my store on Facebook so that I can focus on other things - including Carter. I feel like the weight of the world is on my shoulders. Every little thing stresses me out and rips me apart. To make matters worse, I'm alone without any help. I don't have any good friends here. We are our own island here in Greenwood and it stinks.

One such thing that stresses me out is that many people have questioned as to why Paul didn't go to Memphis with me for the scan. The answer is four-fold: 1) I felt like Carter was doing well and could handle the journey/scan myself. 2) St. Jude only pays for one parent and the patient to travel (and we don't have frequent flier miles or the money for another ticket) 3) Paul has been very fortunate to be able to take so much time off of work for Carter and we don't want to abuse that generosity. 4) We don't have anyone who can take Mason if both Paul and myself are away.

We're doing the best we can - please don't criticize Paul for not being with me. It just adds to my stress level....Quite frankly - I've done the majority of this journey on my own, I'm hurt that people think I couldn't handle the scan on my own, too.

I feel like everyone criticizes us these days - but quite frankly, until you've walked in our shoes, you shouldn't. You probably have no idea what it is like to undergo some major stresses within a one year period (a new job for Paul, a move to a new area, a cancer diagnosis for Carter, loss of my income, etc. etc. etc). I wouldn't wish this journey on anyone. I ask God all the time why He thinks I can handle all of this.....I haven't heard an answer yet. I hope that it's coming soon.

Father God - Hear my prayer. Grant me strength to get through each day. Grant me patience to deal with the trivial issues that seem like mountains. Help me to make this house a home. In Your Name I pray, Amen.

((HUGS!!))

7/15/12
I'm sorry that I haven't written in a while. It seems like every opportunity I have, I am running sales for my store. I'm finally making progress liquidating the summer inventory......then I'll have to conquer the fall/winter inventory from last year that I was unable to sell (because we were at St. Jude).

There have been more bright spots this past week. We got a surprise visit from a Vestry member at our church which included cupcakes (and the boys immediately fell in love with her and the cupcakes!). A good friend from Indian Land and her friend sent Thirty-One gifts for me and donations.....including donations from her son's sixth birthday party (he asked for donations to Carter instead of toys!). I headed to Atlanta for the night to go to the sample sale at the market (and got a little mommy-time). Lots of bright spots to be thankful for these days. Thank you Lord for these blessings.

Carter and I will return to St. Jude on August 13th for his next scan. Please continue to pray - we need this tumor to continue to shrink!

I need to head upstairs for bed. I'm so tired these days....but I think that I can start to see the light at the end of the tunnel! WOO HOO!!

((HUGS!!))
Sarah

Part Four

~

The Beginning of the End

7/28/12
Paul has taken Carter to the ER. Little man has a HUGE belly that is hard as a rock....his tummy is so taut that it looks like a pin prick would pop it! He hasn't been constipated, but we gave him laxatives earlier in the week to see if it would help. It didn't. This coupled with a vomiting occurrence earlier in the week has me paranoid beyond belief. Carter said his back hurt earlier (probably from carrying that belly around!) and said that he wanted to go to the doctor.

Paul has been texting me and the doctor agreed that Carter is asymptomatic for constipation. The doctor ordered an ultrasound and blood work. He wants to check kidney function, too.

Of course, Carter is charming the nurses and making new girlfriends along the way......go.figure!

Please pray - Carter has been doing so well....it shatters me to pieces to know that he's in the hospital again.

Heavenly Father - please keep my baby safe. Please wrap your loving arms around him and hold him close. Please let this be something simple and mundane - I yearn for the simple and mundane. Please keep Carter well. I lift my heart up to you, dear Lord. Amen.

((HUGS!!))
Sarah

7/28/12
Update: There is a build up of clear fluid in Carter's abdomen. We are currently consulting with St. Jude to determine if we need to return to St. Jude to have our doctors there look at it or if this is something that can be addressed in Charlotte at Levine.

Please pray that whatever this is it is not significant and that it is resolved easily.

I'm trying to avoid panic mode.......

Dear God - Please grant me peace. Amen.

7/29/12
Sarah and Carter are headed to Charlotte and they will go to 11th floor at Levine Children's Hospital. Dr. Chad is on duty today and he knows Carter very well throughout this journey. Prayer warriors please spread the word and pray for great news.

7/29/12
Carter will have surgery tomorrow at Levine Children's Hospital to drain the fluid. Once the fluid is tested we will know more. Thank you prayer warriors! Keep up the prayers!

7/30/12
It has been a day! First thing this morning Carter had fluid drained from his belly to be tested. I was able to stay in the procedure room for the duration of it. I honestly amazed myself - I didn't cry when they poked my baby with a needle and inserted a catheter to pull the fluid out! Don't mess with me, I'm a St. Jude Momma!

The fluid was yellow in color, but clear. The doctor took 100ccs of it out and it didn't soften Carter's belly in the least. This should give you a good idea of how much fluid has accumulated in my little man's abdomen.

Our doctor is baffled as to the cause of this and he is testing for everything imaginable including hepatitis A/B/C, another tumor, and an infection of the abdominal cavity. Because so many tests are being done - there are no results as of right now.

The doctor spoke with the neurosurgeons here and they are going to do a shunt series (series of x-rays based on the placement of the shunt) and an MRI tomorrow. This will help them rule out if the tumor is causing issues or if the shunt is causing issues.

We have also discussed draining the fluid. Basically, it sounds like an external bag will be place with a pump on it to help facilitate the removal of the fluid. It must be done slowly as to not shock Carter's system.

I was just interrupted by a surgeon to look at Carter's incision which is draining some - all looks good, though. He will be back in a while to check on it.

While Levine is certainly not St. Jude - it is comfortable being here and we are not having to start over at a new hospital with new doctors. The doctor who is watching over Carter is the one we originally worked with in October and then again in February when we were here for outpatient chemo. We see familiar staff faces in the hallway from Child Life. We even got to ride the elevator with the doctor who placed Carter's Hickman port. Last night our night nurse was a sweet woman by the name of Tessa, she already knew Carter's story because she met our dear friend and former neighbor in work orientation. Not only that, she is a St. Jude Momma herself and so we shared an immediate bond! God has blessed us once again!

It is so comforting to have so many people reach out to me already. People have offered to visit, bring food, give me a break, etc. What a luxury! It is such a gift to feel loved and to have friends nearby. Most importantly, I know that everyone is praying for Carter - which is what we need most.

It's odd in a sense, but I'm not as frazzled by this situation as I probably should be ....I just have a sense of peace about it. I know that God is taking care of Carter and that my little guy is a fighter and we'll get through this battle, too. Honestly - I'm more frustrated that we had one medical bill left to pay and we would have been all caught up! And, we're due back to St. Jude in less than two weeks. Seriously - why couldn't this have waited a week or so? At least St. Jude would have covered the medical bills! Oh well - this is part of the journey. Just when you start to get a little comfortable, a little more relaxed - something else hits.....I need to remind myself never to be comfortable again!

I'm guessing that we'll be here close to a week at this point. I can't envision us being booted out quickly given the uncertainty of the situation. At least I know my way around Levine and can get to the cafeteria and back......without getting lost!

Father God - Please continue to wrap your loving arms around my Carter. Continue to heal his brain and belly. Guide the doctors here to determine what the fluid is bloating his abdomen. Give them the wisdom to relieve the pressure. Grant us peace as we go through the process day by day in our lives to attain answers. Heavenly Father - heal my precious child and make him whole once again. Let him be able to be a normal three year old. Let potty-training be the worse thing that we have to deal with at this point. Smile down upon us, dear Lord, and let us magnify your good works through Carter. I lift my heart up to you dear Lord. Amen.

7/31/12
MRI scheduled for 1pm - Please pray for answers.

((HUGS!!))
Sarah

7/31/12
MRI running behind...won't be until 4pm today.....longest.day.ever.

7/31/12
They finally took Carter back for his MRI about 5pm - we won't have the results until the morning ... Please pray that the tumor has not grown.

I know that the prayers are working because the fluid was negative for infection and for cancer cells!!! WOO!! HOO!! God is good!

I am in recovery with Carter right now - more later when I don't have to type to my phone!

((HUGS!!))

8/1/12
Carter is one miserable little boy and I am one miserable momma.

Please note that Carter threw my phone across the room at a wall and my phone is no longer. I am attempting to get it fixed, but I have no way of getting to a Verizon store at this point.

Dear Lord - You really like testing me, don't you? I can tell.

((HUGS!!))
Sarah

8/1/12
Need to get to sleep - today was a LONG day....but the highlights
included a Bojangles delivery from our favorite area manager,
Joe. He brought enough Bojangles for Carter to eat every day that
we're here!

I am also glad to report that my phone is now working courtesy of
visitors who are tech savvy and knew how to reset an iphone! I
learned something new today!

Please pray that Carter rests comfortably tonight - the poor little
guy is just miserable and pitiful. It breaks my heart.

((HUGS!!))

8/2/12
Shunt revision surgery tomorrow morning at 9:30 am ....I will write
more while Carter is in surgery. Please continue to pray.

8/3/12
It is really difficult to write and be eloquent when you're beyond
exhausted.

Last night we had a horrible experience. The resident on call was
reluctant to give Carter a strong pain medication even though he
was writhing in pain. She gave him Benadryl and Ativan.....neither
of which were enough to relax Carter. This was her third night of
being on the floor - and the third night she continued to evade
giving Carter medication. When I finally was able to convince her
to give Carter some of the pain medication (which is a standard
medication that Carter has been on multiple times), she gave him
a minimal dosage. This at least relaxed Carter, but he still couldn't
sleep. That's when I called for the supervising attendee - and the
resident showed up instead. And needless to say, I unloaded on
the woman. I unleashed the St. Jude Momma inside of me that
I've never had to unleash before.

In so many words I said that if we could put Carter through chemo
and radiation, we really shouldn't be concerned about a strong
medication, should we?

And yes, EVERYONE heard about it.....both from me and our wonderful nurse who understood my frustration over the course of the night/morning.

The best comment came from one of the anesthesia nurses this morning when I told her that the resident said to me that the first dosage was the "standard" dosage. The nurse laughed and said, "Clearly she was mistaken!" She had seen Carter's medication log prior to pre-op and was baffled by the dual minimal dosages.

Carter was blessed to have a special friend ride down to pre-op with him this morning. Carter has taken a special liking to a therapy dog named Windy. She is a collie and only weighs about six pounds. Windy rode in Carter's bed and then came and saw him later this afternoon. She and her owner, Ms. Tucker are both very special people who God has sent to us.

Carter's surgery went well. His shunts were revised from VP shunts to VA shunts, which means the spinal fluid will now drain into his aorta instead of his abdominal cavity. We still haven't figured out why Carter's body has stopped absorbing the fluid, but I'm just thankful that the fluid is infection and cancer free.

Carter also had an external drain inserted into his abdominal cavity. This allows the fluid to drain out of his body in a slow manner as to not shock his little system. The doctors have estimated that Carter has three or four LITERS of fluid. Yes, the poor little guy looks like he's nine months pregnant. I'm praying that by morning he will at least be more comfortable.

Right now Carter is sleeping and receiving a breathing treatment. He's so tired and so sedated that he is wheezing a little bit. The nurses confirm that this is nothing abnormal.

I'm going to bed as soon as I get my laundry out of the dryer (I ran out of clean pjs!). I'm praying that tonight will be a good one for both of us and that we can get some much needed sleep.

Please keep the family of our friend Sheyla in your prayers. She passed away today. She was at St. Jude with us and lived at Target House while we were there. My heart is simply broken. Each time a child we know passes, I feel like I've lost a part of my heart. I know that heaven is gaining the most beautiful angels of all - the innocent and golden.

Father God - Continue to watch over my little boy. Carter told me yesterday that "Jesus is in his heart" and I know it is true. I see Your works every day through Carter. Glory be to you, Lord Christ. Forever and ever. Amen.

8/5/12

I am really trying not to get frustrated and upset....but it doesn't look like we're going to be discharged tomorrow. Poor Carter's white blood cell count is up which means that he's probably battling an infection of some sort. He doesn't have a fever though - and he actually was acting better today. So this news was not expected.

I feel like I'm being tested here. We've had one incident after another with this stay and I keep pressing on and attempting to stay positive. My faith doesn't waiver. I know that God is in control. I know that everything happens for a reason. I know that my son will bounce back from this set-back. It just stinks having to go through it.

Someone once told me, prior to Carter's diagnosis, that the burden I carried weighed heavy on their heart. It made me smile because at the time, I didn't think I had a burden. I still smile at this comment because I still don't believe that I carry a burden. No matter how hard my life may be at times, I know that I am blessed to be Carter's mommy and Mason's mommy for that matter. I was chosen for this journey.

So many people say that I'm the inspiration. It's not me, it is Carter. He is the fighter. He is the trooper. He is the one that keeps me going through the good, the bad, and the downright nasty. Carter is the one that has wrapped everyone around his little finger, including me. I will do anything for this little boy. He is my hero. He is my rock. He is the one that makes me stronger, makes me fight harder, makes me the momma that I am. We have been so blessed on this journey. There are so many people willing to help and to come visit. It was so nice seeing friends this weekend (and this past week) whom I haven't seen in ages. They brought Bojangles, Earthfare, balloons, and goodies...but most of all, they brought love....which is the most incredible gift of all. Love is the gift that God gave to us. It is the ultimate gift which shines as an example for everything. The love that has been given to Carter shines in God's glory - forever and ever.

Please pray harder. Pray louder. Pray from the depths of your soul to the tips of your fingers. Tell your friends, family, coworkers, postman, lawn guy, doctor, and newspaper boy about Carter and his incredible journey. I know that God hears us. I know that is why Carter is still with us.

Father God, I lift my son up to you. When I am weak, you strengthen me. When I am sad, you brighten my day. When I am worried, you calm me. When I am in need, you hold me. Please place your loving hands on Carter and heal him. Let us go home and allow Carter to be a normal little boy again. Allow him to ride his new tricycle, catch baby frogs with his big brother, and bounce on the bed like a healthy little boy. All of the things that make a mother's heart whole. Amen.

((HUGS!!))

8/6/12
I need to sleep - I am one tired momma.

Carter has drained 7 Liters of fluid from his belly now. I will never look at a 2 Liter bottle of Coke the same way again....ever.

I am praying that we'll get to go home on Wednesday. There is some talk of doing another ultrasound on Carter's tummy to make sure that everything looks good.

The good news that we received today is that the doctors at St. Jude have looked at the MRI and they are pleased. Nothing looks too unusual or suspicious at this point. We will still return to St. Jude next week for our scheduled MRI so that the doctors can utilize their MRI machine to compare.

It dawned on me today that by the time I return to Greenwood, half of August will be over and Mason will be starting preschool again. Time flies when you're having fun being cooped up in the hospital.

Today was a good day in so many ways. We were blessed to have many unexpected visitors to brighten what should have been another dull and boring day. Mr. Chad stopped by and spoiled Carter rotten, Officer Jen stopped by and loved on the little man, Rev. Cox sat with mommy for a long time and just chatted, Grandy was here for a short bit before leaving, and Sarah, Jake, and Ms. Candi were here to entertain us. What a blessing!

Carter is continuing to regain his mobility. He did more walking today than he has in a week and that is fabulous for a long list of reasons. He was talking and happy (for the most part), which makes life easier on me, too!

Thank you for your continued prayers, love, and support. I could not do this journey without my prayer warriors.

By the way, I've decided that my new SC plate will either say ((HUGS!!)) or WARRIOR on it .

((HUGS!!))
s.

8/7/12
I drank a chai latte at 3pm and I'm wide awake.....guess I have figured out what will do the trick.....

Please pray that we will get to go home tomorrow. We have one group of doctors ready to boot us out of here and another group of doctors that is hesitant to let us leave.

Up until now the assumption has been that the fluid in Carter's belly was spinal fluid from the shunt. Then one of the doctors heard that Carter had almost eight liters of fluid drained from his belly and found it unbelievable. His questioning of the fluid then sparked debate.

Could Carter's belly really hold that much fluid? My argument is that yes, it could. I say this because I have a large abdominal cavity (even when I was skinnier!). When I was pregnant, I didn't look pregnant until I was basically 7.5 months pregnant and at 8.5 pregnant I looked like I swallowed a bowling ball. Both of my boys were over 9 pounds - theoretically, I should have looked like a beached whale.

So, I digress, my theory is that Carter's belly has never been able to flush the fluid out or it only flushed some of the fluid out. I think that the fluid has been building up for six months since the shunt was placed. It is likely that I'm wrong - but I cannot imagine this child suddenly producing liters of spinal fluid in a short amount of time....and then becoming distended from it.

Anyways, they have clamped the drain to see if Carter's belly swells. If it does, it means that the fluid is something other than spinal fluid. If it doesn't, it means that it was spinal fluid and we've solved this great mystery. I feel like I'm on a bad episode of "House" right now.

Please pray that we are discharged tomorrow. Please pray that this is spinal fluid and not something else.

I feel like we're taking up permanent residency here at Levine. This is not a good feeling! I much prefer the water pressure and temperature in my own shower and softness of my own bath sheets to the hand towels they give you here. The good news is that a) I have a shower in the room and b) I do have warm water. Those of you who have been reading my journal for a while will remember that this is a luxury in comparison to St. Jude!

Carter has been such a trooper. He is tired and cranky, but still manages to put on a smile. Today we went for a walk (well, I walked, he was in the stroller) and Carter said, "God gave me to you and I'm a gift." He said this totally out of the blue and it stunned me. I looked right into his big brown eyes and replied, "Yes, you're the best gift of all."

Heavenly Father, please send us home tomorrow. Please let this be spinal fluid and not something else. Let us rejoice in knowing that this minor setback is over and we can move forward once again. In you name, I pray. Amen.
((HUGS!!))
Sarah

8/8/12
WOO HOO!!! We're going home!!! THANK GOD! and thank you for your prayers! I am packed and ready to go...just need them to pull Carter's drain and WE ARE OUTTA HERE!!

Sarah Bucciero

I thought we were in the clear and that Carter was going to mend. I thought that we would be heading back to St. Jude in a few days. I was so wrong.

Carter slept with Paul the night we arrived home. He was restless and in pain. I called our doctor at St. Jude and requested that we head there today. I needed to get the situation resolved and I was frustrated beyond words.

Our beloved doctor called Levine to touch base and see what was going on behind the scenes. He told me that he would get back to me quickly, so I waited by the phone.....Carter and Paul were snuggling upstairs and Mason was watching television quietly.

I never, ever anticipated the call that I received. The very last test that Levine ran before we were discharged showed that the tumor had travelled down the shunt and taken residence in Carter's belly. It happens less than 1% of the time. Our doctor at Levine had never seen it happen, it was something that he had only read about in journals. Our doctor at St. Jude had only seen it twice.

Dr. Giles told me that there was nothing left that we could do for Carter. Additional radiation would only prolong the inevitable. When I asked him how long Carter had left, he didn't know but said that it could be two weeks or two months.

I took a moment and actually posted in a closed group of women that I was close to at the time. I needed to process the phone call I just had. It was the beginning of the end.....the whisper that I had heard for almost two weeks, the whisper that I refused to acknowledge, the whisper that no mother ever wants to hear.

I had to tell Paul. How do you tell your husband that your son is going to die? That there is nothing left to do for him? He was cuddling with Carter, so I couldn't just walk in and announce it. I composed myself, walked upstairs, and simply told Paul that we all needed to go back to Levine and that Carter needed to have a more permanent drain placed immediately. I told him that we needed to hustle. And when he walked into the bathroom to shave, I broke the news.

There's nothing left for them to do. The fight is over. Carter's journey is over.

We packed in an hour and took anything and everything that we could possibly need. I even packed an outfit that I had bought at the Atlanta Mart a few weeks prior. It was a white jon-jon with beige smocking. When I bought it, I thought that it would be a beautiful portrait outfit but there was a whisper that it would be the outfit that Carter was buried in when the time came. I refused to listen to that whisper, but at the last minute I heard the whisper that told me to take the jon-jon. I listened and packed it.

Paul and the boys drove in a separate car than I did. I knew that I needed to make phone calls, time to process, and selfishly - time for myself.

I cried the entire way to Charlotte (about two and a half hours). I prayed over and over and over again. I spoke to God when I wasn't on the phone speaking to family and loved ones. I begged that He have mercy on Carter. I told him that if He was going to take Carter, to do it quickly so that he didn't suffer. It was the hardest prayer that I have ever prayed.

8/9/12
We are back in Charlotte. Paul and Carter are at Levine's. My heart is numb. This is the beginning of the end.

The sample that they took yesterday showed malignant cells late last night. It is extremely rare, but sometimes malignant cells travel down the shunt.....and this is what has happened in Carter's case. The poor boy just can't catch a break. My mind is still trying to process everything. If we have ever needed prayers, we need them now.

Father God - if it is your will to take my sweet child, please do so in a quick and merciful manner. Hold him close and love him with all of your heart the way that I have loved him with mine. Grant my sweet boy peace and ease his pain. I know that Carter is an angel of yours and that he was here on a mission. I think that mission must be almost complete. Father, I beseech you to grant our family grace during this difficult time. I lift my heart up to you dear Lord. Amen.

8/10/12
So tired. So many thoughts that I want to write about, but I need to sleep. Poor little man is so skinny and frail. My prayer is that if Carter is going to go, that he go quickly and not suffer. We established a scholarship in Carter's name at my alma mater. It

will go to students impacted directly by cancer. I will post details as to how contributions can be made tomorrow. His legacy will live on forever in so many ways.

((HUGS!!))

The days were a blur. I needed to get out of the hospital. It was suffocating me. I had been there for nine days already in August and the thought of being there crushed me.

Carter had a more permanent drain placed. Friends arrived, visited and prayed. We tried to keep Mason involved in a way that he could be with his brother but not enough to understand exactly what was going on …..he played in the toy room, flirted with the nurses, and stayed close to his brother.

There was talk of sending us home on hospice. That whisper was back. It said that it wouldn't be long. It told me to stay at the hospital.

There was a new doctor that afternoon. I sat with her and quietly told her my concern. She understood and told me that she didn't have a problem with us staying and it actually made her feel better, too. It was a relief. It was a blessing.

Carter was slipping away. God was showing him mercy. He was answering my prayer. The angels had arrived.

8/11/12
It won't be long now…. Please pray.

Dear God -
Please take care of my baby.

((HUGS!!))
Sarah

8/13/12
REJOICE and be glad in Him! Carter earned his angel wings and was made whole this morning at 1:20 am. Thank you for your love and prayers.

8/16/12
I don't know about you, but I am celebrating Carter's life with

fire trucks, balloons, Bojangles, white roses, blue ribbons, smiley faces drawn on my hand, and kisses in my pocket...... And then I can hear him say "morning sunshine!" along with his usual diatribe of "well, first off," "probably," and "I fink".. Love you baby boy - I know you are happy and that make makes my heart glad. What have you done to celebrate Carter's life today? :)

((HUGS!!))

8/17/12
This is a poem by Mary Frye (1932) - it has always been a favorite, but it is even more meaningful today:

Do not stand at my grave and weep,
I am not there; I do not sleep.
I am a thousand winds that blow,
I am the diamond glints on snow,
I am the sun on ripened grain,
I am the gentle autumn rain.
When you awaken in the morning's hush
I am the swift uplifting rush
Of quiet birds in circling flight.
I am the soft star-shine at night.
Do not stand at my grave and cry,
I am not there; I did not die.

Carter is with us - every day, every where. He is my sunshine in the morning, and he is the star-filled sky at night. This is not the end my friends, it is just the next chapter......and goodness, do we have a chapter to write!

((HUGS!!))
Sarah

8/24/12
I have so much to write. There are so many things that I haven't told you, things that I need to write down....so many things that scared me before all of this that no longer scare me.

You see, when Carter and I went to the hospital the first time (at the end of July). I kept having this awful thought .....it kept telling me "this is the beginning of the end." I don't know if it was God whispering to me. I don't know if it was mother's intuition.

Regardless, it scared me. I didn't want to acknowledge that it was the beginning of the end. Not when we had finally gotten the brain tumor under control, not when our lives were finally starting resemble normal in some capacity.

What's scary is that even before that, I had this awful feeling. When we were at St. Jude in June and they scheduled Carter's scan for August 13, I had this awful feeling. I wanted to request that the scan be a week earlier or a week later, but I didn't because I thought that I was paranoid or crazy. For some reason, I knew that August 13 wasn't going to be a good date for us.

And the night that I finally went off on the resident ....I failed to tell you that Carter was talking to a little boy standing at our bedside. Carter kept asking "What's your name?" to the little boy. Finally, when I gathered the courage, I asked Carter who he was talking to .....and Carter told me that he was talking to the little boy standing next to the bed and that he wanted to play with him. It was at that point that I told Carter that the little boy was an angel here to help him with the pain....and at that point, the resident walked in and I let my emotions fly.

I think that I knew then...I think that I knew that the end wasn't far away.....but there wasn't anything negative coming from the doctors. We were told that there weren't any malignant tumors. We were told that it was spinal fluid. We believed that this was a minor setback.

When we returned to Levine and Carter had his ultrasound and a more permanent drain was put in place, I let Paul be by Carter's side......I honestly needed a break for a few days after being by Carter's side 24/7 for ten days. I'm so thankful that I did. They needed some Daddy-Carter time.

Saturday I went to the hospital briefly and then I took Mason out to Locust for a friend's birthday party. Prior to that I met with one of the doctors because the plan was for us to take Carter home to the condo in Cornelius. This scared me. In my mind, I somehow knew that it wouldn't be long before Carter was an angel. I told the doctor that I didn't want to take Carter home because I was afraid of him dying in front of Mason...and as a mommy, I still needed to protect Mason as much as I possibly could. Later that afternoon, I went to birthday party with Mason. Shortly after we arrived, Paul texted me and said that Carter's breathing was shortened and that his eye movements had slowed. I went into panic mode and when Paul told me that he was trying to decide if I needed to come back to the hospital, I told him that I was already on my way.

I arrived without toiletries, pjs, or clothes to change into.....I needed to get to my baby.

Saturday night was a long night. It was an awful night in so many ways.....but it was a beautiful night, too. It was Paul, Carter, and me.

Carter was in a lot of pain and the medical staff was attempting to get it in control. He was awake and lucid though - talking to Paul and me about a variety of things.....including the angels that he saw around his bed.

Carter told us that he saw three angels that night. There was a baby, a boy, and a man. We asked a lot of questions and he told us a lot about the angels.

I don't know who the baby was - it may have been one of the babies I lost in miscarriage....it may have been a cousin....it may have been a friend's baby......we'll never know.

Carter talked about the boy. I immediately thought of our friend who had passed just weeks earlier. Carter told me that it wasn't him. I then thought to ask Carter if the boy was our dear friend Jonah. And Carter answered, yes. It did my heart good to know that our friend's grandson was there....Carter also told us that a man was there....in my heart I know that this was my grandfather. I had a dream when Paul and I first got engaged .....and Grandpa told me that "no matter how bad things get, know that everything will be OK." I've used that as my mantra for so many things since then.

Carter was so sweet telling us about the angels. He told us that one had a ball. Another angel had a stroller. But the excitement on his face was best when he told us that the angels had shakes! It was the sweetest thing ever. We kept telling him that it was alright to go to the angels, that they would make him better.....but Carter kept shaking his head "no!".

A PCA pump was ordered for Carter's pain meds about that time and he finally went to sleep.

In the morning our doctor paid us a visit first thing....we told him about the angels.....he commented that "the children who see the angels have an easier time letting go." This brought us both great comfort for Carter's sake.

I need to get to bed....it is late. I am exhausted.....but I will finish the story soon. It has been so beautiful. I am convinced that Carter was an angel of God.

Quickly - less than 1% of malignant brain tumor cells ever travel down shunts and take hold in the abdominal lining......this is one way that I am certain that God wanted to take Carter quickly - for his journey and mission surely must have finished for God to answer my prayers - He took Carter quickly, without suffering and without pain.

I lift my heart up to you, dear Lord.

((HUGS!!))
S.

8/27/12
Sunday morning, Carter's Godparents (Brian and Amy) arrived bright and early...both Paul and I were exhausted, but we were so thankful that they got there to see Carter.

I was smelly and stinky having slept in my clothes without any toiletries, but they didn't care. Thank goodness. I honestly don't remember much of that morning other than thinking that we made it through the night and that I was so thankful for Brian and Amy being able to get to the hospital to see Carter.

They left about the time family started to descend upon us. Paul's mom, dad, step-mom, and brother and sister-in-law were already present. My parents were on their way from Virginia and my brother was on his way from New Jersey.

Sometime during the afternoon I called my mom to see about their whereabouts. Mom's reply was, "I'll call you back, your father just got pulled over." Click. Several minutes later she called back and explained that Dad told the officer in Lovingston, VA that he was in a hurry to see his dying three year old grandson. The officer asked Dad when his last ticket was and Dad said that it had been so long that he couldn't remember. The officer was an angel and sent Dad on his way, warning him to drive safely and be careful. God is good.

Over the course of the day, Paul, Carter, and I spent the majority of the day by ourselves. It was the way Paul and I wanted it. We allowed friends and family to come in for short visits, but we were by ourselves for the majority of the time. One exception was when our friends Tucker and Windy stopped by to visit. Carter woke up during this time while Windy laid by his side. Carter gave Paul and I our last hugs during this brief period of alertness. These were the last hugs we received while Carter was alive.

At one point, Child-Life came in and we did ink hand-prints and plaster casts of Carter's hands. They turned out fabulously and I'm so thankful that we did them. Sweet Carter slept through the entire event. I was never able to do hand-prints of Carter when he was a spry toddler - he wouldn't sit still long enough!

Sunday passed into early evening and my parents arrived - they had time to say goodbye to Carter and spend a little time with him. My brother arrived several hours later to see Carter, too. Paul and I played videos of Mason so that Carter could hear his brother's voice during this time. It is our belief that Carter was waiting for everyone to get there before he said good-bye.

At some point during the day, our rector arrived. I know she was there during the evening hours, but I don't know when she arrived. I do know that she was there until late in the evening.

Late that night Rev. Cox performed essentially what is considered the Last Rites in the Episcopal church and anointed him with oil. We said some prayers for Carter and then everyone left for the night.

It was late. Paul and I went to bed. Paul was asleep with Carter and I slept on the sofa.

I'm not certain why I woke up. I just remember waking up and thinking that Carter wasn't breathing properly. I looked at the clock and saw that it was 1:19. Quickly I started to shake Paul (who was asleep in the same bed as Carter) trying to wake him up. I was so scared that Paul would miss Carter's last breath.

Just as Carter took a huge breath, Paul woke up and turned over. Carter didn't move and I was scared that Paul had missed it. I kept talking to Carter, telling him that it was OK to go with the angels and that I loved him so much and always would. And just when I thought that Carter was gone - he scared the living daylights out of me and took another huge breath.......his last one. The one that Paul got to see.

Once I realized that Carter wasn't going to take another breath, I darted for our beloved nurse, Tessa (and fellow St. Jude mom!). She came in just as the alarms on the machines started to go off. She allowed us time with Carter but told me that the resident on duty was the dreaded resident from the week before. She told me she could get another doctor for me if I preferred and I remember saying something to the extent of it being a wise idea....who knew what I might say to the resident!

And within minutes, as Paul and I sat with our sweet angel Carter, a doctor appeared. Tessa introduced him as "Dr. Carter." It immediately brought smiles to our faces, because we knew that it wasn't coincidence. Although Carter's official time of death by the hospital was 1:35, it actually had been at 1:20am.

Paul and I spent a little time with Carter and then called our dear friend Tim who was staying near the hospital. Poor guy had just gone to bed! He came over to the hospital and helped us pack everything up that night while we prepared to head up to Cornelius without our little boy. We were exhausted, we were numb, and we were thankful that our little boy was whole once again.

The night didn't end then.....still more details to write about, but I'm once again exhausted. I pray that I will be able to catch up on sleep eventually. I don't remember what energy feels like anymore.

((HUGS!!))
S.

8/28/12
Many people have asked me why Carter passed so suddenly....in
retrospect, it was over the course of about three weeks - but it was
still sudden when you consider he had been battling the brain
tumor for ten months. If you don't want to read the details of
Carter's death - please stop reading now. I'm writing this to help
those who need to process and find closure, not to make anyone
upset.

You see, when Carter's belly became distended - we didn't realize
initially that it was from the malignant cells that were planting
themselves throughout the lining of his abdomen. I still have to
laugh when I think about Paul coming home from the hospital in
Greenwood and the doctor there telling him to wait until Monday
and to give Carter some Gatorade in hopes to absorb some of the
fluid (but of course, this doctor didn't know the whole story - and
didn't understand the situation fully).

In fact, our own doctors at Levine didn't understand the fluid
production in Carter's belly fully because the tests kept coming
back negative for malignant cells. There was so much fluid
displacing the cells, that they were difficult to obtain for a positive
test result. That is, until the eight liters of fluid had been drained
and the final fluid test showed the malignant cells. Think about
Kool-Aid. Imagine the cancer cells being the Kool-Aid crystals.
When you add water and stir them up, the crystals go everywhere.
It isn't until you get to the bottom of the Kool-Aid that you actually
can see (or get) the crystals. The cancer cells were the Kool-Aid
crystals.

Essentially what happened was that the malignant cells planted
themselves in the lining of Carter's abdominal cavity and
multiplied. There wasn't a mass creating a single tumor - it was
simply cells, everywhere. These cells created the fluid in Carter's
belly - it was the body's way of fighting the malignant cells. These
cells traveled down the shunt at some point and took hold. This is
something that doctors read about but rarely see. This was the
case with our doctors, they had never seen this happen before - it
is extremely rare.

So - eventually, there was more fluid being produced than could
be drained. And then, Carter's body started to fight the fluid like an

infection (think pneumonia). They could have given Carter an antibiotic, but it would have only delayed the inevitable. At one point I asked the doctor if Carter was drowning - as a former lifeguard, it made logical sense to me to equate what was happening to drowning - and she said, "yes, but we don't like to think about it that way." Shortly before Carter passed, he had a fever of 108 degrees (taken under the arm).

I hope that I'm not being morose or morbid by explaining what happened, but there are many people who need these details in order to process and understand what happened and why it happened so quickly.

I truly believe that it was God who answered my prayers - my little boy never suffered. Yes - it is hard that he went so quickly, but it was God's mercy. Again, I truly believe that God was calling Carter home quickly because Carter's mission was complete here on earth. I may never understand the depth or scope of Carter's mission - but I think we all have a good clue as to what it may have been.

Carter's story is not over....it's just beginning. it's simply the next chapter. He has changed my life. He has changed so many lives. His legacy will go on forever......and I promise, that's not a superlative...I will make sure of it.

((HUGS!!))

P.S.
Dear God - Please make sure that Carter is doing well and not causing too much chaos up there. Please make sure that he doesn't get ahold of a pen because he will write all over himself and the angels around him. If think you've lost something, look in Carter's pocket. If he isn't eating well - let him splurge on Bojangles. He has puppy, ball, and blankie with him, so I'm sure that he's sleeping well at night, but just in case - please sing "Twinkle Twinkle" to him....it helps. I lift my heart up to you dear Lord.....and to Carter, too.

9/7/12
I am sorry that I haven't written in a while - Paul and I are trying to get caught up with life and re-adjust....

I want to continue telling Carter's story and the events of the night he became an angel - I want to remember every detail. I thought about it today. I don't think that I ever kept up with his baby book - a second child, working full-time....it just didn't happen (not that Mason's is much better)....but I want to honor Carter by preserving the details of his passing and the days that followed. It gives me comfort to think of them and to write about them now.

After Paul and I left the hospital, my cell phone rang as we were getting on the highway. It seemed odd - but I answered it because I was in a daze and baffled. The man on the other end of the phone identified himself as an employee of CMC End of Life Services. He was totally genuine and consoling. He spoke gently as to not upset me and asked if he could help in any way. He wanted to know about Carter and his journey and so I openly spoke about my little boy. About the time that I thought that the phone call was over, he transitioned into what almost sounded like a sales pitch. He asked if we'd donate Carter's retinas to help two people.

I am embarrassed to say that I got angry. I had been prepared to donate Carter's brain to St. Jude or Levine for research if they had asked (neither did), but here I was driving with my husband just after losing our son and I'm being asked like it was a last minute sales pitch. Honestly, I can't imagine that after everything Carter's little body had been through (the malignant cells throughout his abdominal cavity), that anyone would want any part of his body. I think that I would have lived in fear that another child would get cancer from the transplant, too. No doctor or nurse had prepared us for this call and it really made me wonder. It wasn't a secret that Carter was dying and no one approached during the 48 hours he was slowly drifting away. I just was in shock....and so was Paul. He got upset about the phone call, too. The man even asked if he could give us a few hours to think about it. NO!!! No means no.....

Just about the time I hung up the phone with this man, we arrived back in Cornelius. Paul and I decided to stay at the hotel where a lot of the family was staying because we didn't want to wake Mason up by coming into the condo in the middle of the night and we didn't want to explain what had happened at that point. We weren't emotionally ready.

Paul pulled up into the registration area of the hotel parking lot and went inside. I was standing outside and came upon one tiny little frog. I knew it was a sign from Carter.

At the beginning of the summer there were literally hundreds of baby frogs in our yard and driveway after it rained. Each time it rained, the frogs returned, but in fewer numbers. Mason had great fun picking them up and putting them in buckets of water. Carter usually hovered over them looking at them intently - trying to determine if he wanted to pick the frog up or not. I remember him saying, "Awww, they're so cute!"

It reminded me of an email that I received back on November 4, 2011 - my dad sent me an email about frogs...

I was told a story about a lady in the hospital who was near death when an area Chaplain came to visit her.

This Chaplain was a very young female with long blond hair. She listened to the lady who was ill and left her a small gift for comfort. It was a tiny ceramic frog.

The next day one of the people from the lady's church came to visit. The lady told her friend about the beautiful young Chaplain who had come to visit her. The friend was so impressed with the way the lady had improved and felt the need to talk to the young Chaplain.

In her search to find the young gal, she was repeatedly reassured that the chaplains are never very young and that there was never a gal that fit the description given.

Upon returning to the lady in the hospital, a visiting nurse entered the room and noticed the ceramic frog. The nurse made the comment 'I see you have a guardian angel with you.'

As she held the little frog we asked why she made the comment and we were informed that the frog stood for:
Forever
Rely
On
God

I called Paul over when he came back outside and showed him the little baby frog.....we didn't have to say anything to each other....we just smiled and knew that it was a sign from Carter that he was doing fine. Why else would there be a single baby frog in the parking lot of a hotel at 3am in the morning?

((HUGS!!))
Sarah

9/12/12
I forgot to add a detail that was told to me by many shortly after Carter's passing. It seems that the Perseid Meteor Shower was the night that Carter went to be with the angels. What a magnificent welcoming for my little boy. I only wish that I had paid attention on the drive home versus talking with the CMC End of Life Services guy.....

I also want to note that there was a Blue Moon in August, too. And yes, I do realize that a Blue Moon is not really blue.....but again - how appropriate that blue was my baby boy's color and it happened in the same month (just two weeks really) after he left his earthly home.

The night of the blue moon I sat beneath the stars and imagined that Carter was smiling down on me.

I digress - back to the rest of the story…

Later Monday morning Paul and I woke up and showered, spoke to the family members we needed to speak to and headed to the condo to pick up my parents.

We had appointments both with the funeral home and with our rector, Rev. Cox at our church.

We took my parents for two reasons. The first, they both are very familiar with the Episcopal doctrine (having been raised in the Episcopal church) and they had knowledge of the cemetery where Carter would be buried in Cincinnati.

Our meeting at the funeral home was long - but they were fabulous about going over every single detail and making sure that they did everything that we wanted. Mr. Hartsell is an amazing man and he treated us like we were the only event that week (which was not the case!).

We later headed over to our church and spoke with our rector. I love her dearly. She has been such a part of our journey....and has always been there to talk with me and help me think. I will never forget when she came to the hospital and stayed with me for hours in early August (when we thought the fluid was clear of malignant cells). I will never forget telling her that as a cancer mommy you hear of children passing from the very beginning - but in the beginning, these are children that you don't know. As you continue on the journey, the deaths become closer and closer. The child you knew in the clinic, the child you saw in the hallway, the child who was a friend of a friend. As the journey continues, it becomes your friends....the older boy that Carter loved from down the hall, the child who was diagnosed just before Carter, the child who was diagnosed just after Carter.....it's like a vise getting tighter and tighter.

Again, I digress. We talked about how we wanted the memorial service to be a celebration of Carter's life. We wanted everyone to leave and feel good about Carter's angelic mission here on earth. So that is what we planned - hymns that were uplifting, a children's sermon, and Bojangles in the parish hall afterwards. What more could a momma want?

It was later that night that my dad told me about this crazy idea he had....only it wasn't that crazy. He reminded me that Carter was an honorary fireman and that it would be appropriate according to fireman's protocol for Carter to be delivered to the church on a fire truck. I remember thinking - how am I going to ask the West Stanly Fire Department to bring Carter's casket on one of their fire trucks to the church? Needless to say, the WSFD is amazing and didn't even question it - they just said that they would make it happen. How's that for amazing? Not only that, but unbeknown to me, they stayed up until 2am the night before Carter's memorial painting their helmets baby blue for Carter.

Monday was a very, very long day for Paul and me.

It didn't dawn on me until almost eleven o'clock at night (I know because that is the time that I posted on FB) that Carter was one of seven children to die of cancer that day. 46 children are diagnosed with cancer every day and 7 die every day ......cancer is the leading cause of death by disease in children.
Heavenly Father - Tonight I pray for the 46 mommas who found out that their babies have cancer today. Tonight I pray for the 7 mommas who lost their babies today. I pray for their families. I pray for their friends. I pray that they, too, were greeted by the angels like Carter. I pray for those who are just starting this journey and need the love and support of their friends and families. Most importantly, Father God, I pray that all of these families know you or come to know you over the course of their journey. Welcome them with open arms and let them feel your warm embrace. In your name I pray. Amen.

((HUGS!!))

9/13/12
I will probably post a few times today....it will help me get through the day...please bear with me!

A Prayer for Carter

On Monday, August 20 of this year, we gathered under a canopy at Gate of Heaven Cemetery in Cincinnati, Ohio. Carter's casket was in the center, surrounded by all of his family and several close friends,

Just prior to the commitment of Carter's remains to the Earth, the Reverend Susan Lehman asked if anyone wanted to say something. No one, with the exception of my dad, wished to speak.

My dad had asked to offer a prayer for Carter, but before he did, he set an expectation for everyone at the service.

He told everyone present that Carter had an emphatic way of saying grace, and if you ever had that opportunity to do so with him, you knew that at the end of the prayer, he always finished it with an enthusiastic "Ahhhhh-men!" Dad asked that at the conclusion of his prayer, we honor Carter accordingly.

Sarah Bucciero

Reprinted here is Grandy's prayer:
> *Holy, gracious and loving Father,*
> *we thank You for the gift of Carter,*
> *and for the love he shared with us*
> *during his brief time in this world.*

> *Father God,*
> *In the joy of Your Creation,*
> *You gave to us, the gift of Life,*
> *In the birth of your son, Jesus,*
> *You gave to us the gift of Love*
> *without condition,*
> *and in His death and resurrection,*
> *You gave to us the gifts of*
> *forgiveness and life everlasting.*

> *Fulfill now unto your faithful child,*
> *Carter Joseph,*
> *Your Resurrection promise.*
> *Lift him up on eagles' wings and*
> *bring him to Your nearer presence.*
> *Throw open wide the gates of Heaven*
> *and bid him enter in,*
> *embrace him in the arms of your abiding*
> *love and give him ((HUGS)) each day for*
> *all eternity and beyond!*

> *Let his pockets overflow with soft, warm kisses*
> *and may he rejoice this day, and always,*
> *in the company of angels.*

> *All this we ask in the name*
> *of our Lord and Savior, Jesus Christ.*

> *Ahhhhhhhhhhhh-Men*

((HUGS))

P.S. Many of you have asked where I learned to pray......I think that my dad's prayer answers that questions! ((HUGS!!))
9/13/12
Carter's Bucket List
1. Go to the zoo/petting zoo....feed the animals
2. Ride Thomas the Tank Engine
3. Go to a Clemson football game
4. Go to the beach
5. Swim in the pool
6. Ride the Toy Story ride at WDW
7. Go to Walt Disney World
8. Have a girlfriend.....or two, or a hundred
9. Ride a tricycle
10. Go on a cruise
11. Go to the Bahamas
12. Fly in a plane
13. Travel to Florida, Georgia, North Carolina, South Carolina, Tennessee, Mississippi, Alabama, Virginia, West Virginia, Pennsylvania, Maryland
14. Sit in a race car
15. Make a gingerbread creation with top Memphis area chefs
16. Be the Duckmaster at the Peabody Hotel in Memphis
17. Meet Eric Trump
18. Win Lauren Alaina's heart
19. Eat as much Bojangles as possible
20. Win the heart of every person possible.
21. Be an honorary fireman
22. Be Mr. January
23. Go to Mommy's College
24. Teach doctors that "sick" kids don't always act sick.

((HUGS!!))
Sarah

9/17/12
Early on August 14th my mom and I headed to my favorite florist in Albemarle, Harwood's Florist. We met with Claude, the owner and he knew exactly what I wanted and how to do it. He just needed the details. The first flowers I ever received from Harwood's was when Mason was born.......I fell in love with the arrangement and Paul only sent me flowers from them from that

point forward. The flowers were once again perfect for Carter's visitation and memorial.

From there we went to visit one of my best friends. I needed to see her at her workplace in Albemarle. She was one of the first people outside of our family to hold Carter. Her family has always been special to us, and I just needed to cry with her a little bit.

Mom and I headed to Tailgators for a quick lunch. We were early and missed the lunch crowd. I have to say that it was kind of nice to be incognito .....until we walked out and saw one of our favorite Bojangles buddies having lunch there on his day off!

Mom and I then went over to the funeral home to deliver Carter's outfit.

We then headed back to Locust to pick up Mason.....he was so excited to be able to spend time with his old friends.

Many have asked how we told Mason about Carter earning his angel wings. On Monday night we took Mason on a walk out by the dock at my parent's condo. We sat down on the dock and started talking about Carter and how much we loved him. Paul and I simply explained that much like Mommy had to take Carter to St. Jude to get Carter better, Jesus had to take Carter far away to make him better. Mason was able to tell us that Jesus had taken Carter to heaven. It was perfect in so many ways....there were ducks swimming all along the dock and we joked about "sitting on ducks" and Carter being the Duckmaster at the Peabody. God was with us. Carter was with us. Peace was with us.

((HUGS!!))
Sarah

9/20/12
The Wednesday after Carter became an angel, I spent the day alone. It was something that I needed to do on some level. I needed to think. I needed to remember. I needed to grasp my new reality.

I headed to my dermatologist (because my skin was showing the stress and age of the past ten months).....and then I headed to

South Park Mall. You see, we left home with just minutes to pack...I never thought that I would be packing for my son's funeral. So I needed three outfits - one for the visitation, the memorial, and the burial. I needed shoes. I needed make-up. I needed Spanx .....you name it, I needed it. It took all day, but it helped me think and re-group.

I may have been born in Cincinnati.....and raised in Chicago, Philadelphia, and Northern Virginia....but I've been south of Manassas, Virginia since college....which means I have spent more of my life in the South now than in the North......and that means I knew enough to know that I needed to pull myself together in order to see the hundreds of people during the visitation and memorial. I bought my shoes a size to big because I knew they would swell over the course of the events and I didn't want to have to take them off. I could almost hear my Mimi guiding me through the process of what I needed to do (she passed in 2001). I know that all of this may sound odd - but it was a surreal day for me in many ways.

The only day that I can compare this to was the day that my friends and I had to shop for an outfit to bury my matron of honor in when she passed in 2005......nothing was good enough for her then and I felt a similar sense while shopping. Nothing would be good enough for my baby boy. I needed to honor him. I needed to look beautiful for him. I needed to continue to be strong for him. I guess this sounds narcissistic, but after ten months of not caring what I looked like....I finally wanted to look beautiful for my little boy.

It took me all day - but I found three dresses, two pairs of shoes, jewelry to wear, Spanx.....got my nails and toes done and put together a facade to meet and greet hundreds over the course of three events.

I cried numerous times over the course of this day and told Carter's story, too......but I was praying for grace. I needed to be strong, to be graceful, to be able to tell Carter's story.....and God once again answered these prayers. Or, at least I think so ...

I heard that some of my friends thought that I wasn't really being "me" at the visitation and at the memorial.....that I was too strong, that I was too graceful, that I was too reserved......and maybe this was true....but maybe it was God's gift that I was simply able to make it through these events without any type of medication. To see people I didn't know would be attending, to see people that I hadn't seen in years, and to see people which evoked raw emotion from me.......maybe God once again gave me the strength and grace that I prayed for to make it through these days....

Wednesday was my gift. It was my solace. It was my way of preparing for the unknown. I am thankful that I had some time by myself and some time to think and pray.

God is good. He always has been and He always will be......Wednesday was His gift to me. He knew what I needed and He provided, once again.

((HUGS!!))
Sarah

9/27/12
So today has been helpful - it has made me mad about Carter's death....they tell me that this is part of the grieving process

You know what I'm mad about? I'm mad that we finally got Carter's brain tumor under control and yet somehow there were malignant cells that traveled down his shunt into his belly.

I'm mad at the ignorant people who don't appreciate their children and who judge others while they are grieving.

I'm mad that we ran out of white roses to give out at Carter's visitation because I underestimated how many people would come.

I'm mad that I haven't had time to write about the hundreds of people who came to celebrate Carter's life with us, at the funeral, internment, and the visitation.

I'm mad that more people didn't get to see the beautiful site of my baby's casket riding on the fire truck ....the firefighters riding on the back with their Carter blue helmets ensuring his safe passage to the church and back.

I'm mad that more people didn't get to know Carter and his story.

I'm mad that more people didn't get to hear him say things like "pumpernickel", "stethoscope," and "well, I fink that probably."

I'm mad that I am not going to know just how brilliant my little boy could have been.

Most of all - I'm mad that ANYONE would judge a mother of a child with cancer.....and it has happened time and time again on this journey. I have tried to be graceful and kind and transparent, and yet it isn't enough for some people.

Have I snapped? Probably.

But I am NOT mad at God. Never have been and probably never will be - God didn't do this.....

God - Please get me through this grief and pain that I am feeling tonight. Hold me close and help me feel Carter close to me. Let me feel your warm embrace and hear your sweet whispers. Cradle me with love and let the memories sing me to sleep. In your name, I pray. Amen.

9/28/12
Goodnight sweet boy - I hope that you aren't hurting the way I am right now. I pray that blankie is keeping you warm and that you are holding puppy and ball tight like you always did. I will never stop fighting for you .... I have made every step of this journey public and I will continue to do so .... To show the good, the bad, and the ugly of what it is like.... So other parents can be prepared for what might happen to them.

I will see you in my dreams little man..... That is, if I can get to sleep!

((HUGS!!))

10/1/12
I keep trying to find time to sit down and write about the final events during the week Carter became an angel. I am still trying to unpack the house, get it decorated, get it cleaned, do fundraising for Moped to Memphis, and have time to be with Paul and Mason.

I think that people assume that everything is normal because Carter is no longer here and that my life must be dull and boring. If anything, I am realizing that it was the grace of God that I got through the summer when I was attempting to do most of these things AND take care of a sick child.

The visitation was on Thursday evening at Hartsell Funeral Home. It went from 6-9 pm and we literally had hundreds of people attend. It meant so much to me that people drove from Williamsburg, Raleigh, Columbia, Greenwood, and places up and down the East coast to be there. Some people could only come for the visitation and literally saw us and drove home the same evening. It was such an overwhelming feeling to know that friends would visit us when we needed them most.

There were people who attended the visitation that I hadn't seen in years. I thought some people had forgotten about us and moved on in their lives, but they were there for us. It was mind-boggling to see people round the corner in the line. There were familiar faces and faces I had never seen before. Complete strangers came to pay their respects to us because they had been reading about Carter's journey and praying for him. Former students, teaching colleagues, and former principals came to hug me and cry with me. I had no way of anticipating who would be there and it meant the world to me.

I ordered a spray of 250 white roses to cover Carter's casket and two vases of 50 white roses flanked it. As each person went through the line, I gave them a rose to have as a memory of Carter. I wanted each person to have a little piece of the journey to take with them. Unfortunately, we had more than 350 people attend the visitation and I ran out of flowers to give out. It made me so sad to know that there were people who would be going home without a rose. I actually gave my rose to someone so that they could have one. I am still upset with myself for not ordering more.

That being said, I am proud of myself that I had the foresight to buy my heels a size too large! I was able to keep my shoes on the entire night. I know that this sounds petty, but I kept my shoes on at my wedding the entire night and I wanted to keep my shoes on the entire night of my child's visitation. Silly things like this help me smile and giggle about the event. Carter loved to put on my shoes and I felt like if I took them off, he'd want to put them on and try to walk around. One thing that I found is that a sense of humor helps get through the difficult moments. I never have taken myself too seriously and this is simply an illumination of who I am.

The beauty of the night is that it wasn't sad, at least not for me. It was glorious that I was able to see so many people and thank them for being a part of our journey. I laughed, I sobbed, and I was at peace that evening. I could feel God's loving arms wrapped around me, holding me tight and granting me comfort.

The morning of Carter's memorial service we packed so we could stay at the hotel with family and friends and then got ready to go to the service. It was chaotic on one level, but calm on another...an oxymoron at its best.

We arrived at the church early, around noon I think. There were very few people there and we were able to go into the parish hall without being "discovered" by the masses. There were still a lot of questions and uncertainties that I needed to address. I felt as if I were walking on clouds, yet very present in the situation. And no, I was not medicated at any point in time during the week of Carter's death - other than a sleeping pill at night to ensure my sleep!

I remember being overwhelmed when I saw I few unexpected faces prior to the service....it didn't dawn on me that they would be there for the service. It meant so much.

Since Carter was deemed an honorary fireman at ((HUGS!!)) for Carter Day in April, my little boy was escorted to the church on a fire truck, just like any other fireman. The small white casket looked so sweet and innocent when it arrived. But I choked back tears when I saw the helmets of the firemen had been painted Carter blue. Both Mason and Carter received Carter blue fire helmets on ((HUGS!!)) for Carter Day. I couldn't help the tears from flowing when I saw them.

I remember Mason being so excited to see the fire truck. He tried so hard to be good, but he knew that something was wrong that day. We tried to prepare him prior to the service, but I don't think that anything that we could have said or done would have prepared him.

We paused outside of the church for the prayers by our beloved rector, Nancy Cox. The pallbearers, the male family members, all wore Carter blue ties to distinguish them in a subtle manner. Mason wanted to pull me down the aisle as the casket was processed. I remember thinking that I should pick him up, but it was all that I had in me just to get down the aisle behind the casket.

And, of course, the seating arrangements didn't go as planned...everyone wanted to sit next to someone .....it was the least of my concerns but it bothered me nonetheless.

Rev. Cox gave the children's sermon - it was based off of the children's book, Waterbugs and Dragonflies. This was actually a surprise to me because I thought that she was going to talk about a caterpillar turning into a butterfly. I am grateful that she spoke of dragonflies though.....It was that morning that I ventured to the hairdresser to have my hair fixed for the memorial service....when I pulled out of the parking lot, a dragonfly flew across my windshield four times - as if it were saying hello. I acknowledge the dragonfly by saying, "Hi Carter, I know that's you. I love you." So you can imagine my surprise when she started speaking about dragonflies and waterbugs during the children's sermon.

When Mason went to the front of the church for the children's sermon, he sat further away from everyone than I expected. And he did a good job until he heard, "Dragonflies don't speak waterbug." It was at that point that his bottom lip curled downward and he looked to the ground. He didn't cry, but when I beckoned for him to return to me, he did so eagerly. He was distraught and I gladly handed over my iphone so he could watch Netflix and My Little Pony. I didn't want my little guy being upset during the service and at least this kept him distracted.

Our family friends, were all readers in the service. They all did a beautiful job.

Communion was so special because everyone received communion and then passed me on their way back to their seats. So many squeezed my hand to let me know that they were there for me. So many faces that I hadn't seen in such a long while, and so many others that were so familiar. It was so beautiful.

I know that I need to finish writing about the memorial, but I am exhausted and need to sleep. Sleep is one thing that I don't seem to get a lot of these days - regardless of whether I take a sleeping pill or not. I cannot afford to get sick and I need to at least give my body a rest. I'm so sorry that I cannot finish writing tonight. Perhaps I will be able to in the morning.

((HUGS!!))
Sarah

10/15/12
I remember the moment you arrived.
I remember the joy you brought to our eyes.

I remember the snuggling, the cuddling, the kisses, and the hugs.
I remember the happy times, the fun times, the dirt and the bugs.

I remember the chemo, the ouchies, the bites.
I remember the lovies, the happiness, the moments of light.

I remember naked babies, shaving with daddy, and new hair.
I remember the sky, the stars, and the night you went there.

Every star was shooting across the dark sky
Everyone was praying that you'd hold the angels' hands close
Every angel was ready to help you across

Baby boy, I remember, the night you arrived
Baby boy, I remember, the night that you died.
Baby boy, I remember, each night I held you dear.
Baby boy, I remember, because I loved you so - even when the end was near.

******

Carter's story didn't end there. It continues each and every day. His story is told and he lives on because of it. It hasn't been an easy journey. A mother's grief never ends. It changes, but it never ends.

One thing that I have learned is that time doesn't heal, it doesn't have that ability. Only love can heal. Love is the piece of the story that was there throughout the entire journey and continues to be a part of the story. It was there before Carter was diagnosed. It was there propelling me forward each and every day while he fought for his life. And now, love helps me get through each and every day.

I have learned how to celebrate Carter's life. It has been an important lesson on this journey. I continue to speak his name, tell his story, and share his pixie dust.

I am a St. Jude Momma and this is my love story.

Author's Note:

It has been six years since Carter left us to play with the angels. My life has changed dramatically since his death. I have learned to celebrate life and I have learned so much about myself. I have walked away from many toxic relationships including one with the college I attended. That is why the name is not mentioned in this publication.

While I have maintained the message of the journal, I have removed many references to people whom I no longer have contact with or and do not wish to include. While I have not added any additional journal entries, I have removed a few. I hope you understand. I have also attempted to contact all of the St. Jude Mommas, friends, and others who are mentioned in this book. I understand that reading your name in a Caring Bridge journal is one thing, seeing it in print is another. Thank you to each of you who allowed me to share your name. You're a part of Carter's story.

Please also know that this journal and book aren't perfect, just like life. I have relied heavily on the generosity of friends as beta readers, editors, and designers. This is a book that comes from a place of love, I would appreciate it if you would love the mistakes, too.

It has taken me all of these years to compile my journal and to write this story. It has been emotional and difficult. Every time I would read or write, it took me back to the journey and I re-lived it. I still cannot read this without crying.

I keep trying to figure out how to close this story, but you see, that's impossible. The story isn't over. Carter's story lives on through his storytellers and the fundraising we do in his honor. He lives on through pixie dust, dragonflies, Bojangles' and sweet tea. He is never far from my thoughts and always in my heart.

((HUGS!!))
Sarah

57756330R00135

Made in the USA
Columbia, SC
13 May 2019